A Visitable Past

MARGARETTA M. LOVELL

A Visitable Past

Views of Venice by American Artists 1860–1915

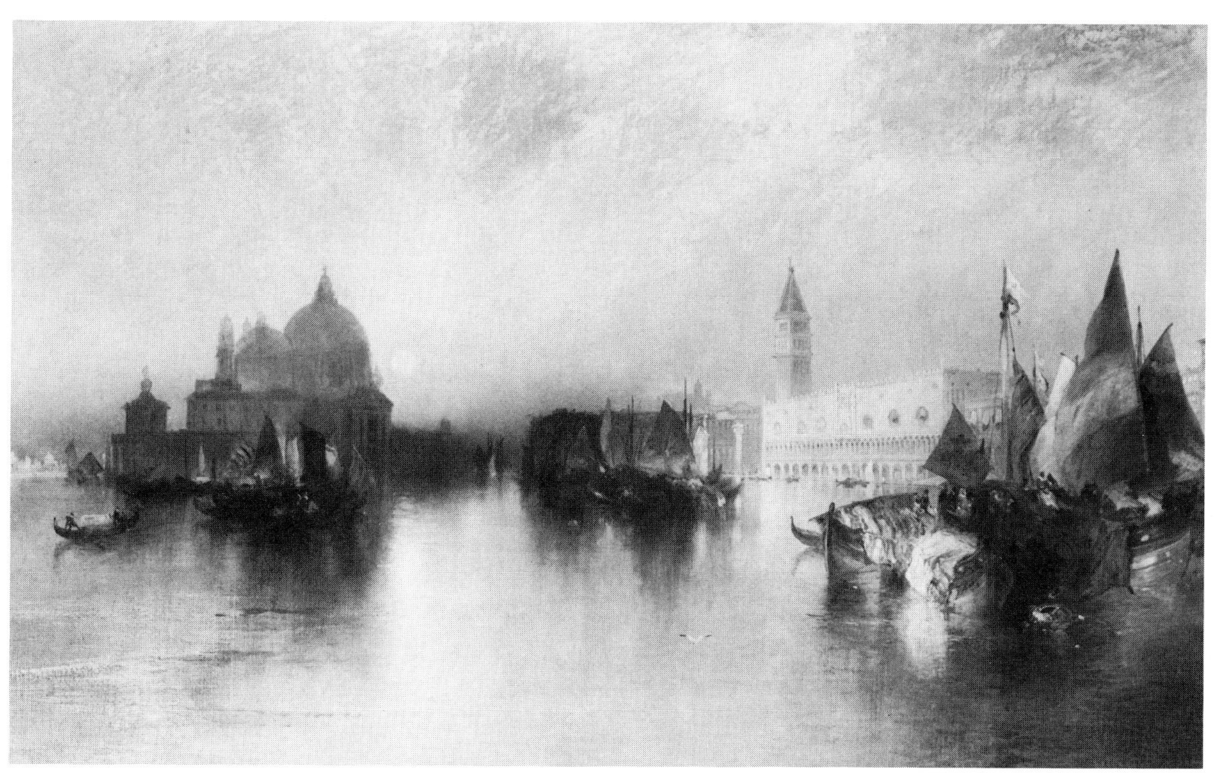

The University of Chicago Press
Chicago and London

Margaretta M. Lovell is assistant professor of art history at the University of California at Berkeley.

For Stephanie and Holly

The University of Chicago Press, Chicago 60637
The University of Chicago Press, Ltd., London

97 96 95 94 93 92 91 90 89 54321

Library of Congress Cataloging-in-Publication Data

Lovell, Margaretta M.
A visitable past : views of Venice by American artists, 1860–1915
/ Margaretta M. Lovell.
p. cm.
Bibliography: p.
Includes index.
ISBN 0-226-49412-8
1. Venice (Italy) in art—Catalogs. 2. Art, American—Catalogs.
3. Art, Modern—19th century—United States—Catalogs. 4. Art, Modern—20th century—United States—Catalogs. I. Title.
N8214.5.I8L69 1989 88-10021
760'.044994531—dc19 CIP

CONTENTS

ILLUSTRATIONS

PLATES *following page 116*

FIGURES

PREFACE

This study focuses on a large and various group of images of Venice by American artists, works that seem to have perplexed scholars in their traditional quest for the American character of American art. These works constitute a definable set, however, and their very existence comments upon the larger quest for an American culture in interesting, if indirect, ways. They are not as well known as those iconic celebrations of nature with which we are most familiar in nineteenth-century painting, but neither are they topographical exercises set in a merely alien locale. They pursue complex goals, interesting interrogatives, and they do so in such numbers, with such a concentration of energy that it seems curious that they have heretofore eluded both the art historical and the cultural historical canon.

Nineteenth-century American paintings of urban subjects are rare in spite of the example set by the French from midcentury in their enthusiastic painterly investigation of Paris. Given this apparent reluctance to pursue urban pictorial problems, this single substantial venture into architectural subjects triggers the curiosity of those interested in American interpretations of architectural space and structure. The present study is an investigation of the meanings that can be discovered (and *how* those meanings can be discovered) in these artists' several approaches to this singular urban subject.

The facts of this Venice-viewing phenomenon, matters concerning artists' biographies, tourism, and popular culture, are discussed in another work, an exhibition catalog entitled *Venice: The American View, 1860–1920.*[1] The current work moves in another direction—toward close analysis of visual texts within the context of the universe of works as a whole.

Because this is primarily an interpretive work, a narrative of the discovery of meaning in relationships, the examples discussed have been chosen to explicate most clearly those structures and juxtapositions. But the study began as an investigation of the entire corpus of Venice images, and the nature of the works dictated the shape of the analysis from the outset. The images discussed are, then, deliberately representative of the types of views produced and also exemplary of the artists' approaches to finding meaning in their subject and creating meaning in their interpretation. That some of the most talented artists found in Venice the occasion for some of their most creative, aesthetically successful thinking and painting is a fortunate but not surprising fact which, I hope, will contribute to interest in this study and in the subject as a whole.

Beyond an investigation of American late nineteenth-century interpretations of Venice, of the past, and of the fact of belatedness of which they are a symptom, this book also centrally concerns itself with issues of theory and approach. It assumes that objects contain within their structure significant and decodable attitudes, or as Jan Mukařovský has put it:

> The understanding that the artistic sign establishes among people does not pertain to *things*, even when they are represented in the work, but to a certain *attitude* toward *things*, a certain attitude on the part of man toward the *entire* reality that surrounds him, not only to that reality which is directly represented in the given case. The work does not, however, communicate this attitude—hence the intrinsic artistic "content" of the work is also inexpressible in words—but *evokes* it directly in the perceiver. We call this attitude the "meaning" of the work only because it is rendered in the work objectively by its organization, and it is therefore accessible to everyone.[2]

The argument that objects, and images of objects, are encoded with intellectual postures that are culturally suggestive, even eloquent, links the art object to its context in a manner unobtainable in most models of art historical investigation. Specifically, this study suggests that by thinking in terms of modes we can enlarge the ways in which we usefully analyze and understand pictures. I have found it useful to borrow the critical vocabulary of Northrop Frye because his model for a protagonist-based reading of literature seems provocatively apt. But using other terminology, another scaffolding, one could discover and discuss the same distinctions. The concept of the mode helps to reveal and describe distinct languages of posture and tone with which the artist has selected and endowed not only his subject but also the fictive beholder. The syntax of each mode differs from that of the others and, in some cases, comments on the assumptions and conditions of the others. They are interdependent and relational.

Theoretically the model discussed here is applicable to a broad range of art historical issues and subjects. Its particular appropriateness in this context is made clear by the immediate presence of the artistic and cultural predecessor. Here we have Americans commenting on Europeans, painters commenting on architects, and all revealing preoccupations that extend beyond issues of rendering into an understanding of the past and an acute consciousness of artistic and cultural belatedness.

ACKNOWLEDGMENTS

Few aspects of writing a book are as pleasurable as going over one's intellectual accounts and ruminating on the ledger of indebtedness from which it has inevitably been drawn. The encouraging mentors, the challenging colleagues, the patient curators, the supportive friends are too numerous ever to be reasonably and sufficiently acknowledged. But I trust I shall be able to return their assistance in kind, if not to them, then to others.

Several to whom I am directly indebted for their assistance on this project include those who have read portions of the manuscript and given me their advice on matters large and small: Carroll Brentano, Robert Herbert, Joseph Koerner, R. W. B. Lewis, Jules D. Prown, and Bryan J. Wolf. Without their assistance, guidance, and encouragement many errors and lapses would undoubtedly have remained in the text. One reader to whom I owe a special debt of gratitude is Jonathan H. Lovell, whose supportive questioning and patient listening have contributed to the book's content and its readability. I reserve to myself responsibility for its flaws and omissions.

For financial, mechanical, and research support I am grateful to numerous institutions and individuals who assisted in the realization of this text. These include the Gladys Krieble Delmas Foundation and the Barra Foundation, the Inventory of American Paintings Executed before 1914 (National Museum of American Art, Smithsonian Institution, Washington, D.C.), Linda Graham and Wendy Ruppel, and Barbara McCorkle, map curator, Yale University, all of whom lent valuable and timely assistance for which I am deeply grateful.

ONE

The Splendid Common Domicile

The Venetian Subject

For a short period during the late nineteenth and early twentieth centuries American artists painted, etched, and drew thousands of views of Venice. The subject of those views, or interpretations as they may more accurately be termed, is Venice's architecture, its open spaces, and, occasionally, its populace. The sheer volume of these images, the considerable number of artists attracted by the subject, and the extraordinary quality of their work prompt questions concerning the meaning of this interest and the significance of these works. While these images portray a topographical reality, they also incorporate an interpretation of Venice's mytho-historic past and appear to point, indirectly, to an interpretation of (or at least an interrogation of) the artists' own contemporary age.

There was no Venetian subject in American art during the eighteenth or the early nineteenth century, and there is very little one could call a Venetian subject in American art of the post–World War I years of the present century. These images, then, constitute a finite set, a broad, deep, and wide-ranging group of works, but a set nevertheless bounded by the cultural concerns, aesthetic energies, and market forces of a discrete era. As such they offer us two opportunities: a window on the larger subject of the meaning of Europe to Americans, and a case study in deciphering modes or methods of artistic presentation and interpretation. In both directions—that leading to cultural history and that leading to art history—any analysis of the period 1860–1915 marks a path both complex and eventful. On the one hand we are presented with a particularly rich episode in the ongoing saga of the relationship between American and European culture—a saga better understood as mutual exchange, education, discovery, and rediscovery than as a linear and charged "developmental" account of dependence and independence—and on the other, a critical moment in the introspective artistic dialogue concerning the nature and meaning of picture making.

As landscape painting rose in significance during the nineteenth century, supplanting the primacy and absorbing many of the attributes of history painting, the subgenre of cityscape rose also in importance and saleability. Although the best known American landscapes of this period record the semiprimeval wilderness zones of the American continent, scenes of the Old World, both urban and rural, were recorded in great numbers. To some extent these latter works have been passively and actively suppressed by subsequent generations purchasing pictures and writing histories with nationalistic enthusiasms and an embarrassed eye toward the concept of indebtedness to European roots. But it is clear that during the late nineteenth-century period, rival mythologies of frontier innocence and European experience often stared at each other across the expanse of an urban parlor, reflecting the owner's easiness with both visions as mythic, as alternatives to and as explications of his or her own nonrural, non-European quotidian experience.

The American enthusiasm for images of Venice is not explicable by any easy reference to the influence of John Ruskin (*The Stones of Venice,* 1851–53) or Lord Byron (*Marino Faliero,* 1820, *The Two Foscari,* 1821, and canto 4 of *Childe Harold's Pilgrimage*, 1818). It seems to be one aspect of a deep interest in exploration of the past, and especially those aspects of the past that were seemingly absent from (or antithetical to) contemporary American political, moral, and aesthetic life. Venice, seemingly frozen in historical time, provided an alternative point of view, one remote in time, place, topography, and culture. Effectively shut down as a society and washed by tourists as by the sea since the eighteenth century, Venice seemed to offer literal transposition of its visitors into an unreal semitheatrical world. That this aquatic city was seen as an arena of discovery and of self-discovery as potent as the pristine natural world of western mountains (so much more familiar to us in painterly, literary, and historical accounts of exploration) is made clear by the works themselves. It is important to note that the interest in things Venetian confined itself, aesthetically speaking, to paintings and works of fiction. Surprisingly few structures built during this era of literal architectural imitation used Venetian models.[1] Apparently these three-dimensional realizations reached too far beyond the fictive, intruding with strained theatricality into the fabric of American reality.

In practical market terms, the European subject in general and the Venetian subject in particular were products of a distinct cultural aura. George Inness, Jr., records a trend as well as a biographical fact in his brief account of the reasons for his father's long sojourn abroad: "Concluding that foreign subjects would be more saleable than domestic ones, Williams and Everett [Boston art dealers] induced my father to go abroad, agreeing to take his pictures at stated sums. So in the spring of 1870 we sailed for the Old World."[2] Many artists, sensing the meager marketability of "domestic," or local, subjects, went both east to Europe (that scene of centuries of human history surviving and experienceable in architecture) and west to panoramas of natural history (dramatized and popularized by the work of John C. Fremont, Francis Parkman, Jr., and Alexander von Humboldt). That contemporaries could perceive analogies between these two subjects is suggested by the naming of natural phenomena with architectural terminology and the abstracted use of those terms in such titles as Albert Bierstadt's *Domes of the Yosemite.*[3] Here the evocative terminology of grand religious architecture is synthesized with the extraordinary evidence of aeons of titanic natural forces. The two histories, natural and human, both readable in the surviving stones, are yoked together and interpreted in terms of each other. "In fact," Bierstadt wrote as early as 1859, shortly after his first western painting expedition, "we have here [in the natural scenery of the West] the Italy of America in primitive condition."[4]

The domes of Venice, unlike those of Yosemite or those of other European cities, were sited in a unique environment which made the city an eccentric subject even within the canon of European sites. The distinctiveness of Venice as an artistic subject lay in the unusually uneventful nature of its natural environment. No massing of trees, no fallen trunks, no rolling hills, winding roads, or robust mountains could set off its man-made elements. Only sky, water, structure, and people were available to the artist as subjects or combinations of subjects. This elementary, restricted vocabulary of forms was to some artists an insurmountable handicap. "Tree" landscape painters such as George Inness and "mountain" landscape painters such as Thomas Moran had great difficulty with pictorial organization in Venice. Nor was the restriction one of vocabulary only. The lack of an expanse of land meant that aerial perspective as a pictorial device was largely unavailable to the artist. Some artists, such as James McNeill Whistler—who had no dependency on these natural forms or organizational devices to shed—blossomed as landscapists in Venice.

It is perhaps surprising that given the narrow range of possible pictorial events most artists of this period voluntarily eliminated one of these principal pictorial ingredients—human figures. One of the possible reasons for this retreat lies in the extraordinary potency of structure. Architecture and architectural space are human in their creation, and we tend to read them even more than landscape elements as human surrogates. They are containers of human expression as well as vessels of human experience. And in Venice where the primary dialogue was with the past—best represented in its aged and palpable stones—the contemporary population (both tourist and native) was either irrelevant or useful only as antithesis.

Venice was not, of course, a uniquely American subject. During the second half of the nineteenth century Spanish, French, English, and German artists also flocked to the city. Many of their works have much in common with those of American painters, for they too were intensely interested in the investigation and analysis of the past. But one group of American paintings of Venice—that which I have termed ironic—appears to have no European counterpart and points directly to distinctly American concerns. What Venice offered all of her observers was a personal glimpse of the past in a rapidly modernizing world. What these paintings, taken together, offer us is a "case" as Henry James would put it, an instance, of wider movements and issues. The responses of each of these artists differed, but the fact of willful confrontation with historic presences is a constant, interesting in itself.

There are reasons why Venice makes an especially good case, why it serves as a readable touchstone or index of artistic and cultural developments better than other places. More than any other principal city of Europe, the city we see today is the Venice that John Singer Sargent (1856–1925), James McNeill Whistler (1834–1903), Maurice Prendergast (1859–1924), Henry James (1843–1916), and their contemporaries experienced. The water level has risen, the physical fabric of the city has been ravaged by external forces, a very few new buildings have appeared, but no new construction or razing has changed the scale or shape of the principal buildings or spaces. No new boulevards, ring roads, office towers, or overhead utility lines alter our experience of the city. Even the lampposts have remained unchanged. The Victorian artists in their turn could have looked on Venice's past and felt that—with the notable exceptions of Napoleon's creation of the vast public gardens and the noisome speed of the vaporetti—the city they experienced had been largely unaltered since the sixteenth century. Part of the attraction and significance of Venice, it seems, was as much in this mere fact of miraculous frozen preservation as in the physical facts and spaces so preserved.

Venice is a masonry city. It is built of brick and faced with marble and stucco. Its building began—for our purposes—in the ninth century and was essentially complete by the early seventeenth (with the important addition of the Church of Santa Maria della Salute in the late seventeenth century). It is built on islands, but from most waterborne vantage points there is no sense of island or land at all. As abruptly as cliffs plunging into Norwegian fjords, the architectural facades meet navigable waters. The character of this shift in medium, unmitigated by beach or walkway, is distinctly Venetian. In contrast to the pedestrian scale of Amsterdam which is the result as much of its canalside two-person-wide walkways as of its architectural proportions and features, Venice's scale is unpedestrian. Size, including the architecturally projected image of the human frame, is dictated by space and structure alone. Because the buildings hug the canal edges and abut snugly upon one another, the interior open spaces in the islands, the campi, have the character of completely man-made interior spaces. With no distant horizon filled with hills or orchards or fields to dispel the illusion, these flagstone spaces seem roomlike, rooms for giants but rooms nevertheless. Many have remarked upon this architectural inversion, this interior aspect of exterior space, especially in the Piazza San Marco. Henry James describes that enormous "room" as "a great social saloon, a smooth-floored, blue-roofed chamber of amenity" and a "splendid common domicile."[5] Scale, it seems, is a more fluid commodity in Venice than in most cities, more susceptible to arbitrary arrangement and treatment. Painters were particularly sensitive to this aspect of the city.

The principal civic space—the primary stalking ground of these artists and the space that will centrally concern us here—is indicated in figure 1, a detail of an 1847 Venetian map.[6] It is comprised of ecclesiastical, administrative, residential, and civic buildings. The oldest structure is the ducal chapel, San Marco, with its five swelling domes (*A*). Like many churches in Venice and unlike the principal palaces, it fronts on land, that is, on a piazza rather than on water. Its approach is marked by three enormous sixteenth-century flagpoles. To the south is the Ducal Palace (*B*), Gothic on its two principal facades. Its third facade, that facing the Rio di Palazzo della Paglia, was constructed during the Renaissance period as were the prisons (*C*) and the Bridge of Sighs (*D*) which connects these two prominent structures. The Procuratie Vecchie and the Procuratie Nuove which enclose the Piazza San Marco on the north and south sides were built primarily in the sixteenth and seventeenth centuries (the short western end dates from the Napoleonic period). Their handsome arcades shelter pedestrians equally from sun and rain. A fifteenth-century clock tower (*E*) punctuates the skyline in the northeastern corner of the Piazza and establishes a north-south axis with the Piazzetta. The tallest and most striking landmark from a distance is the 324-foot-high Campanile (*F*). The brick tower capped by a gilded copper roof which appears in most of these images is the sixteenth-century original; it collapsed in 1902 and was completely rebuilt by 1912. Few images record this central area or this distinctive skyline without its commanding presence. The serenely Renaissance Libreria Vecchia (*G*), designed by Jacopo Tatti, called Sansovino (1486–1570), frames the Piazzetta and forms the second portal to this huge civic "room." Two massive granite columns serve to dignify this entrance. The westernmost is surmounted by a statue of Saint Theodore standing on a crocodile (*H*). He faces landward, as does the bronze winged lion of Saint Mark on the other pillar (*I*).

The Molo, a grand paved dock fronting the Bacino di San Marco (see figs. 2 and 3), is linked

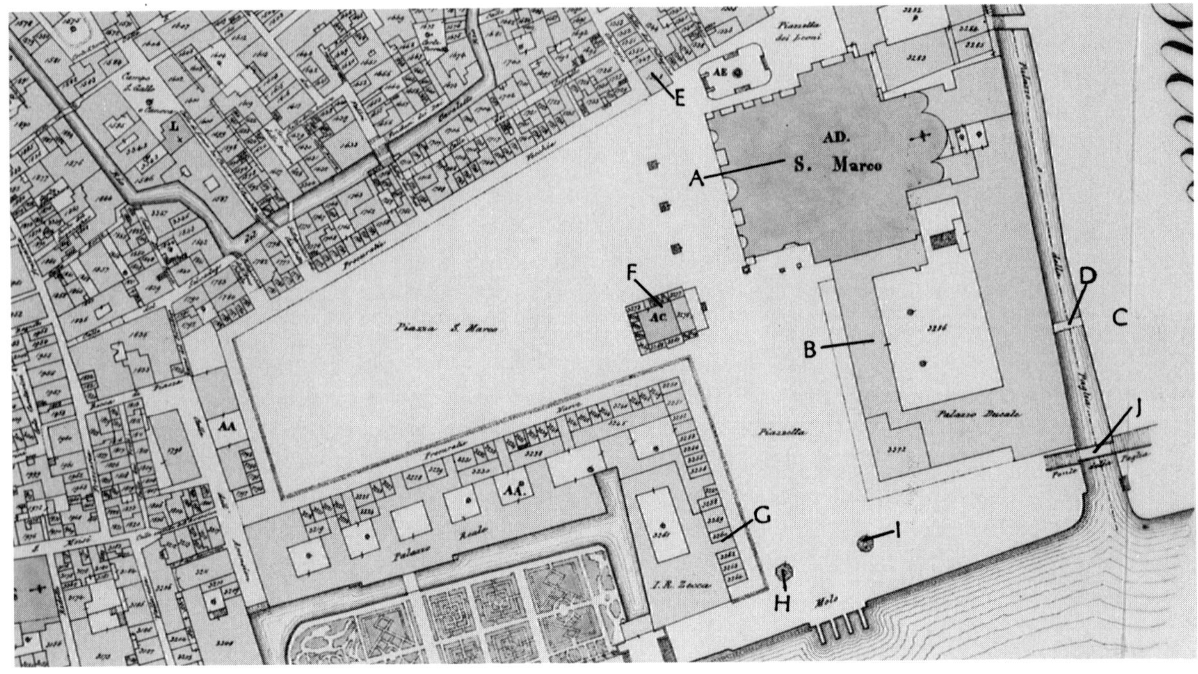

A. Church of San Marco
B. Ducal Palace
C. Prisons
D. Bridge of Sighs
E. Clock Tower

F. Campanile
G. Libreria Vecchia
H. Saint Theodore pillar
I. Winged Lion of Saint Mark pillar
J. Ponte della Paglia

Fig. 1. Map of Piazza San Marco, Piazzetta, and principal structures, from *Mappa del Comune Censuario di dorsoduro porzione della città di Venezia . . . 1847*, Yale University Map Collection, New Haven, Connecticut.

with its broad eastward extentions (the Riva degli Schiavoni, the Riva di Cà di Dio, the Riva San Biagio, and the Riva dei Sette Martiri) by a series of white marble bridges. The first bridge, the Ponte della Paglia (*J*), stands close to the Ducal Palace and parallel to the Bridge of Sighs. From the Molo one sees in the middle distance to the south the island church of San Giorgio Maggiore (*K*), designed by Andrea Palladio (1508–80), with its attendant monastery buildings and imposing campanile. In the far distance to the southwest is a second Palladian church, Il Redentore (*L*), on the Giudecca. To the west one sees the buildings of the Customs House on the Punta della Dogana and, just beyond, the exuberant baroque church of Santa Maria della Salute (M; Baldassare Longhena, 1598–1682), its multiple white domes marking the entrance to the Grand Canal. This canal bisects Venice and is the site of its principal palaces. It is crossed by three large bridges, the new Accademia and Railway Station bridges (built in 1854 and 1858 respectively) and the sixteenth-century Rialto.

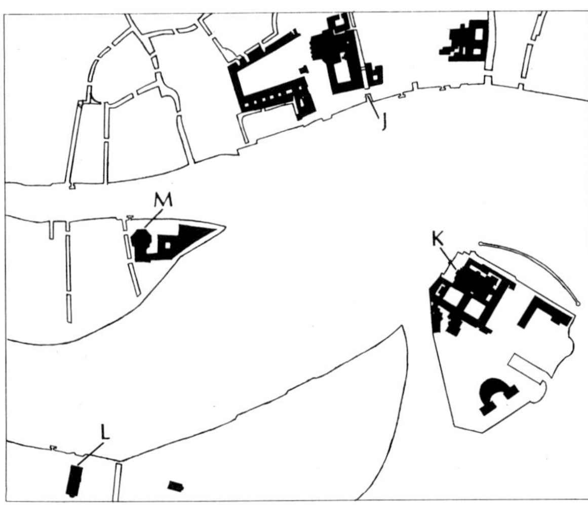

J. Ponte della Paglia
K. San Giorgio Maggiore, Andrea Palladio
L. Il Redentore, Andrea Palladio
M. Santa Maria della Salute, Baldassare Longhena

Fig. 2. Map of Venice with principal churches visible from the Molo indicated.

Each of these structures was studied and interpreted, mapped and imaged repeatedly throughout the nineteenth century. The salient features and relationships of these monuments were preknown to visitors through descriptions, photographs, paintings, and prints, so that the novice's experience of these public spaces in Venice had as much the character of a familiar scene reconfirmed as of a remote novelty to be mastered. During the decade of the 1880s, the peak of picture making in Venice when more than a hundred foreign artists were active in the city, Venetians must have come upon painters—with campstools, easels, and white umbrellas—perched in every corner of this celebrated civic space. Curiously, few artists—even during this era noted for its introspective paintings of picture making—captured images of their counterparts engaged in the act of interpreting the city.[7] Most eschewed the inclusion of figures altogether and riveted their attention on the immediate subject of urban structure and their ultimate subject—the past.

Modes

The fact that so many artists descended on Venice during that relatively brief period, setting themselves the task of interpreting the same richly associative and well-known visual "texts," provides us with a wide-ranging group of images. In this we are presented with an opportunity for locating meaning not only in individual achievement but also in a vast array of relationships—relationships between the work of contemporaries, between nineteenth-century artists and their predecessors, between nineteenth-century images and the city they record, and between artists and their cultural context. The project of building a model of these relationships, of mapping them, as it were, in three dimensions, challenges traditional art historical approaches. Neither monographic issues, nor a focus on primacy ("firstness"), nor even the larger theoretical patterns developed by the founding fathers of the discipline, seem well tooled for this enterprise.

The life-and-works approach abstracts the individual artist from his milieu except at those points when temporal event, physical accident, and psychological perception are interpreted as causative. The attempt in most monographs is to see the "cause" of art in the sequential events of a life and to string these events on a chronological thread, an attempt that necessarily sacrifices the complexity of fact, event, and causation inherent in a synchronic view of the same moments of achievement and treats with a certain willed innocence the post-Freudian model of the human mind. And while its subtext—the issue of primacy—definitely links the monographed artist to his counterparts, its focus on the critical valuation who-did-what-first endangers the enterprise of locating an interpretation of how and why artists, as a group, find meaning in certain genres, subjects, techniques, and metaphors. Primacy—the belief that the most important aspect of an object is its order of creation—has acquired a kind of sacredness in art historical studies, privileging and heroicizing the eponym at the expense of overall pattern, and in this enterprise it follows the lead of the influential (and market-oriented) systematizer Bernard Berenson, overlooking the significant critiques of his contemporary Leo Tolstoy and of our contemporary Fernand Braudel.

Perhaps the most eloquent theoretician of the relationship between invention and convention, that issue at the core of monographs, surveys, and period studies in art history, is George Kubler. In *The Shape of Time* he suggests a model of art historical development centering on the concept of a prime object, an artwork of ingenious originality that affects the universe of objects like a pebble thrown into a still pond; the ripples represent successive dilutions of the central idea.[8] This model of art historical occurrence is extremely useful but presents two difficulties. In its postromantic Western bias toward the individual and toward the original, the powerful reactionary tug of images and objects toward generic, nearly anonymous, crystallizations of known forms (a tendency perhaps best exemplified in the long history of Asian art) is de-emphasized and de-valued. Secondly, when oversimplified, the model appears to imply the isolation of art historical incident from its larger culture, explaining an object and finding its causes in prior visual incidents. The difficulty here is that the object is perceived in terms of mimicry and its study focuses on the discovery and retrieval of precedent.

While it is probable that an artwork is not caused by its precedents (as Shakespeare's *Othello* cannot be said to be caused by Giraldi Cinthio's *Hecatommithi*), it can be made possible, or as Harold Bloom might maintain, impossible, by its precedents.[9] The nature of the relationship, whether one of identity, or denial, or rivalry, is more complex than it is often perceived to be. Bloom would see in Kubler's ripples not only weak poets (or artists) but also the struggling presence of the belated strong poet who must come to terms, in an elaborate aesthetic psychodrama, with the predecessor. Mimicry is not his strategy, but rather he engages in a kind of aggressive evasion. Kubler and Bloom both devise

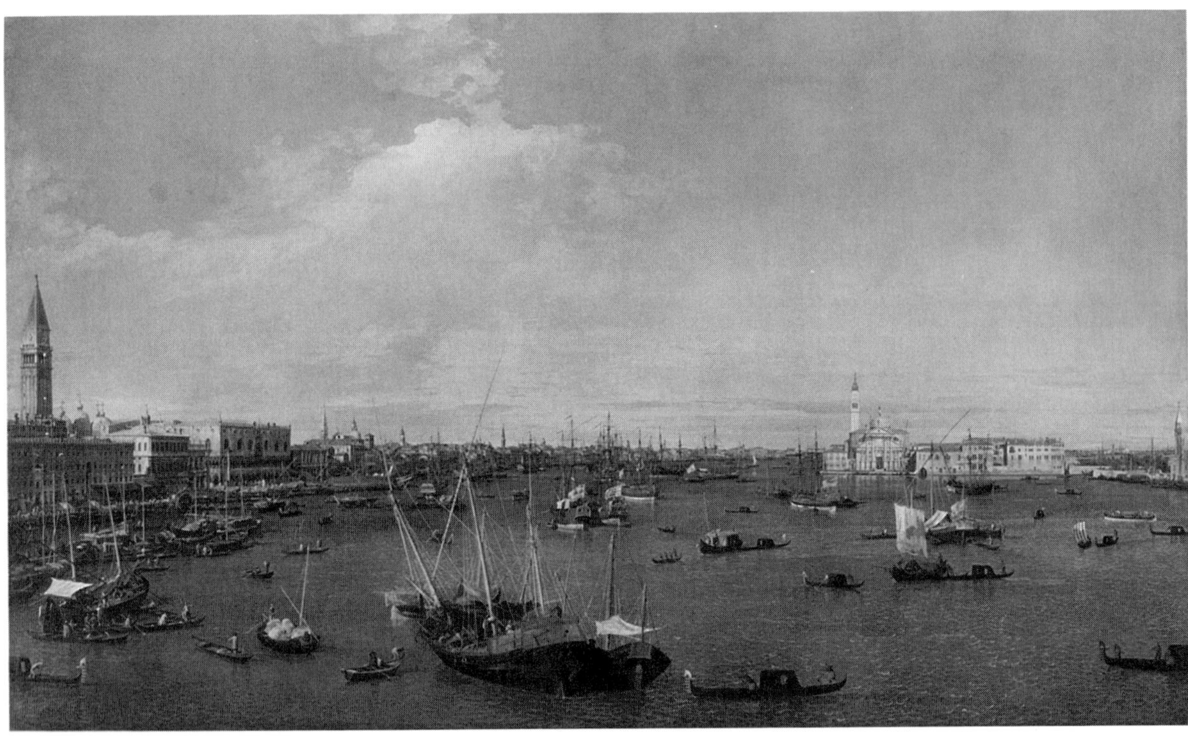

Fig. 3. Canaletto [Giovanni Antonio Canal], *Bacino di San Marco, Venice*, 1745, oil on canvas, 49″ × 80 ½″, Museum of Fine Arts, Boston, Abbott Lawrence Fund, Seth K. Sweetser Fund, and Charles Edward French Fund.

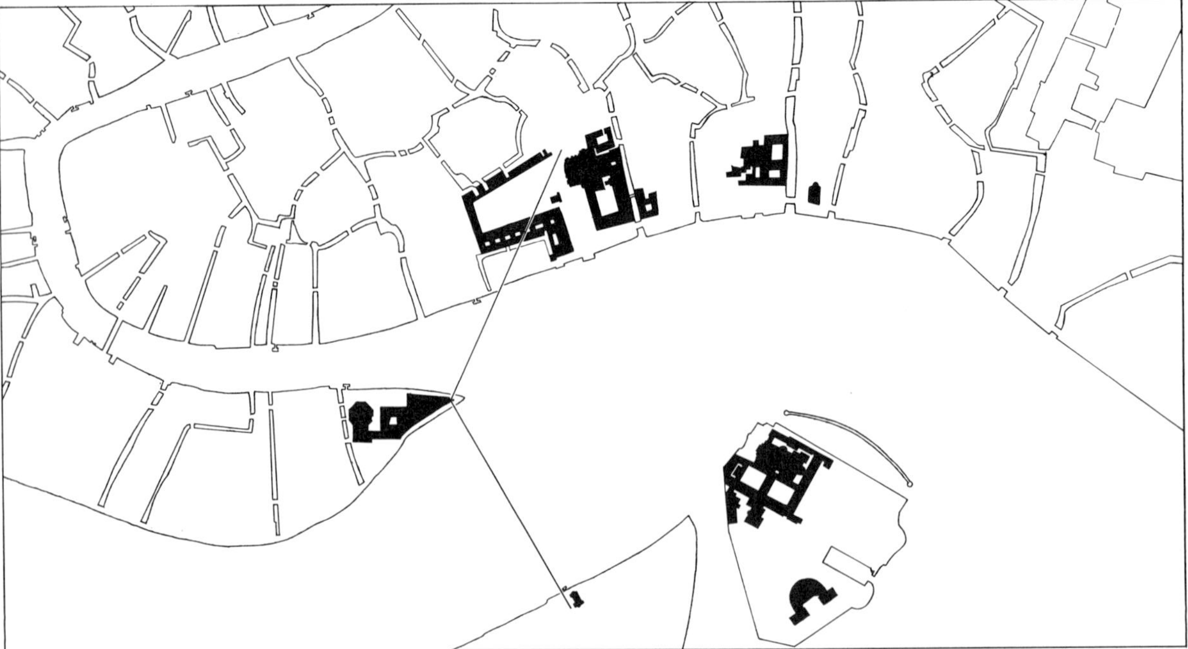

Fig. 4. Cone of vision in Canaletto, *Bacino di San Marco, Venice* (fig. 3).

and abstract general principles from specific occurrences, they speak to relationships that they see as essential and recurrent. And while both imply a temporal armature, neither imbeds his elegant analysis of works or principles in a broadly historical or cultural warp and weft.

Of the influential art historians who have stepped back to view both overall pattern and underlying structure few have done so as impressively as Heinrich Wölfflin in *Principles of Art History* (1915), a study in which he sets out to establish and articulate fixed laws of expression and development in the evolution of Western forms. Wölfflin does so using the dynamic polarities of northern (linear) and southern (painterly) art—reminding us that he was of the generation of Thomas Mann—weaving a binary pattern in which "epoch and race interact."[10] He moves swiftly beyond Berensonian connoisseurship into the analysis of meaning in style, shifting the ground of art historical taxonomy. While his paradigm works especially well with the set texts of the discipline painted, built, and sculpted during the fifteenth through the seventeenth centuries, it falters as a tool of explication and analysis when applied to art since 1870. For Wölfflin the locus of differentiation and discrimination is in the art product; the object itself has certain fixed qualities. A larger analytical structure that would take into account not only the character of the object but also the projected persona of the perceiver would be more versatile, more useful, especially in our consideration of the art and design of the last century.

If we are to read artworks with an eye on culture it seems useful to look beyond monographic fallacies and Kublerian prime objects, to look at artists and artworks not singularly but in groups, observing them work out telling and similar problems. But by focusing not only on Wölfflinian issues of technical rendering but also on point of view (to literalize a term that is usually used metaphorically), another dimension can be added to our understanding and analysis of images. Point of view encompasses several disparate but related elements: the viewer's vantage point, that point above the ground plane from which the scene is viewed, the location of the horizon line within the picture, and lastly, the distance and the cone of vision between the artist's eye and the perceived objects. Of these elements, the last—that which I term the cone of vision—appears to be especially significant. The cone's tip is the perceiver's eye, its direction is horizontal, or directed somewhat up or down, and its field includes everything in its path at whatever depth. Its artificial nature is underlined by the fact that while it mimics natural vision, the cone is usually conventionalized by painters as a crisply four-sided pyramid, usually horizontal in format (echoing our greater lateral than vertical vision), in which precise focus is available throughout the field. In his selection of a vantage point and a cone of vision the artist places himself (and his painting's perceiver) both figuratively and literally in a distinct and readable relation to the world before him—a relation that has meaning in itself.

Painted landscape and cityscape views, even those that appear topographically faithful, are, of course, not only conventionalized imitations of the act of sight but also fictions in terms of their subjects. Each is necessarily an interpretation, a fictive manipulation of elements present before the canvas. The nature and configuration of this manipulation is guided by attitudes (not necessarily conscious or articulated) present in the artist's mind. And a careful reading of these images through close attention to pictorial elements—point of view, subject, composition, medium, technique, and scale—can suggest a reading or an interpretation of these culturally as well as personally eloquent attitudes and premises.

The matrix of meaning, then, includes the observer (who views and interprets the image), the protagonist (that persona with which the artist has endowed the viewer on the one hand and the primary pictured subject on the other), and the subject (those resonant architectural, meteorological, and human elements included, arranged, and rendered for specific effect). Taken together in symptomatic clusters, these characteristics follow distinct patterns, or to borrow a term from Northrop Frye, modes. While Frye, in his seminal essay "Historical Criticism: Theory of Modes," was theorizing about literature, not pictures, the two fictive enterprises—the pictorial and the literary—have much in common and his perceptions are pertinent to the central question here: how did Americans perceive and interpret Venice, or to phrase the question differently, how do these artists construct meaning in these images and in this context?[11] Frye focuses his discussion on the relationship of the protagonist to other characters and to the laws of nature. If we take for the pictorial protagonist the architectural subject about which the artist arranges his image, an apt analogue in pictorial terms is possible. For instance, the central actor in the *Bacino di San Marco, Venice* (figs. 3, 4) by Canaletto (Giovanni Antonio Canal, 1697–1768, Italian)—to take a familiar image—is the prosperous, architecturally framed Bacino. The relationship between the imaged interpretation of this key waterway and the laws of nature on the one hand, and the surrounding structures, natural elements, and people on the other hand, has an analogue in the relationship between a hero, his fellow characters, and the rules of the natural world which they inhabit. Beyond this there is a distinct parallel between the literary authorial voice and the painterly point of view. Canaletto, for instance, in this painting takes the voice and prospect of the omniscient narrator.

Specifically, Frye posits five sorts of fictions, classified according to the hero's power.

> 1. If superior in *kind* both to other men and to the environment of other men, the hero is a divine being, and the story about him will be a *myth*. . . .
>
> 2. If superior in *degree* to other men and to his environment, the hero is the typical hero of *romance*, whose actions are marvelous but who is himself identified as a human being. The hero of romance moves in a world in which the ordinary laws of nature are slightly suspended: prodigies of courage and endurance, unnatural to us, are natural to him . . . enchanted weapons, talking animals . . . violate no rule of probability once the postulates of romance have been established. . . .
>
> 3. If superior in degree to other men but not to his natural environment, the hero is a leader. . . . This is the hero of the *high mimetic* mode, of most epic and tragedy.
>
> 4. If superior neither to other men nor to his environment, the hero is one of us: we respond to a sense of his common humanity. . . . This gives us the hero of the *low mimetic* mode, of most comedy and of realistic fiction. . . . On this level the difficulty in retaining the word "hero" . . . occasionally strikes the author. . . .
>
> 5. If inferior in power or intelligence to ourselves so that we have the sense of looking down on a scene of bondage, frustration, or absurdity, the hero belongs to the *ironic* mode. This is still true when the reader feels that he is or might be in the same situation, as the situation is being judged by the norms of a greater freedom.[12]

Frye immediately adds a temporal dimension to his analysis: "Looking over this table, we can see that European fiction, during the last fifteen centuries, has steadily moved its center of gravity down the list" (p. 34). It might be argued that painting has also clearly "moved its center of gravity" in a similar progression, but for the purposes of the present study, encompassing a much more modest slice of time, we will temporarily lay aside developmental questions and consider our period as a synchronic whole. Frye makes it clear that these modes often overlap, and hybrid genres exist such as those in which "it is hardly possible to separate the mythical, romantic and high mimetic strands" (p. 35). However, in most cases the genus to which a work belongs can clearly be understood. In the body of material investigated in this study, a pattern of images analogous to several of Frye's modes is discernible, archaic forms (high mimetic and romantic) coexisting with the low mimetic which Frye takes to be the dominant voice of this late nineteenth-century period, and a few examples of the ironic mode which Frye identifies with serious fiction of the twentieth century.

While different modes exist simultaneously, each period has a dominant mode exerting a kind of pressure on the fiction maker in terms of his or her choice of mode. The mode is simply a specific aesthetic expression of general habits of structuring real and representational experience, habits broadly, even unconsciously, expressive of cultural environment. It is consistent with the artist's model of how social, physical, and political reality works or should work. An artist works in one mode or another not just because of accidents of training, exposure, or free invention but because it is consistent with an unstated, even unexamined, personal and cultural point of view. That these unconscious mental scaffolds exist, that they are limited in number, and that they are, with effort, discoverable and articulatable is the premise of such modern observers of culture as Claude Lévi-Strauss: "If, as we believe to be the case, the unconscious activity of the mind consists in imposing forms upon content, and if these forms are fundamentally the same for all minds—ancient and modern, primitive and civilized (as the study of the symbolic function, expressed in language, so strikingly indicates)—it is necessary and sufficient to grasp the unconscious structure underlying each institution and each custom." For him, the scholar's "goal is to grasp, beyond the conscious and always shifting images which men hold, the complete range of unconscious possibilities. These are not unlimited, and the relationships of compatibility or incompatibility which each maintains with all the others provide a logical framework for historical developments, which, while perhaps unpredictable, are never arbitrary."[13] As the mind is consistently a pattern maker, then each custom, institution, or, one might add, mode has its own structure, its own rules, assumptions, and power, and these frameworks are discoverable and meaningful. From this perspective, the analysis of fictions, of course, becomes an indirect analysis of mental realities.

During the period that Venice was a subject of interest to Americans, the dominant mode was low mimetic but, reflecting and expressing the fundamentally unhomogeneous character of Western thought during the late nineteenth century, other modes were also simultaneously evident and significant in the productions of these artists. The spectrum of types of interpretations of the city is extremely wide, more various than seems at first apparent or than we would—given even a good acquaintance with late nineteenth-century America on the one hand and Venice on the other—easily imagine. This lack of consensus about how to look at Venice gives us our subject.

Of the five modal categories, only the first, the mythic, is absent from our pictures. In a broader sense, there is a mythic (that is, god-story) ingredient in all these images because they deal with a protagonist, Venice, which is often taken to be superior in kind to (or at least exotically remote from) other cities and to the laws of nature. However, myth here does not constitute a differentiating mode.

Frye's second category, romance, does have a translatable counterpart in such a work as *View of Venice* (fig. 5) by Thomas Moran (1837–1926).[14] It is clearly a "world in which the ordinary laws of nature are slightly suspended," as the Salute on the left is seen from an entirely different prospect than is the Doge's Palace and Campanile on the right (fig. 6). Consistent with the characteristics of romance the lighting and color effects are heightened, the time of day is transitional (in this case sunset), and the tone is one of pleasurable pathos. Images in this category will be discussed with epic, as they belong less to pure romance than to what Frye calls a "sentimental" or "later recreation of an earlier mode," and thus incorporate intermediary epic elements. Our discussion, then, with the exclusion of the mythic mode and with the inclusion of romance parenthetically (in its "later recreation" romantic form) within the high mimetic, will be limited to three modes: high mimetic (including romantic works as a subcategory), low mimetic, and ironic.

High mimetic or epic fiction concerns a protagonist of a higher order than ourselves but one which is subject to the order of nature. Returning to the Canaletto *Bacino* briefly, it is useful to note the characteristics of the epic mode which it exemplifies. The viewer's vantage point is high, in this case thirty to forty feet above the water level. The cone of vision (fig. 4) is broad (about 135 degrees), and the format is a stable horizontal rectangle. The buildings and spaces included are recognizable and monumental. An oblique view of the Ducal Palace and a fully frontal portrait of San Giorgio Maggiore frame the busy Bacino and the arc of the Riva sweeping into the distance. The lateral edges are clearly demarcated by the imposing Campanile San Marco on the left and the more modest campanile of Le Zitelli on the Giudecca to the extreme right. Weather conditions are benevolent. Our high vantage point emphasizes the comprehensibility of the prospect, aids in the recognition of its monuments, and projects a sense of well-ordered, comprehensible social order. The viewer, especially in these epic views, begins to take onto himself some of the characteristics of the field surveyed. This empathetic appropriation or identification with the fictive character is not unlike that of a viewer of Shakespeare's history plays; one feels oneself to be walking socially (and perhaps intellectually) on stilts. Surely the viewer here is superhuman; he is taller than any human and the breadth of his vision is extraordinary. He becomes a second protagonist himself. He can in fact only be a Titan or a building.

In the low mimetic mode Frye reminds us that "we respond to a sense of his [the protagonist's] common humanity, and demand from the poet the same canons of probability that we find in our own experience." Low mimetic images constitute the majority of those made of Venice during this period; literally hundreds survive. The form invites invention, and as we would expect, there are a wide variety of subtypes within the larger type de-

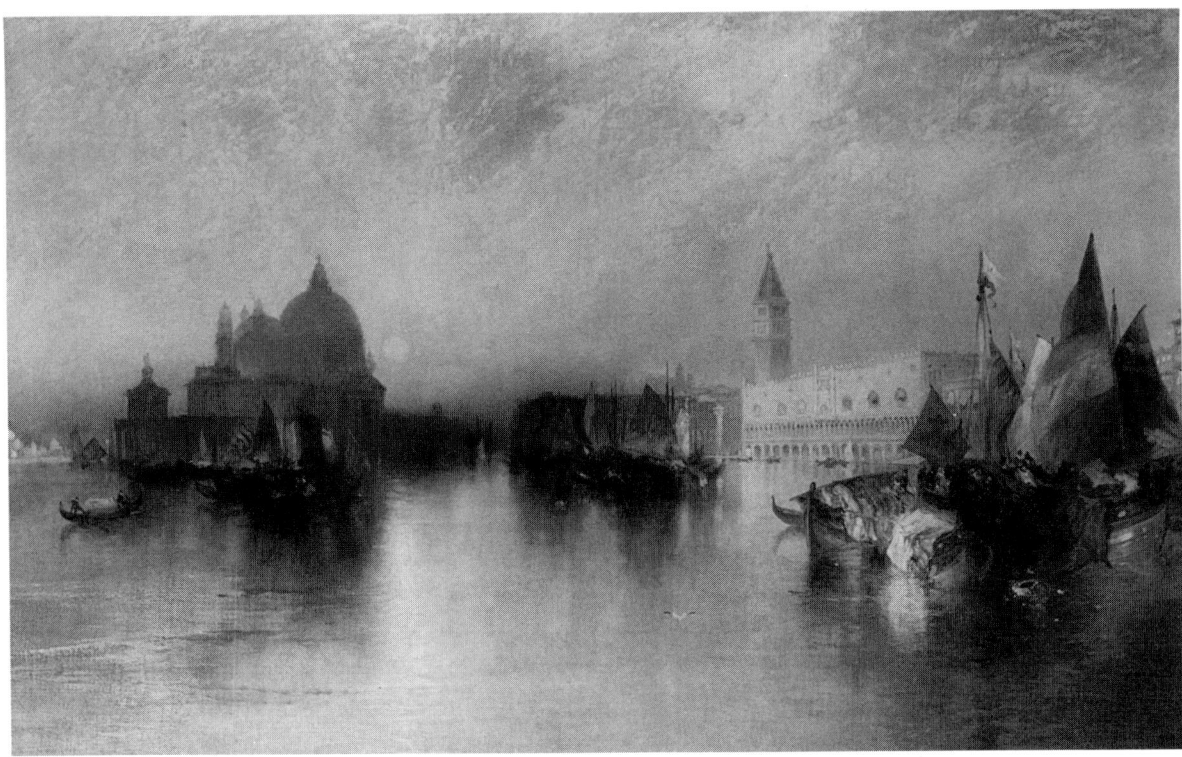

Fig. 5. Thomas Moran, *View of Venice*, 1895, oil on canvas, 16½″ × 26½″, Wellesley College Museum, Wellesley, Massachusetts.

fined by subject and point of view. Many of the principal characteristics of the low mimetic form are evident in an etching *The Doorway* (fig. 7) by Whistler.[15] Unlike the epic Canaletto, this image is small in size (11⅝″ × 8″) and modest in medium. The widespread use of etching, watercolor, and pastels during this period can be seen as a discovery of the versatile nature of these minor media, and as one aspect of a general retreat from the monumentality associated with oils.[16] Whistler's cone of vision in *The Doorway* is narrow and invites a vertical format, giving the image a sense of confinement and concentration. The point of view is low and entirely human. The viewer seems to be seated or standing on an opposite threshold.[17] In terms of subject, recognizable monuments are studiously avoided in favor of an inconsequential human incident framed by an interesting and historic but unrecognizable architectural fragment. As Frye notes, there is some difficulty in using the term "hero" here. Other types of low mimetic images stress different aspects of the mode, but generally they are modest with respect to scale and vantage point and often mimic spontaneity and informality

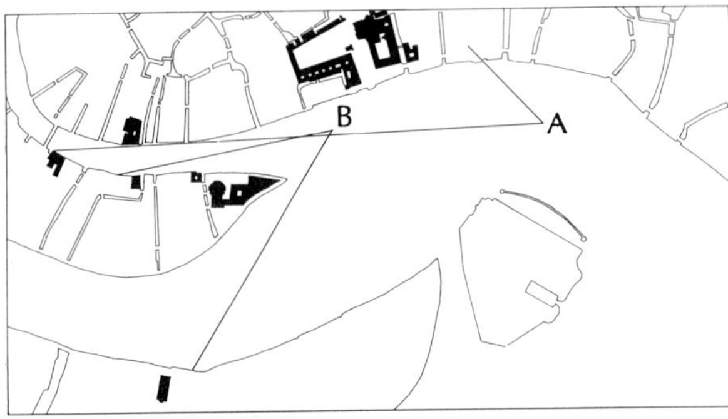

Fig. 6. Cones of vision in Thomas Moran, *View of Venice* (fig. 5).

in their technique. They rarely depend directly on a subject with ascribed value, trusting to art alone to create value from an inherently random, and valueless, slice of daily life.

The focus of this study is on meaningful differences, on the ways in which artists confirm and manipulate our modal expectations. These strategies are thrown into particularly high relief when the subject is Venice, a known "text" of acknowledged value. The character and significance of these

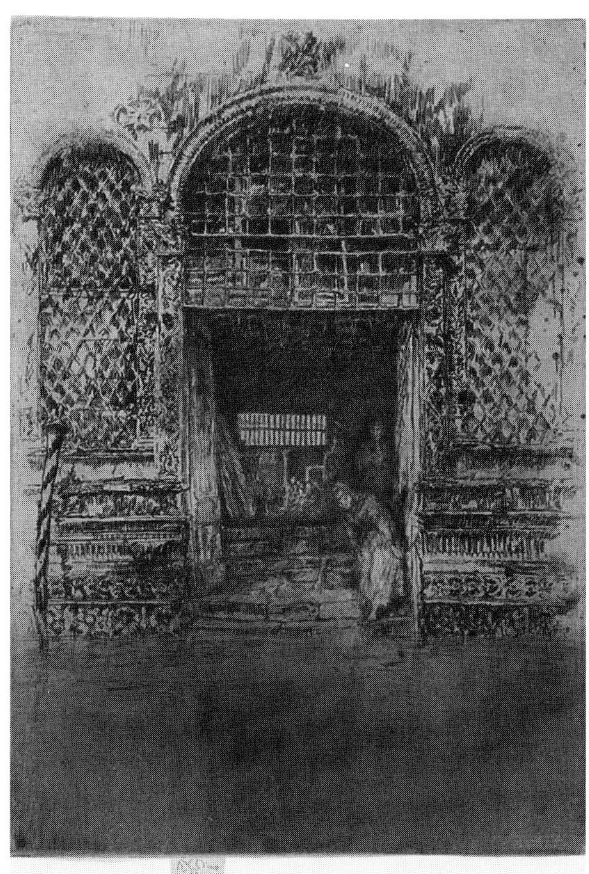

Fig. 7. James McNeill Whistler, *The Doorway*, 1879/80, etching, 11⅝" × 8¹⁄₁₆", Collection of Julius L. and Anita Zelman.

differences can be clarified by a brief look at three further examples of American works. *Venetian Scene (Palazzo Dario)* (fig. 8), by Joseph Lindon Smith (1863–1950) is a high mimetic (or as we may variously call it, epic) image of one of the best-known buildings in Venice, a gem of a palace located on a prominent reach of the Grand Canal (see fig. 37).[18] It is a concentrated "portrait" of the early Renaissance Palazzo Dario (ca. 1480), portrayed with its full inventory of clustered windows and entwining circles of colored marbles. While the observer's point of view is lower, more intimate than that in Canaletto's *Bacino,* the subject, nevertheless, retains its full dignity and identity. Just as the subject is identical with its title, the format of Smith's image mimics that of the structure. In fact, the building crowds the frame, filling it with intricate visual incident, and by this avoidance of juxtaposition with sea, sky, or taller buildings, gives it stature beyond its size, monumentalizing it. *The Cà d'Oro, Venice* (fig. 9) by Robert F. Blum (1857–1903) takes its name, like the Joseph Lindon Smith *Palazzo Dario,* from a notable palace on the Grand Canal, but unlike the Dario picture, here the artist does not confirm our knowledge about the appearance of the gaudy palace; he does not order his canvas around the shape of the building's facade (see fig. 10). Instead he cleaves the distinguished palace in half and insists that it share space, and hence be equated with, other structures and incidents. At the mouth of the alleyway (emphasized by its centrality and the vertical format of the image) four naked boys irreverently swim. The Cà d'Oro here is not the extraordinary timeless monument we expect. Instead it is a site for the unextraordinary in daily life. By shifting not so much the subject but the treatment of subject, by manipulating the cone of vision, Blum has created not only a different tone, but he has slid us, the audience, into a radically different mode. From the posture we feel ascribed to ourselves as protagonist-perceiver in the Smith image (heroic, dignified, and orderly), we feel altered to a vernacular, low mimetic self in the Blum—our attention is differ-

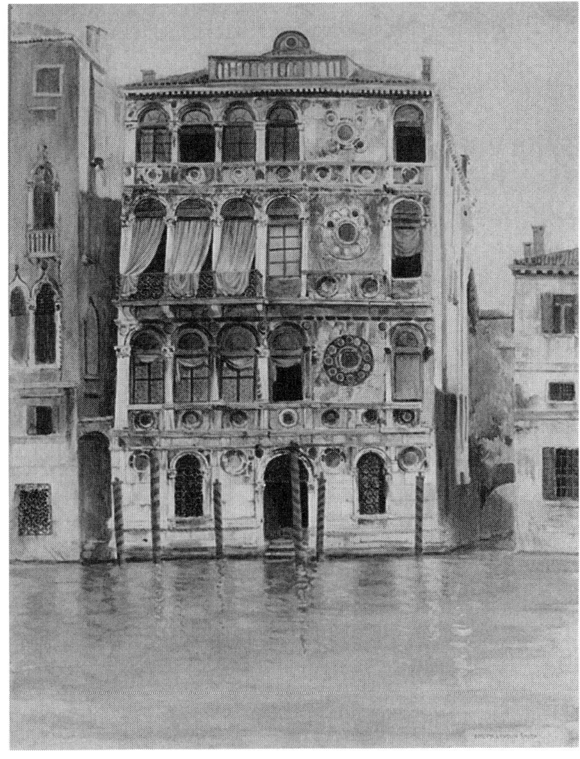

Fig. 8. Joseph Lindon Smith, *Venetian Scene (Palazzo Dario)*, ca. 1894, watercolor on paper, 19¼" × 14", Metropolitan Museum of Art, Gift of the Estate of Mrs. Edward Robinson, 1952; see also fig. 37.

ent, our sense of ourselves and of the external world of incident and history is different. Vision is not used to confirm the known, established, valued fact, but to explore, through random acts of sight, our commonality with quotidian experience *even* under the shadow of the monument.

Our final mode, the ironic, is characterized by a portrayal of the world as more absurd, disorienting, and fragmented than we sense it to be even though we "might be in the same situation, as the situation is being judged by the norms of a greater freedom." An image of Venice that suggests this ironic vision is Sargent's view of yet a third palace, the Palazzo Balbi, also on the Grand Canal, called *Doorway of a Venetian Palace* (fig. 11).[19] Our point of view is low, much lower than average human height, and visually we are disconcertingly, damply, in the water. The picture space is cramped; Brobdingnagian mooring posts and architectural openings seem entirely out of scale with our point of view. The building is seen at an oblique angle, gesturing toward a very different direction than that of our approach. Post and facade extend above our cone of vision, and we can only guess at their completed form.

When compared with the high mimetic *Palazzo Dario* (fig. 8) of Joseph Lindon Smith, and the low mimetic *Cà d'Oro* (fig. 9) of Robert F. Blum, the radical nature of *Doorway of a Venetian Palace* and its comment on the other two modes of palace viewing become apparent. The Palazzo Dario is seen frontally and completely, its dimensions dictating the format and frame of the picture; a careful inventory of its two-dimensional facade is given. In *The Cà d'Oro* the artist's eye had slid off the monument's facade, centering the image on an aperture, a zone of daily, ahistoric Venetian life. The palace is present and recognizable but sliced and yoked into a low mimetic world of alleys and naked boys. In Sargent's visually anonymous palace the juxtaposition that Blum labored to achieve between historic structure and present human incident is absent. The image is straightforward, objective, uninterpretive, and visually elegant; it is we ourselves and not any external actors who provide the eye and perspective of the naked swimmers. In a sense, ours is an ignorant eyeball, seeing only what it can see and knowing no more than it can perceive from an ordinary, even subordinary, perspective.

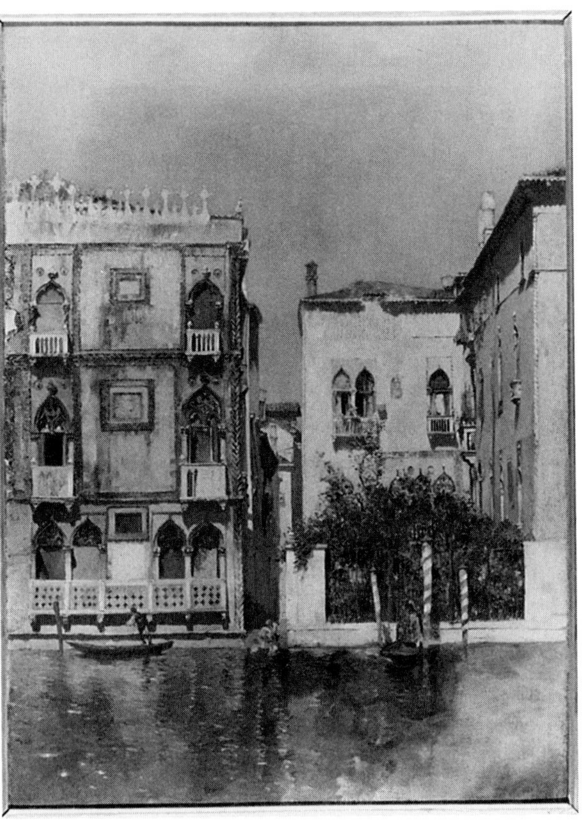

Fig. 9. Robert F. Blum, *The Cà d'Oro, Venice*, ca. 1880, oil on canvas, 26″ × 18¼″, collection unknown, formerly the Brooklyn Museum.

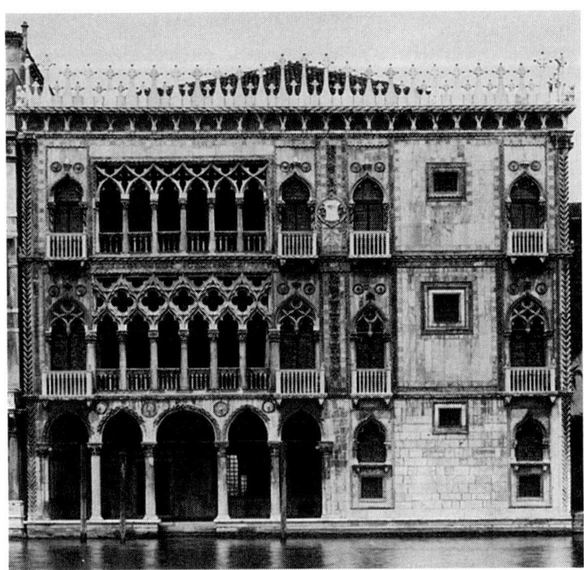

Fig. 10. *Cà d'Oro, Grand Canal* (before restoration), ca. 1900, photograph, Alinari/Art Resource.

This study is a focused analysis of specific groups of pictures in these three modes. Each has its own characteristic set of subjects, points of view, tone,

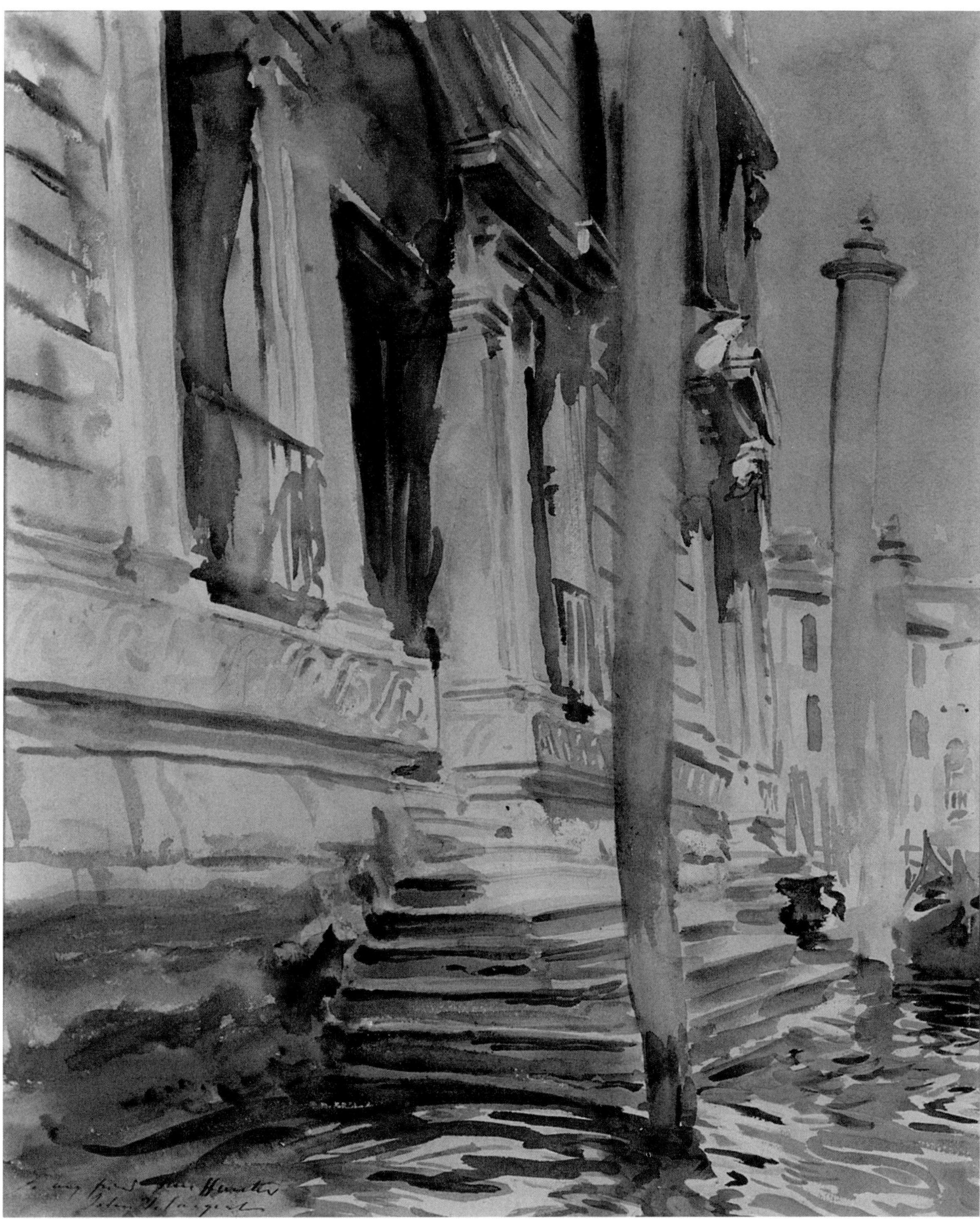

Fig. 11. John Singer Sargent, *Doorway of a Venetian Palace*, ca. 1906–10, watercolor, 23″ × 18″, Westmoreland Museum of Art, Greensburg, Pennsylvania.

and pictorial strategy. From this richly various record we can explore the what and how of American Venice-viewing and, by implication, investigate the possibilities of a modal reading of images on the one hand, and on the other, glimpse a shadow portrait of contemporary anxieties, postures, and desires concerning space, structure, social experience, and history.

TWO

Nobility and Hierarchy: The High Mimetic Mode

A Sense of Possession: The Venetians

Mimesis is, of course, the imitation of reality. This secondary, imitation reality, usually miniaturized or otherwise condensed and always organized, we usually term a fiction. All mimetic forms, then, are fictions, partly captured (reality mimicked) and partly invented (reality ordered, miniaturized, and given finite borders). The high mimetic mode captures and creates fictions within certain boundaries of human experience and imagination. In Frye's analysis, the "hero of the high mimetic mode, of most epic and tragedy" is "superior in degree to other men but not to his natural environment."[1] The heroic protagonist and his fellow characters have higher political and social power than is familiar to us in our own experience, but are, nevertheless, bound by natural physical laws. Their situation is made particularly acute and significant by their high station, and in this respect the artist is dealing with quantities of ascribed value—as a prince or a duke or Achilles or Saint Francis. Translated into pictorial terms, this means that in the high mimetic mode, the artist's representational effort centers around recognizable and significant subjects, treating them in a serious manner. (The use of these figures and objects with comedy, bathos, or irony immediately alters the mode.) "High," of course, does not measure the ultimate value of the work of art, only the ascribed value of its subject and the tone of its representational treatment.[2]

A tone of high seriousness invests most pre-nineteenth-century images of Venice. When Venetians painted their city they created self-assured, self-dramatizing works incorporating a sense of confident command over and possession of these extaordinary civic spaces. While images of the city of Venice were not produced, in and of themselves, until the eighteenth century except in cartographic and decorative works, they do appear importantly as backgrounds in many of the earlier Venetian history and religious paintings. In general, the cityscape in these pictures serves as a defining and enabling framework for the central human action. In *The Procession in the Piazza, San Marco* (fig. 12) by Gentile Bellini (1429–1507), the ritual, epic

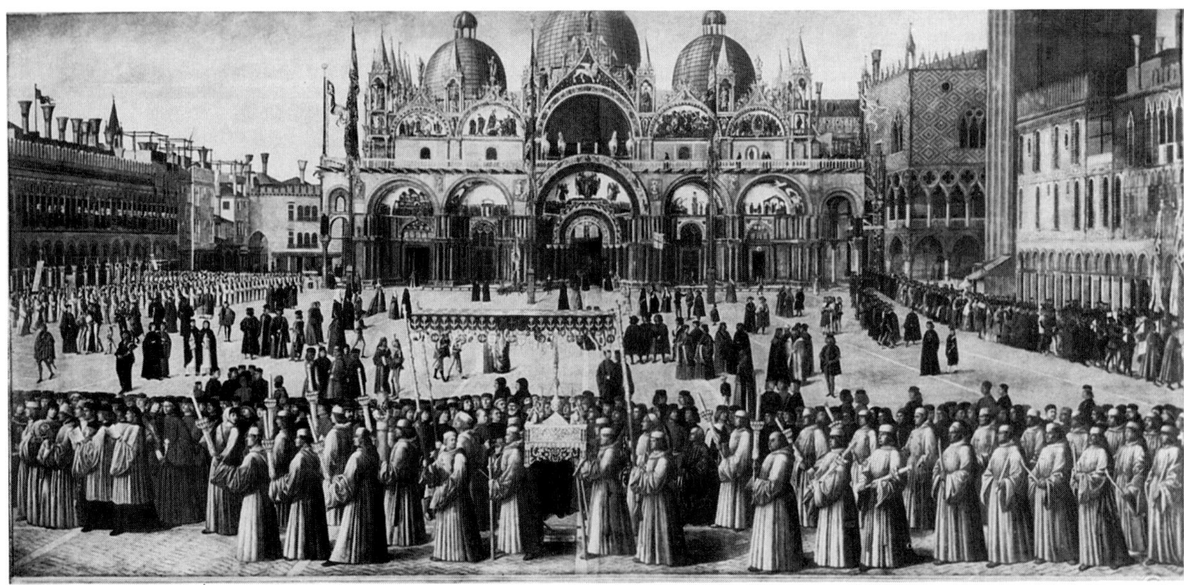

Fig. 12. Gentile Bellini, *Procession in the Piazza San Marco*, ca. 1496, mixed technique, 148¾″ × 372½″, Accademia Venice.

character of the scene is defined as much by the expanse of the Piazza and the exuberant facade of San Marco as by the expressions, positions, and motions of the human characters. Characteristic of the high mimetic or epic mode are devices that contribute to a general sense of order and a heightened sense of visual experience. One's view is broader in scope and better in quality than in ordinary experience. And here, as in most high mimetic paintings, the time of day and weather conditions are not marginal or adverse. However, the sunlight streams in on the scene from a point almost due *north* (see fig. 13), a logical impossibility probably dictated by a desire to keep the foreground faces sunlit, clear, and readable. Of course Bellini could have reversed the procession instead of the sun, but social fact seems to have been stronger than natural fact. In this we see a slight skewing of the laws of nature, which seems to be permissible in high mimetic fictions. It is an alteration of natural fact different in kind from that of the mythic mode in which such marvels as the levitation of human figures and the appearance of ghosts and gods intrude into the scene. In posture and organization, point of view, and subject, Bellini's *Procession in the Piazza San Marco* is a model of painting in the high mimetic mode.

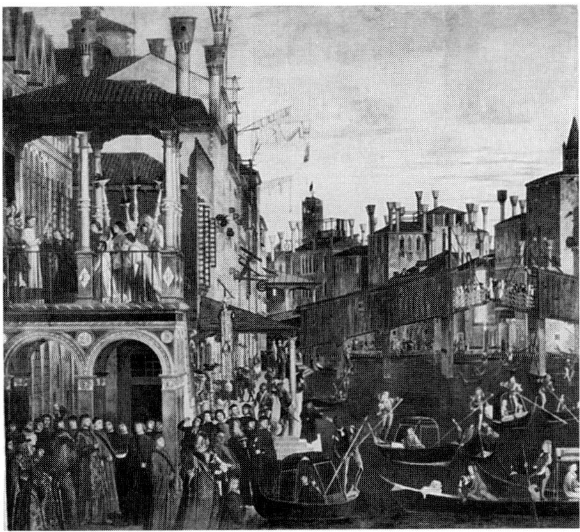

Fig. 14. Vittore Carpaccio, *Legend of the True Cross: Healing of the Demonic*, 1494, oil on canvas, 164½″ × 175″, Accademia, Venice.

In some instances, elements of low mimetic threaten to take over a purportedly epic picture. Bellini's younger contemporary, Vittore Carpaccio (1455–1525) in his *Legend of the True Cross: Healing of the Demonic* (fig. 14) sites the miracle near the old wooden Rialto bridge. The vantage point is low, and the principle action has been set off center to the left and unusually high on the canvas. Although the incident recorded is far from ordinary, randomly moving gondolas, drying laundry, and a vernacular architectural setting all contrast with the basically epic nature of the incident. As this instance makes clear, the artist's freedom to manipulate the modes and to baffle the viewer's expectations is one of his most powerful tools. However, the commonest pictorial vision in the fifteenth century was the epic or heroic mode in the classic form of Bellini's *Procession.*

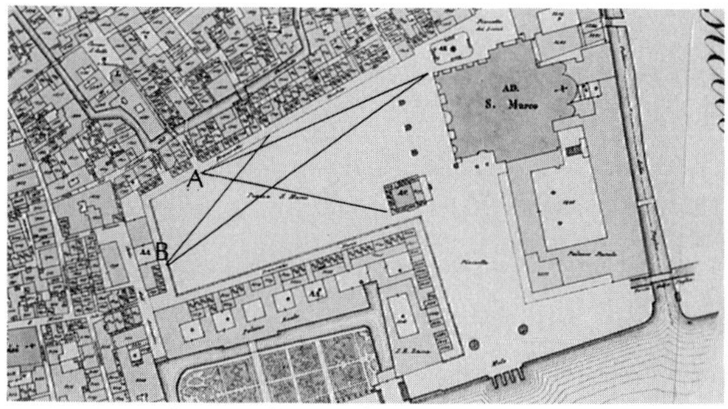

A. Vantage point for principal section of painting
B. Vantage point for left-hand side of painting
and pseudo-vantage point point for the whole composition

Fig. 13. Cones of vision in Gentile Bellini, *Procession in the Piazza* (fig. 12).

Venetians occasionally used their city's literal fabric as a setting for, and a participant in, images in the mythic mode. These large-scale (presentation) paintings include divine beings, superior to other mortals and to such natural laws as gravity. Jacopo Tintoretto (1518–94) in his *Doge Alvise Mocenigo Presented to the Redeemer* (fig. 15) and *Doge Pietro Loredan Praying before the Virgin* (fig. 17) inscribes the fabric of the city (as well as the personage of the doge and ecclesiastical attendants) onto the religious superstructure of the culture. The effect of placing these hovering celestial beings in literal context with mortal humans and terrestrial space is to confer upon that space and those humans superhuman experience. In the *Doge Alvise Mocenigo* the fictitious room in which the action takes place is located in the clock tower, about thirty feet above the ground. Beyond the doge is the Piazzetta, framed by the Ducal Palace on the left and the Libreria on the right, and beyond it the Bacino alive with shipping (fig. 16). It is not surprising that the artist deleted the two pillars at

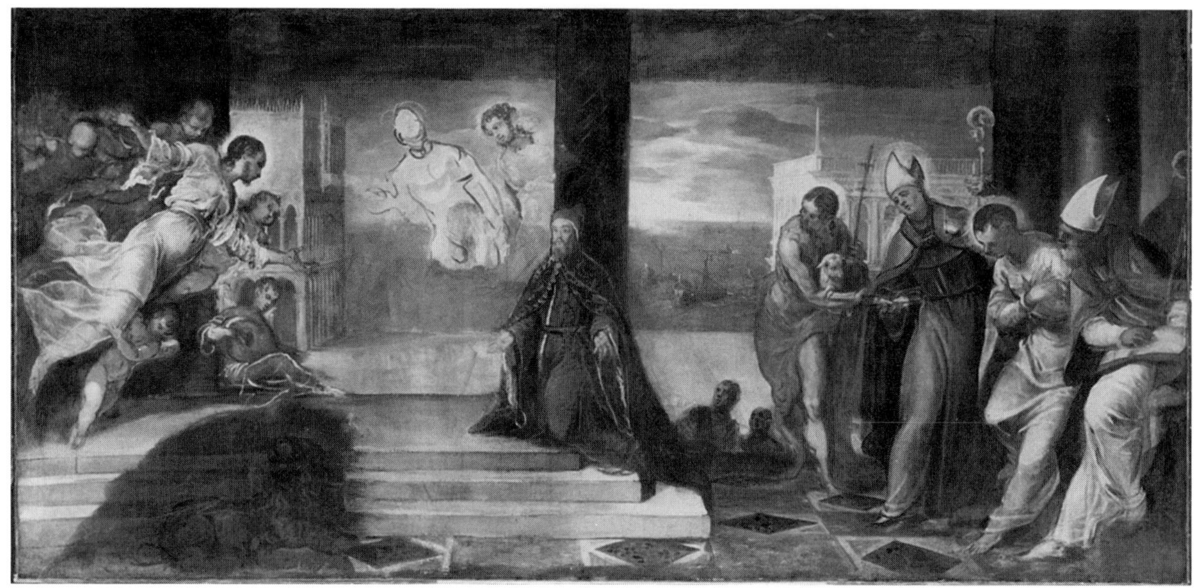

Fig. 15. Jacopo Tintoretto, *Doge Alvise Mocenigo Presented to the Redeemer*, n.d., oil on canvas, 38⅝″ × 78¼″, Metropolitan Museum of Art, John Stewart Kennedy Fund, 1910.

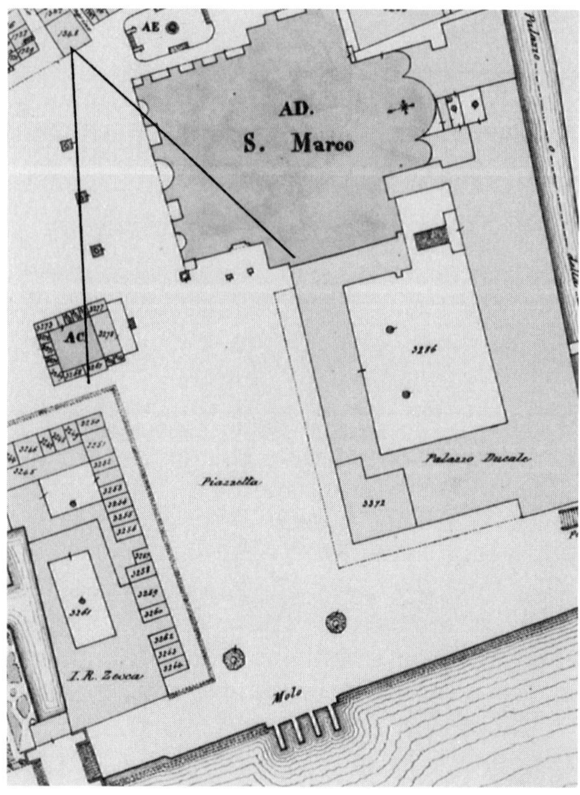

Fig. 16. Cone of vision in Jacopo Tintoretto, *Doge Alvise Mocenigo* (fig. 15).

the portal to the Piazzetta, but it is curious that two secular buildings have been included and the three religious structures in this vista—San Marco, the Campanile, and San Giorgio Maggiore—have been eliminated. Either the artist was after the effect of a grand and familiar civic (not religious) space or—more likely—inclusion of these religious buildings would have structurally violated the rules of the mode.[3] In *Doge Pietro Loredan* a constellation of holy figures surround the doge, who kneels at the far end of the Piazza (see fig. 18). Framed by the clock tower on the left and the Campanile on the right, San Marco is prominently placed, its domes echoing the doge's head. Reality has been adjusted here in two characteristic ways: the church's central portal has been aligned with the central dome, and the Campanile has been shortened to allow the inclusion of its full height. These alterations point to basic structuring principles: completeness of form (especially in the vertical dimension), frontality, and symmetry. It is probable that the exclusion of the Campanile from the markedly horizontal *Doge Alvise Mocenigo* picture (fig. 15) was prompted by a reluctance to truncate the tower. From a vantage point deep within the

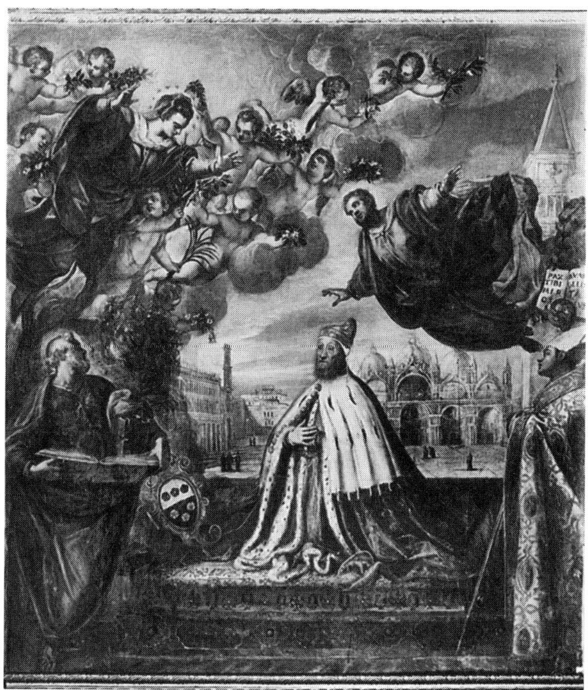

Fig. 17. Jacopo Tintoretto, *Doge Pietro Loredan Praying before the Virgin*, n.d., oil on canvas, Sala del Senato, Palazzo Ducale, Venice.

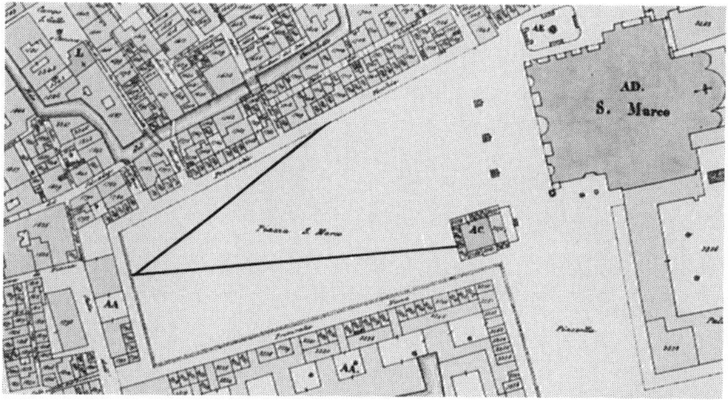

Fig. 18. Cone of vision in Jacopo Tintoretto, *Doge Pietro Loredan* (fig. 17).

fictitious room it would have appeared (without base or roof) as an inexplicable mass of brick, continuing without closure both above and below the frame. This effect wars with the "rules" of visual syntax that we can see operating in works in the mythic and high mimetic modes and would have been as "unthinkable" to Tintoretto as it was thinkable and interesting (as we shall see) to artists in the late nineteenth century.

In *Piazza San Marco* (fig. 19) Canaletto painted an image from the same vantage point as Tintoretto's *Doge Pietro Loredan*. It is as characteristic of his age, its patronage system, and its underlying concepts about space, history, and social order, as Tintoretto's is of his. Most emphatically, the architectural space is no longer an attribute of the human drama; it supplants and, to some degree, stands in for the human drama. This synecdochic substitution of the architectural context for a central human action is the first in a series of increasingly oblique shifts in vision. The specific alteration visible here is a function of a general secularization which made the mythic mode impossible, a specific descent in Venetian fortunes and a consequent remoteness from celestial proximity, and, in a parallel development, the ascendency of landscape as a primary painterly genre. Perhaps more important, the Canaletto preserves much of the earlier vision; significant changes are evident, but the mode is, in the broadest sense, continuous. He chooses buildings of ascribed value and renders them with a celebratory, positive tone, a stable horizontality, and a sense of frozen time. The structures are complete, seen frontally from a high vantage point and in a clear unambiguous light. However, unlike Bellini or Tintoretto, he does permit the central dome to slide out of alignment with the central portal, a topographically accurate inclusion which points to a tolerance for asymmetry and a modicum of disorder even within the epic mode.

In another sense this painting is a symptom of a dramatic shift in audience. As a principal goal on the Grand Tour (that prescribed excursion through past events and past glories as much as through geographic space) Venice had managed to maintain prestige despite its loss of power.[4] In *Piazza San Marco*, the figures have shrunk in proportion to the architectural setting, they turn their backs to us and to the light source. Our eye slides off them easily. The architecture in this picture can be read less as an attribute of present action and significance (as in Bellini or Carpaccio or Tintoretto) than as a visible souvenir of past heroic action and significance. At least in part defined and encouraged by tourism, Venice continued to stage splendid pageants, festivals, and regattas in the eighteenth century. Often sited on the Bacino San Marco or the Grand Canal, they were the subject of many of Canaletto's canvases. However, unlike Bellini's *Procession*, in these images the architecture is primary and the human event secondary.

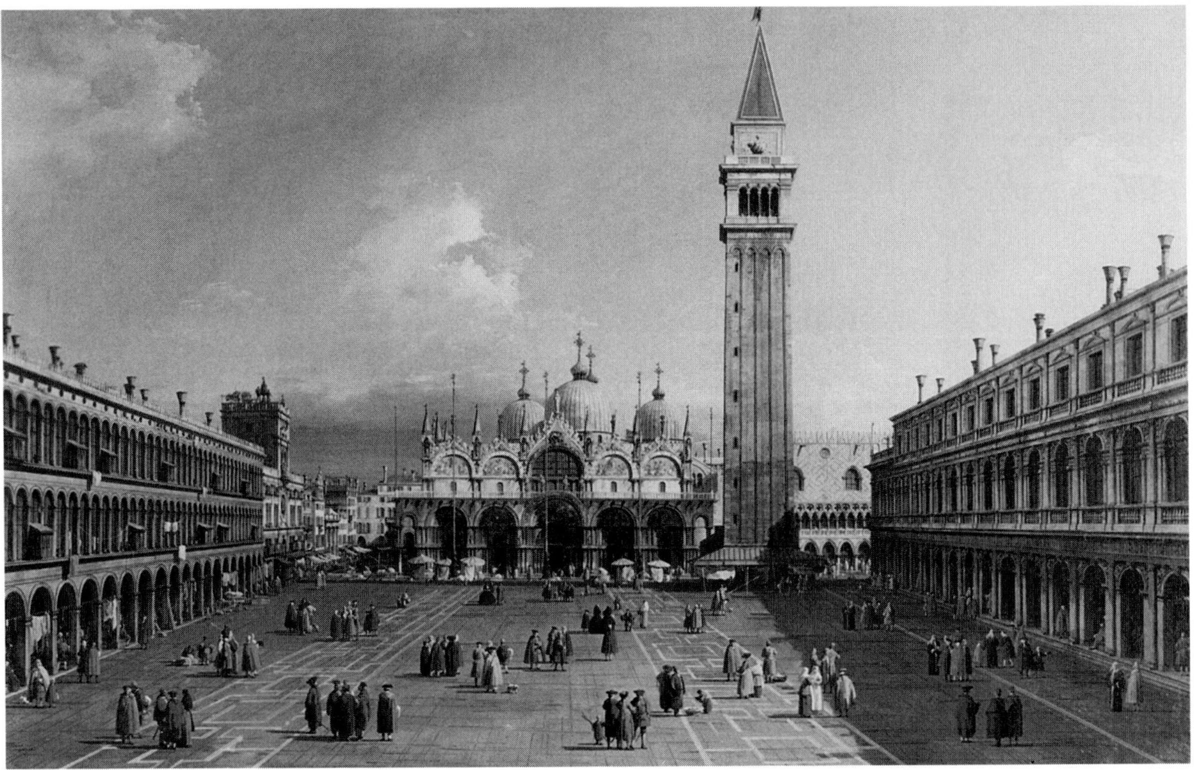

Fig. 19. Canaletto, *Piazza San Marco*, ca. 1730–35, oil on canvas, 30″ × 46¾″, Fogg Art Museum, Harvard University, Cambridge, Bequest of Grenville L. Winthrop.

In a few paintings, notably *Campo San Vidal and Santa Maria della Carità*, known as *The Stonemason's Yard* (fig. 20), Canaletto moves close to a low mimetic mode. Portrayed in the foreground are sheds, blocks of unworked stone, examples of vernacular architecture in picturesque disrepair, and working Venetians going about their daily tasks. The cue that we are tourists (or epic observers) and not stonecutters ourselves is provided by our elevated point of view with its consequent breadth of vision. We see beyond the raw unworked stone and daily human toil to its realization in the ordered timelessness of architectural achievement across the canal.

In all of these works by Venetians, Venice was interpreted as a city of monumental architecture, high noon, and benign weather. The tone is ceremonial or celebratory and serious, although in the work of Canaletto's younger contemporary Francesco Guardi (1712–93), there is a new note of drama and nostalgia in glowering skies, theatrical chiaroscuro, and shimmering impasto. For all these artists, the spaces of Venice and its inhabitants are comprehensible, and the images themselves are ordered and rational in their stable horizontality and careful sense of closure (especially in the vertical dimension). These images give the viewer a sense of command over a broader field of vision than he can normally see. They focus on recognizable sites, they suggest a comprehensibility of sense data beyond ordinary sense perception, and they invest the scene with a tone of seriousness and grand consequence.

A Sense of Loss: The Romantics

The romantic vision of Venice—best seen in the work of Joseph Mallord William Turner (1775–1851, English)—retained the high mimetic elements discussed above and added the emphatic dimension of time. For as mimesis is the imitation and fictionalization of the real, the basic romantic alteration is in the focus within the concept of reality itself, away from surface manifestation and toward an inner or an other or a former reality. The quest for this inner reality involves simultaneously an intensification of perception of the outer world and a radical acceptance of the subjectivity

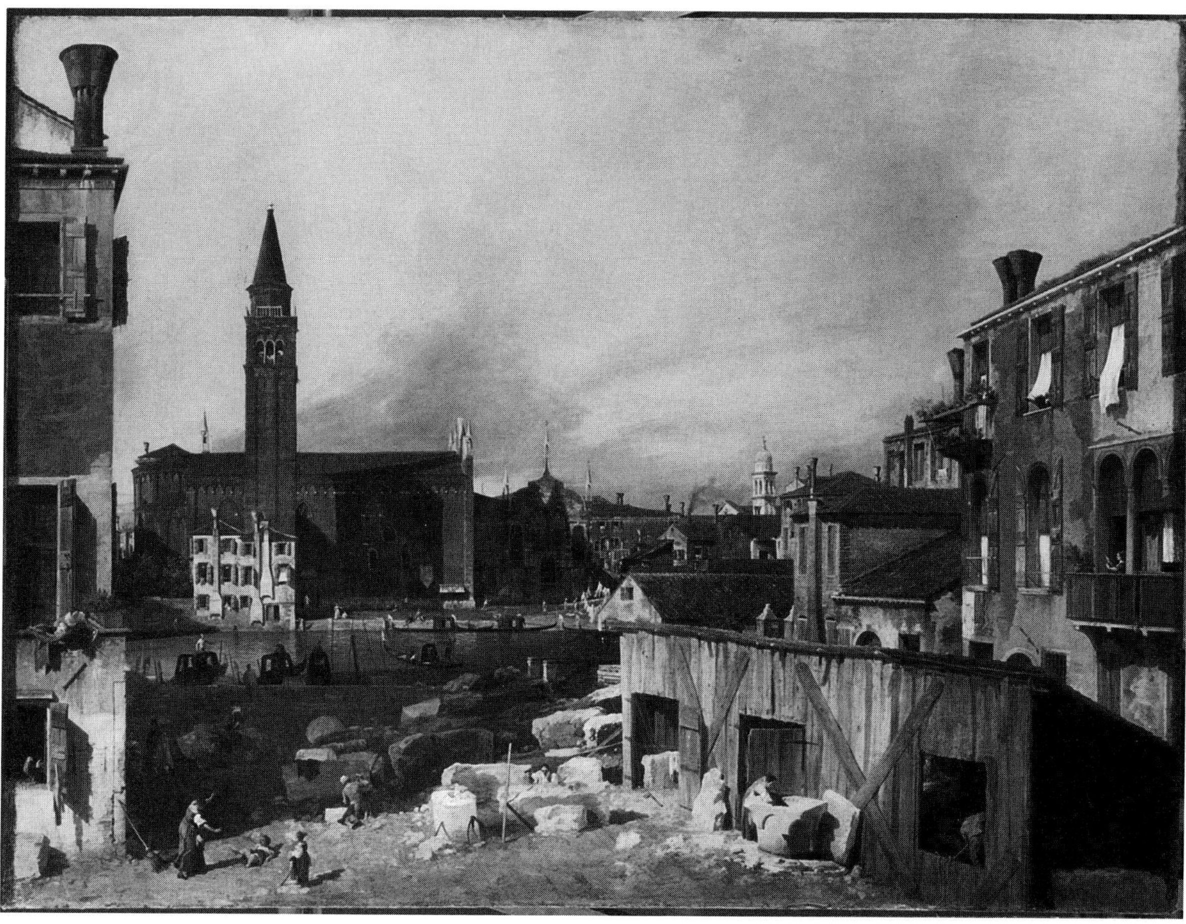

Fig. 20. Canaletto, *Campo San Vidal and Santa Maria della Carità (The Stonemason's Yard)*, 1729–30, oil on canvas, 48¾″ × 64⅛″, National Gallery, London.

of that perception. But its point of initiation and of arrival, of "the saving moment, . . . is backwards into lost time," as Bloom puts it.[5] The present is contingent and is invested with value only insofar as it incorporates and resists its temporal displacement. The creation and the experience of the romantic artwork, then, includes and implies an experience in hindsight of an episode or epic remembered, framed within an artistic tradition (a mode) that is consciously historic. But time, even civic memory, is difficult to portray. For this reason, many images in the romantic mode include a specificity of weather, and time of day, or season (although season is almost impossible to portray in Venice), especially of marginal moments: sunset (elegiac), sunrise, storm gathering, or storm passing. The specificity of time emphasizes the fact of time and the fact of loss (even in the face of artistic creation). And loss is, above all, the note struck by the romantics. Never far from the surface of the artwork is a sense of Venice's extraordinary past, the immensity of her gains and the immensity of her losses.

In *The Grand Canal, Venice* (fig. 21), J. M. W. Turner has, in one of his many images of Venice, taken a point of view about ten feet above the surface of the Grand Canal and, looking to the east, portrayed the principal waterway of the city in the late afternoon. The view is calculated, even strained, to include the most significant structures within this prospect. On the right is the white portal of the Salute with the set-back Seminario Patriacale and reddish customs buildings beyond, terminating in the small but dramatic tower and statue on the Punta della Dogana. This last structure has been turned ninety degrees for easy recognition. The image is—as is often the case in the high mimetic mode—synthetic. This right or south side of the Grand Canal has been viewed from point A on the map in figure 22. The other side

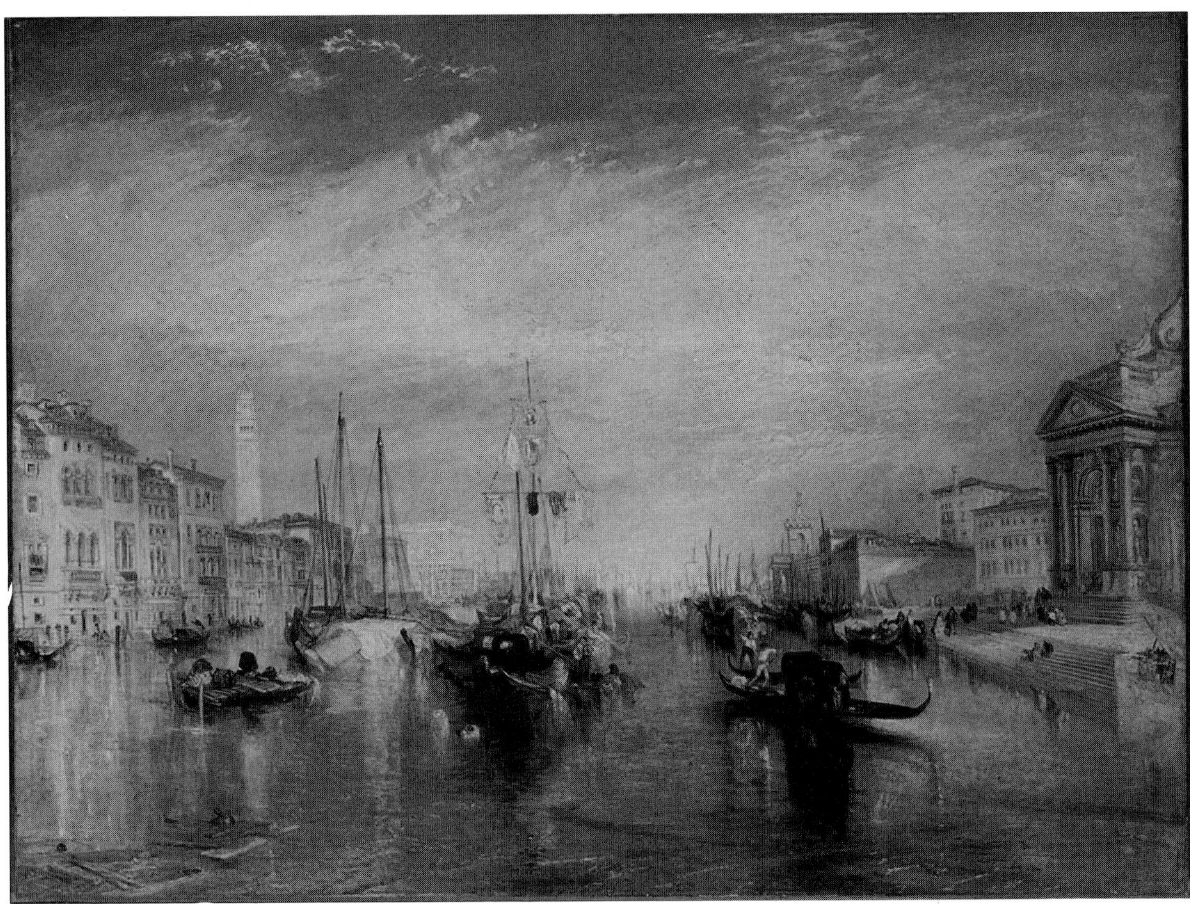

Fig. 21. J. M. W. Turner, *The Grand Canal, Venice*, 1835, oil on canvas, 36″ × 48″, Metropolitan Museum of Art, Bequest of Cornelius Vanderbilt, 1899.

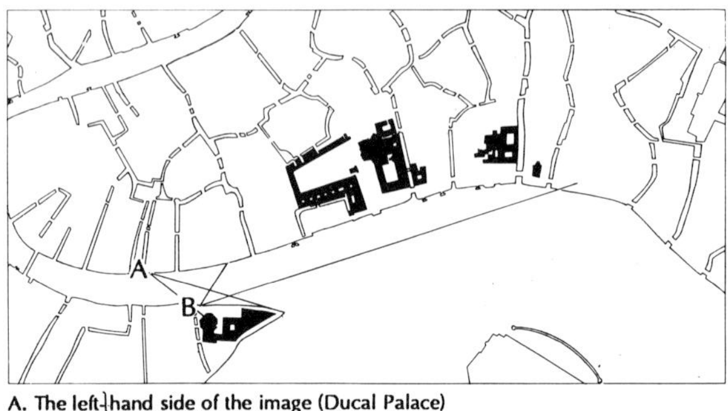

Fig. 22. Cones of vision in J. M. W. Turner, *The Grand Canal* (fig. 21).

of the Grand Canal has been viewed from a point on the Salute landing *B* and includes the Doge's Palace, the Campanile (somewhat elongated), and a parade of palaces including that known as "Desdemona's house." In the center of the image is a deep void and a group of boats and gondolas, one sporting a mast hung with brave but tawdry banners, a framework that mimics the gesture of the Campanile on the left and the shape of the Salute pediment on the right. This banner rig, unlike any of the other pictorial elements, is parallel to the picture plane. It arrests our visual progress into the center of the picture and forces a comparison with the carefully plotted architectural framework. Unlike the Canaletto scenes, here the boats are stationary and the blue-green water is alive, itself an actor in the drama, with its deep and palpable reflections. The insistent banners in this context seem less to be celebrating any current event than shadowing and reflecting (as the water does here physical substance) glorious past festivals and naval victories more in keeping with the civic space pictured. The tone of epic space and epic celebration is mixed with a magical and pensive melancholy.

In a far more dramatic and complex way Turner has captured a sense of the past and of the heroic and of the poetic in his *Juliet and Her Nurse* (fig.

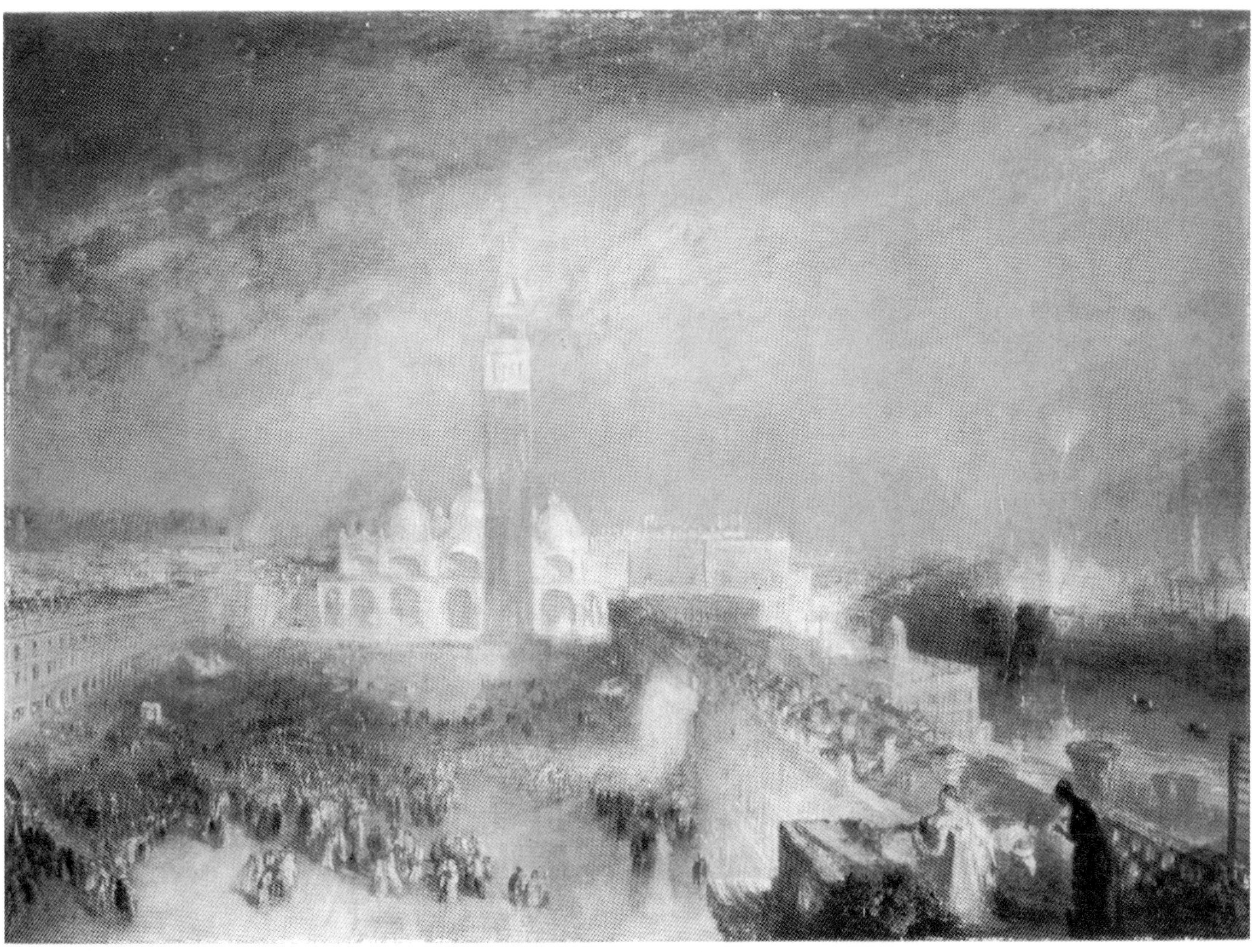

Fig. 23. J. M. W. Turner, *Juliet and Her Nurse*, 1836, oil on canvas, 35″ × 47½″, private collection.

23).[6] Removing them from their "native" Verona, he has set their drama in Venice, selecting the same prospect of San Marco across the full length of the Piazza that was used by Bellini in his *Procession* (fig. 12), Tintoretto in *Doge Pietro Loredan* (fig. 17), and Canaletto in *Piazza San Marco* (fig. 19). However, he has raised the vantage point to about seventy feet. We look at the scene from a (nonexistent) structure in the southwest corner of the Piazza. A few feet down and to the right the figures of Juliet, her nurse, and a small black cat stand on a balcony overlooking the crowded public square. As in the Bellini painting, the artist has reorganized topographical reality (while also seriously rearranging the fictive reality of Shakespeare's play) and departed from the optical laws of nature. Bellini's alterations moved his image toward ordered symmetry and visual clarity; here Turner has manipulated space and light to produce a sense of tension and of heightened, suprasensory experience. By our high and central vantage point (within the same fictive building Juliet inhabits) Turner suggests, even insists, that the viewer become a sympathetic participant in the giddy panorama. The scene sweeps through ninety-five degrees, from the Procuratie Vecchie on the left, across the broad piazza and the black void of the Grand Canal to the Church of San Giorgio Maggiore on the extreme right. The only object taller than the viewer's vantage point is the soaring (shifted) Campanile of San Marco which, with its brightly erect mass, interrupts the church's elongated facade. Although most of the illuminated buildings seem to glow from within rather than to reflect any consistent solar, lunar, or stellar light, it is probable that the buildings to the north and east are to be seen as lit by a setting sun. Figures in the Piazza are illuminated by a glowing "fire" light on the facade of the Procuratie Nuove and by a second unseen bright source of light beneath our feet. Beyond, in the Bacino, fireworks light the horizon.

On these irregularities of site, topography, and light, contemporaries commented critically, so much so that John Ruskin (1819–1900) was raised, as he put it, "to the height of 'black anger.' "[7] As Ruskin makes abundantly clear, Turner's pictures are, in his eyes, metaphors or similes suggesting essentials beneath and beyond the matter-of-fact dross of a factual world. He "changes and combines, giving effects without absolute causes . . . seizing the soul and essence of beauty, without regarding the means by which it is effected."[8] Clearly the biggest change and combination is the removal of Juliet from Verona to Venice, a relocation prompted by the absolutely poetic and eminently heroic nature of the latter city in the romantic imagination. Turner is here making an analogy between the splendor and fate of Romeo and Juliet's passion and the splendor and fate of the Queen of the Adriatic. Juliet is only possible in Venice, only suitably balconied in Venice. Turner has departed from the text in this singular respect, but he has literalized the insistent metaphors of fire (for love and hatred) that thread through Shakespeare's play. He has, in fact, manipulated the entire fictive story, retaining only the essential "given," ascribed, and recognizable values of the two protagonists—Juliet as the tragic heroine of Shakespeare's most poetic play and Venice as the most splendid exterior stage set of a grandly poetic event.

Retaining the resonance of the recognizable superstructures of Venice, such romantics as Turner layered overstatement and heightened sensory experience on factual reality to suggest invisible realities and Ruskinian "enchantments." For most, the range of reference includes a temporal dimension and a sense of loss within that sense of time. This is not seen in a deterioration of the physical fabric of the city (as in the low mimetic mode) but in the heightened use of color, dramatic light, transitional times of day, and a tone of pensive melancholy. There is little present action, but the heroic architecture insists that there was heroic action and ambition in this place in the past. Memory and association are evoked in the recognizability of the structures pictured, and a lapse of time is often underlined by a dramatic juxtaposition of modern (picturesque but diminished) inhabitants with their monumental context.

Of the Americans who worked in this mode, none was more prolific than Thomas Moran. First achieving public attention as a recorder and interpreter of the geologic wonders of the American West, Moran's sketches and paintings of Yellowstone helped to create a national consciousness of the American wilderness and were instrumental in the congressional push for a national park system.[9] However, the taste for large heroic landscapes of exotic western scenes paled as the century waned, and Moran found Venice his most saleable subject. During two relatively brief visits to the city (1886 and 1890) he made sketches which provided him with decades of paintings; there are, in fact, more extant Moran paintings of Venice than of any other subject.[10] Like *View of Venice* (fig. 5) and *Splendor of Venice* (pl. 1), they dwell, for the most part, on the principal structures bordering the Bacino—the Salute domes, San Giorgio, the Doge's Palace, and the Campanile. These forms are often heightened, lengthened, or inflected out of normal perspective to afford the viewer a better or grander prospect. Gypsyish fishing boats with vibrant orange-red and yellow lateen sails, gondolas, and a few palace clusters complete his syntax of forms. The compositions are asymmetrical and, in most cases, deviate so much from topographical reality as to be unmappable.[11] Moran's synthetic architectural landscapes are set off, indeed enveloped in larger expanses of sea and sky than are visible in the work of Tintoretto or Canaletto. Because of the romantic emphasis on time and therefore on unusual and marginal lighting situations, a wider scope is given to the sea and sky to express weather and time of day. In *View of Venice* (fig. 5) and other instances the principal source of light, the sun, is included within the image, dramatizing the fact of sunset, riveting our attention on the fact of light, altering local color, and throwing much of the imaged scene into theatrical silhouette. As in most Moran compositions the sky occupies the upper two-thirds of the image and the sea the lower third—a stable, classic arrangement which absorbs even a riot of color with equanimity. In many respects, these two works (and Moran's entire Venice oeuvre) are like the Turner of *The Grand Canal,*

Venice (fig. 21). They are unlike the Turner of the *Juliet* painting (fig. 23) with its specific literary frame of reference and its vertiginous point of view, and equally unlike the Turner of *Festive Lagoon Scene, Venice* (ca. 1840, Tate Gallery, London) in which the stable horizon line is dissolved in a whirling spiral of chromatic mist. Moran seized upon Turner's more classical compositional geometries, his color, and his brushwork. The aura of nobility and consequence with which Turner endowed his subject, the juxtaposition of human stasis and natural dynamism, and the luminous glow in the sympathetic sea and sky clearly captured Moran's imagination as Turner's more radical compositions did not. That Moran's Turneresque enthusiasm for a heightened, rarefied vision of an extraordinary city was shared by others, in fact was popular, is suggested by the fact that an 1898 Moran view of Venice was published in an edition of twenty-two million on a color calendar.[12]

The *Splendor of Venice* (pl. 1) is unusual in Moran's oeuvre, indeed in the whole canon of Venice views, in its inclusion of the figure of an artist. Darkly silhouetted in the left foreground, a painter works intently at an easel in the prow of a moored gondola. It is curious that it is Moran who conjures up this apparition of the *plein air* artist, placing him within the context of a painting whose studio creation is underlined by inconsistencies in light source, topographic infidelities, and an aura of heightened, synthetic visual experience. It is a picture about another kind of picture making, a fiction about another type of fiction making. But with the introduction of this figure, the painting becomes both an experience in itself and a mediated experience. That we are asked to view the scene through the eyes of this surrogate, to appropriate his persona, gives the scene both a greater immediacy and a greater sense of dislocation between time present and the wished-for memory. Hunched and attentive at his task, this figure underlines the change from Bellini's *Procession in the Piazza*—in which Venice is a place to be and to act—to the nineteenth century when Venice is primarily, in the artists' eyes, a place to perceive and remember. In his essay "Nature," Ralph Waldo Emerson remarked, "If the king is in the palace, nobody looks at the walls. It is when he is gone, and the house is filled with grooms and gazers, that we turn from the people, to find relief in the majestic men that are suggested by . . . the architecture."[13] In Moran's painting the era of princes has clearly passed, and we are positioned as one of the "gazers"; we are intent on the spectacle suggested by "the walls" but no longer enacted by the populace. At best the Venetians furnish a picturesque foil to the majesty suggested by the locale. All nineteenth-century artists in Venice were conscious of their role as "gazers," as observers who saw one thing and knew, or thought they knew, or remembered (in the sense that the tale of Venice's past was a public memory) another. Their responses to this simultaneous consciousness of present and past varied considerably from those like Moran, who strove to evoke a sense of history, a dramatization of time embodied in noble structure to those (we shall call them ironic and discuss them later) who appear to repudiate a knowledge of Venice as a context for prior and nobler deeds. But Moran—and most other gazers, both artists and their lay public—focused on an insistent note of grandeur and epic memory.

Other artists, less well-known than Moran, who recorded an equally romantic interpretation of Venice, include George Loring Brown (1814–89) and David Neal (1838–1915). Their paintings, while vested with the haunting sense of time, especially time lost, that we associate with high mimetic romanticism, express this preoccupation with temporality differently from Moran and from each other. Brown's painting *On the Grand Canal, Venice* (fig. 24) is a view from the Accademia bridge looking east toward the Salute. On the left the Palazzo Cavalli Franchetti and Palazzo Barbaro figure prominently, and on the right a very white and elongated Salute is spotlighted against a threatening sky. A retouched wet-plate photograph taken between 1850 and 1860 by an unknown photographer, entitled *Moonlight on the Grand Canal* (fig. 25), may indeed be the source for this and other Brown paintings. That the same light effects would do, with very little adjustment (especially in the palace facades), for morning light, moonlight, and breaking storm demonstrates the versatility of these artists and photographers as well as their will to avoid the common light of day. Both artist and photographer here depend more heavily on special light effects (and the resonant name "Venice") than on the specific architectural or spatial qualities of the scenes portrayed. The sense of loss at the passing of the heroic moment has been completely

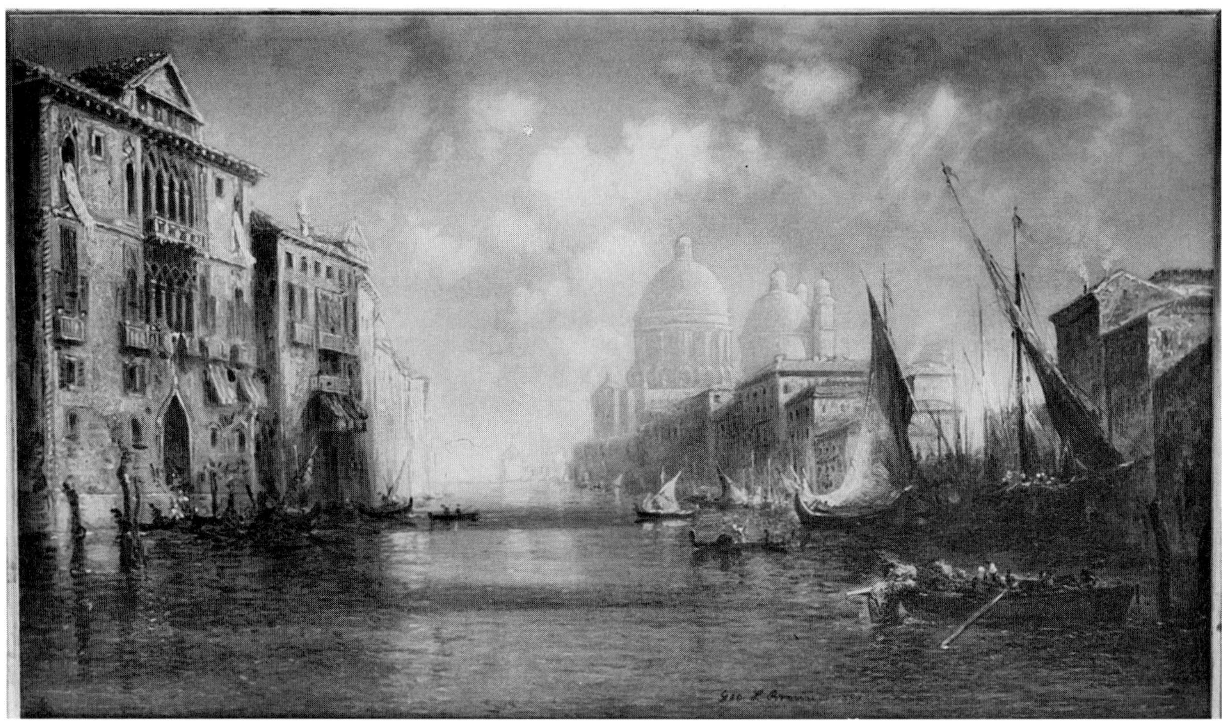

Fig. 24. George Loring Brown, *On the Grand Canal, Venice*, 1880, oil on canvas, 11½″ × 20″, St. Johnsbury Athenaeum, St. Johnsbury, Vermont.

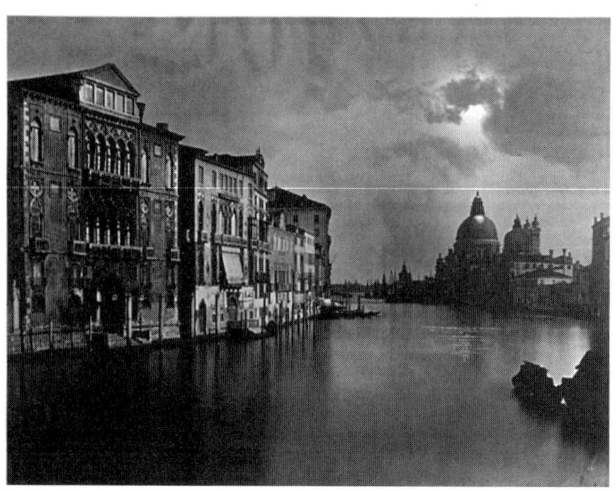

Fig. 25. Carlo Naya (attributed), *Moonlight on the Grand Canal*, ca. 1850–60, retouched wet-plate photograph, Metropolitan Museum of Art, Estate of Emily Delafield Floyd, 1961.

translated into visual pleasure in the elegiac mood. These are less, in a sense, pictures of Venice than pictures of an internal state of reverie (invested with a languid charm) for which Venice is the objective correlative.

More closely related in concept to Turner's *Juliet* is the romantic fiction that literalized the past. Not simply remembered, here the past is brought forward, costumed so to speak, and given the stage. David Neal's *Interior of Saint Mark's, Venice* (fig. 26) portrays a seventeenth-century wedding party at the iconostasis, near the pulpit, with meticulous and accurate detail.[14] This act of summoning up past human glories to people the ancient space (which one *can* experience in the flesh) is simply to fill out the canvas, to complete the "reading" of the stones. Venice was, above all, a dramatic stage set.

Neal's painting points up a significant difference between the painterly and the literary treatment of Venice. Here we are given in pantomime a noble, handsome couple joined in matrimony—a point of commencement, of felicity. The literary treatment of Venice (and here I include histories, guidebooks, popular fiction, and literature proper) is short on weddings. As in James Fenimore Cooper's *The Bravo* (1831) Venice is usually seen as the site and symbol for most forms of earthly wickedness: tyranny, murder, conspicuous opulence, and licentiousness. Even Mark Twain, the great puncturer of European legend, showed himself, in *Innocents Abroad* (1869), not untouched by the Gothic reputation of Venice. even while pointing up the physical realities of sewerish canals and mildewed facades he reveled in the *idea* of Venice as a delicious haven for iniquitous plots,

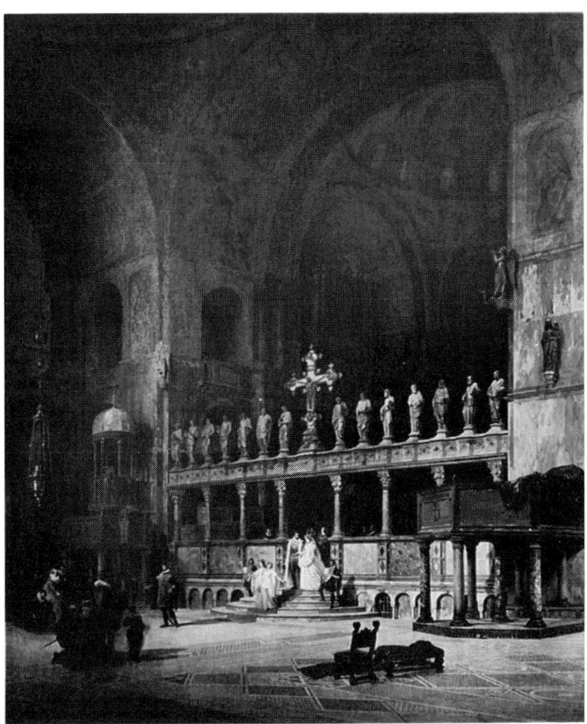

Fig. 26. David Neal, *Interior of Saint Mark's, Venice*, 1869, oil on canvas, 72½″ × 58⅛″, Art Institute of Chicago, S. M. Nickerson Collection.

foul treacheries, and hideous torture. For him and many other nineteenth-century visitors, Venice personified the extravagance and wickedness of European, or to put it more as they might have felt it, of pre-American human experience.

For many, Venice had the magical quality of being *the* city in which plays (especially tragedies of coercion, murder, and melodrama) seemed likely to leave the theater and act themselves out in the streets. This view of Venice as a city of masqueraders is clearly and centrally useful in such works of imaginative literature as Edith Wharton's "A Venetian Night's Entertainment" (1903). As in most of Wharton's Italian subjects, the story is set in the past and involves a situation of captivity and coercion. Its action revolves around a pun on the title's "Entertainment."[15] The city becomes a stage on which the real and the impossible collude and conspire to give the reader and the narrator their several "entertainments" in the inhospitable entertainment the young protagonist finds in this curious city. And the whole commedia is invested with a sense of pervasive wickedness which is a central aspect of Venice's literary reputation. A general theatrical detachment from "reality" and an intricate perfidiousness of character are two Venetian givens which the author here exploits for literary capital and utilizes for specific invention.

Why then, if we assume that Casanova and Byron were equally in the minds of the painters and their patrons, do the images—even those in Neal's play-acting spirit—avoid trials, inquisitions, and prisons? It is possible that the discrete physical *things* of terror do not survive (with the possible exception of the remarkably underpainted Bridge of Sighs), or that Venice's physical space, without chasms or rushing torrents, has no architectural space that adequately suggests terror. Or perhaps the sheer physical allure of Venice simply overwhelms any sense or memory of human wickedness or agony. In more complex terms, the answer seems to lie indirectly in Frye's definition of romance as a mode "characterized by the acceptance of pity and fear, which in ordinary life relate to pain, as forms of pleasure."[16] The lurid events of Venetian history were not threatening, either by analogy or by imaginative projection. They are simply read as exciting, and therefore—by the alchemy of our mental processes—as pleasurable. The painters go more directly to the pleasurable, to the mood of pensive melancholy and the languid charm, knowing that their audience knows Venice's reputation and can supply the intervening steps of great herioc action and great horror. The painters, in that sense, lean on the writers to help supply their meaning.

Pleasurable, then, these romantic paintings are, dealing as they do in a theatrically special reality in which light—exact to time of day and mental state—is used as a visual metaphor for time. They deal largely in images of recognizable monuments seen from a height and within a broad cone of vision. Their tone is one of high seriousness. Venice was, to Turner, Moran, Neal, and other romantics, more than anything else, a poetic place, that is, not a prosaic place. Juliet's "The orchard walls are high and hard to climb /And the place death, considering who thou art" (II, ii, 63–64) *ought* to have been set in Venice. And orchard walls are far too modest for a hero of Romeo's stature, and the whole, after all, a public spectacle of highest theatrical magnitude, not a private tryst.

Poetry, however, was not the language of the contemporary world by the 1880s, and Henry James felt moved to defend it or at least to note its passing, fictively, in *The Aspern Papers* (1888). Set in

Venice because only in Venice could the forces of poetry meet, or possibly triumph over, the forces of the contemporary world, the tale is based on James's discovery "that Jane Clairmont, . . . the intimate friend of Byron and the mother of his daughter Allegra, [was] . . . living in Florence . . . up to our own day [1879]."[17] In James's translation of these facts into his fictional narrative, the aged Juliana Bordereau, once the beloved of the immortal lyric poet, Jeffrey Aspern, lives in an antique palazzo in Venice. Her flamboyant history, her fabled beauty, her secretive dignity she shares in common with the venerable city, "there being absolutely no refinement of the mouldy rococo in human or whatever other form, that you may not disembark at the dislocated water-steps of almost any decayed monument of Venetian greatness." For James it was not the bare awareness of antiquity or the venerableness of Venice that was striking as it was to Ruskin, but rather the contiguous continuity with his own period: "We are divided of course between liking to feel the past strange and liking to feel it familiar; the difficulty is, for intensity, to catch it at the moment when the scales of the balance hang with the right evenness."[18]

James contrives his short novel to revolve around a collision—psychological, moral, and historical—between the two ages in the persons of Juliana and the journalist narrator known only as the "Publishing Scoundrel." Juliana is—however fossilized—a palpable link with the golden age of personal and artistic poetry, of Turner's vision, while the narrator is the emissary of de-Byronized modernity. For James the newspaper was *the* pernicious instrument of the modern world. It erased the poetic age and instituted the age of prose. Juliana retains her secret inviolate before the onslaughts of the Publishing Scoundrel, as Venice maintains her mystery and charm in the face of tourists and guidebooks. In *The Aspern Papers* the essence of the matter is a historic affair of passion and betrayal between a beautiful woman and an immortal poet. The reenactment of this affair between a middle-aged antiquarian and the pathetic spinster niece a half century later in the 1870s is comic, pitiful, prosaic, anything but poetic. The novel itself belongs to the ironic mode; it is told by a narrator who sees, in fact, only a small part of the story he tells, but it illustrates the intensely poetic nature of Venice to even such a modernist sensibility as James's. The tale is set in Venice precisely, we are led to feel, because only there could the past and the poetic defend themselves and survive. The removal of the tale from Florence to Venice signals here (as in the case of Turner's *Juliet*) the greater suitability of this site—with its poetic reputation and its resistance to contemporary modernity—than that of the original city. Venice is for James "a palpable imaginable *visitable* past" and thus only here can the past and the poetic actually triumph over Publishing Scoundrels and intrusive prosaic modernity.[19]

A Repossession

In the mid-nineteenth century a certain J. Harris etched a map of Venice that was published by J. J. Harper of New York under the title *Venice as It Appeared A.D. 1765* (fig. 27). It is a modest but early and very suggestive example of an American rendering (albeit a borrowed rendering) of Venice. It was, in fact, pirated from an eighteenth-century Italian map which was itself an updated version of a sixteenth-century view. Bird's-eye-view maps of this type were common in the seventeenth, eighteenth, and nineteenth centuries, and they seem to point to certain ways of seeing that are not unconnected with general habits of mind about the organization of physical reality. Before airplanes, helicopters, and balloons, such views were of course only imaginary, experiments in reality organization, not records of perceived prospects. The Harris view shows the entirety of the city and includes three-dimensional renditions of most of its buildings. It shares many of the characteristics of the Canaletto and other high mimetic cityscapes discussed above, taking the point of view and the demand for order one step higher.[20] Like them, it is characterized by completeness, order, and above all, comprehensibility. The temporal and poetic elements of the romantic views are absent, as the event portrayed is spatial and essentially timeless. In *Venice as It Appeared A.D. 1765* the waterways and wharves, the church towers and open spaces are seen as individual elements and as a complicated but comprehensible series of relationships. Whether it is topographically accurate is unimportant. That it gives the viewer a model of civic space—and by extension, of civic life—as an ordered and graspable entity is important. It is a miniaturization and a simplification and a clarification.

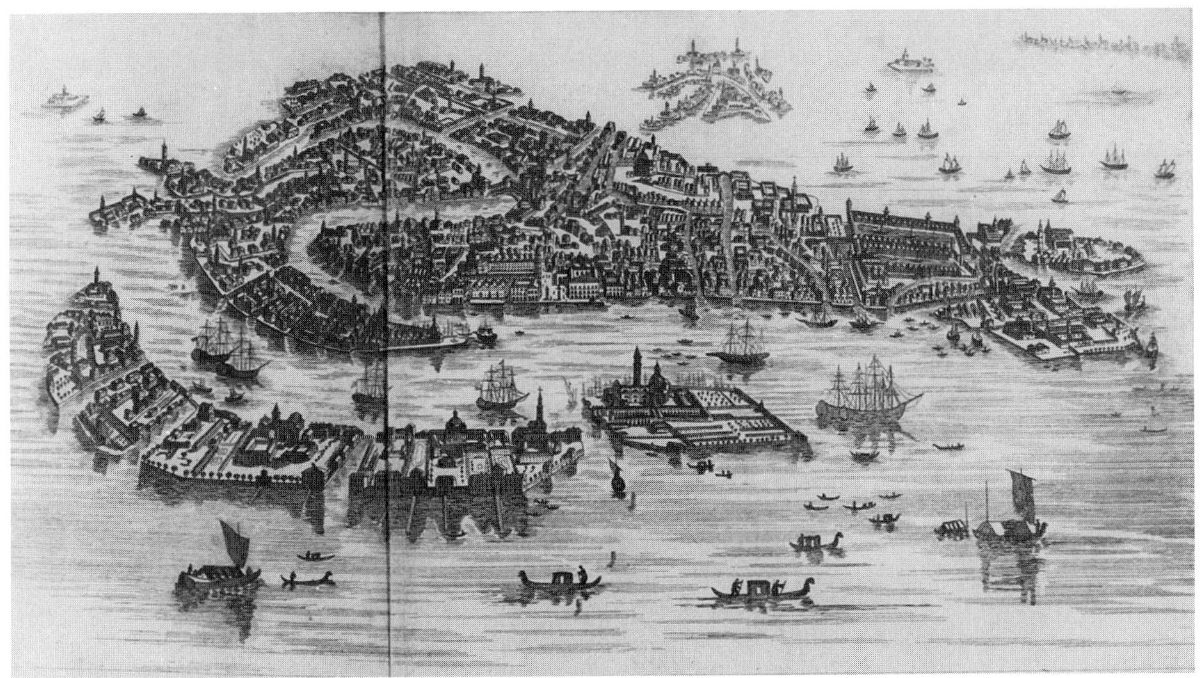

Fig. 27. J. Harris, *Venice as It Appeared A.D. 1765*, ca. 1850, etching, 6″ × 9⅜″, Yale University Map Collection, New Haven, Connecticut; see fig. 37.

And it is by such image making that one can appropriate or intellectually possess—or, in this belated nineteenth-century version of the high mimetic, repossess—the physical reality of Venice and the qualities that it represents.

For Levi-Strauss, the reading of a map or a work of art has a curious, almost unsettling relationship to understanding:

> What is the virtue of reduction either of scale or in the number of properties? It seems to result from a sort of reversal in the process of understanding. To understand a real object in its totality we always tend to work from its parts. The resistance it offers us is overcome by dividing it. Reduction in scale reverses this situation. Being smaller, the object as a whole seems less formidable. By being quantitatively diminished, it seems to us qualitatively simplified. More exactly, the quantitative transposition extends and diversifies our power over a homologue of the thing, and by means of it the latter can be grasped, assessed and apprehended at a glance. . . . In the case of miniatures, in contrast to what happens when we try to understand an object or living creature of real dimensions, knowledge of the whole precedes knowledge of the parts. And even if this is an illusion, the point of the procedure is to create or sustain the illusion, which gratifies the intelligence and gives rise to a sense of pleasure which can already be called aesthetic on these grounds alone.[21]

For Lévi-Strauss, reading a map or a work of art in which there has been a reduction in scale seems to reverse the viewer's "natural" process of understanding. If, however, we look at the artwork empathetically, from, as it were, the point of view of the artist, the fact that it comprehends, takes into account, and discriminates among a vast array of phenomena while preserving relationships perceived between individual instances, then the artist's activity, what Lévi-Strauss would call his or her "process of understanding," is not unlike that of the scientist or the anthropologist, readable by others only in reverse, that is, from ordered principles to underlying instances. In other words, anthropologizing and painting are analogous order-oriented activities. However, this line of reasoning does raise the question of the nature and origin of order itself. As one animal taxonomist put it, "Scientists do tolerate uncertainty and frustration, because they must. The one thing that they do not and must not tolerate is disorder. . . . It can well be questioned whether the order so achieved is an objective characteristic of the phenomena or is an artifact constructed by the scientist."[22] And by extension, by the ordinary human. As Lévi-Strauss argues, the primary aspect of the mind is its will to order. As we have seen, the will to order, to take upon oneself the posture of comprehension and completeness, is a primary characteristic of the high mimetic views we have been considering. That it is not a universal value will become clear when we take up the low mimetic and ironic modes.

Just as the Harris map permits the entirety of Venice to be "grasped, assessed and apprehended at a glance," American views of wide areas of the city and portraits of its individual monuments render it both comprehensible and, in a sense, possessable. They are descendants—in scope, subject, and tone—of Bellini's and Canaletto's images and point to a preservation of the high mimetic mode into the nineteenth century, or, to be more accurate, they represent an active repossession of an earlier interpretation of the city.

Most American paintings in the herioc mode focus not on the whole city but on individual buildings. Most seize upon one monument, isolate it, center, and portrait it, carefully delineating its well-recognized features. Artists who recorded this aspect of their experience of Venice include such well-known painters as Maurice Prendergast, the less well-known Samuel Colman (1832–1920), Walter Launt Palmer (1854–1932), Francis Hopkinson Smith (1838–1915), and an unknown folk artist from New York State. One particularly noticeable aspect of these works is the not infrequent gulf between the ascribed value of the building pictured and the achieved value of the work of art.

The view that was selected for *San Giorgio Maggiore* (pl. 2, fig. 37) by Samuel Colman is not quite frontal but slightly oblique. As Rudolf Arnheim reminds us, "An oblique orientation does not fail to convey its particular expression to the viewer. This is true especially for architectural renderings . . . because a picture freezes the viewer's station point and bestows significance upon the slant. If the draftsman shows the building at an angle in order to avoid the uninformative flatness of the head-on view, he also characterizes it as turned away, dwelling in a world of its own, minding its own business. The oblique position of the building suggests that if anybody wants to approach it, he must provide his own bridge, look for the entrance, and seek out the rules of the place in order to comply with them."[23] And certainly this view is archly remote. Yet, by the same turn, by virtue of its miniaturization and completeness, it endows the viewer with a sense of possession. Colman has framed Palladio's celebrated structure in cool, remote, and timeless isolation. In his image of the church, the portrait one sees, by reflection, of Colman's model of reality (or his conception of what reality ought to be) is not far from that which is evident in Bellini's *Procession.* Hierarchy, unity, symmetry, balance, and order prevail. In fact, Colman's two treatises, *Nature's Harmonic Unity: A Treatise on Its Relation to Proportional Form* (1912) and *Proportional Form* (1920), point to exactly these as ruling principles of tangible reality. In an authoritarian tone ("for the great law of numerical harmonic ratio remains unalterable") Colman delivers the message that the world is, in fact, comprehensible, orderly, and symmetrical.[24] Within the context of this image Colman expresses this symmetry, this sense of a basic binary scientific order, by restricting his palette to a pair of color opposites: blue and orange. The two hues define structure and sails on the one hand and sea and sky on the other; they intermingle in the reflections on the water, the shadows on the structures, and in the sunset sky, vibrating against one another with various, well-modulated intensities. The effect is one of well-regulated harmony, unity, and binary balance.

More typical of these high mimetic images in respect to point of view is the flatly frontal elevation of the Rialto Bridge in *Venice* by an unknown New York State painter (figs. 28, 37). Passing over for the moment our surprise at finding a painter so completely innocent of the uses of perspective attempting a cityscape, especially this cityscape, the bridge itself is rendered as most artists have rendered it, flatly lengthwise. When a folk artist (especially a nineteenth-century American folk artist) paints or stitches an image of a horse or a shoe, these objects will be shown almost always in their broadest dimension. This is the view that is most descriptive; it shows the horse with its complete inventory of attributes—four legs, a head, and a tail—all visible and recognizable.[25] By analogy, a daisy will be seen in plan, so to speak, and a tulip in elevation, as these are the views in which the objects' distinguishing characteristics are most vis-

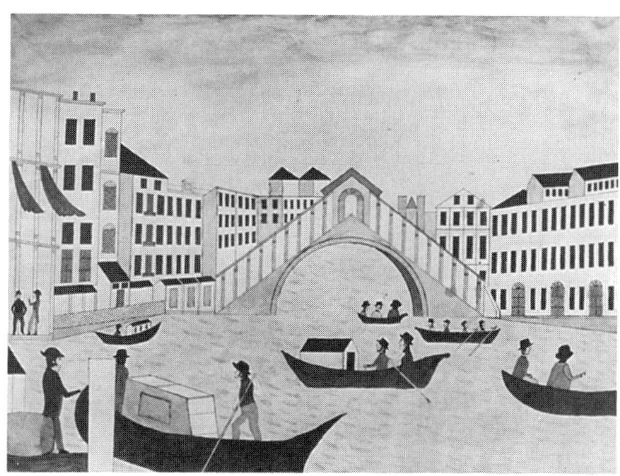

Fig. 28. Unknown, *Venice*, ca. 1840–60, watercolor, 14¾″ × 19¾″, New York State Historical Association, Cooperstown; see also fig. 37.

ible. A building or structure, then, to be shown in its most characteristic pose, will usually be shown whole and frontally, the viewer's line of vision perpendicular to the facade. This is not how structures are experienced, of course, but it is how they are remembered, and there is a great deal of the mnemonic device in these high mimetic views of Venice. They are views of expectations confirmed, of traveling memories remembered. The frontal elevation of a bridge or building is essentially two-dimensional and suggests little about the three-dimensional volume contained within. We do not know from this image, for instance, that one of the remarkable things about this sixteenth-century bridge is that it is seventy-two feet wide, accommodating shops along both sides. What is important for this artist, clearly, is that it is a single-arch span (the lift of the hump greatly exaggerated here), that it is in an urban setting, and that small, peopled boats row under it. As disappointing as the idea is, it is probable that the artist who painted this view did not leave America. The fact that the structures flanking the bridge seem to be reversed, and that the shutters that are invariably green in Venice are here red, point to the probability that this view was made from a print (of such a painting as Guardi's *View of the Rialto,* National Gallery of Art, Washington, D.C.). However, the use of a print in this case, and of a photograph in the case of the Brown painting (fig. 24), point to an inevitable fact of Venetian views—all are preknown and preinterpreted; all artists have some awareness of how it was "done" before. This Rialto also points up the fact that whatever liberties a high mimetic artist takes with his subject, he must key his visual syntax carefully; he must cluster those elements without which the object is unrecognizable and with which the whole balloon of associations will, for the viewer, rise freely and grandly.

Other images in this portrait mode include the *Palazzo Dario* (fig. 8) by Joseph Lindon Smith, discussed earlier, and *The Salute at Noon* (fig. 29) by Walter Launt Palmer. Both render Grand Canal monuments with an unambiguous heroic frontality. Unlike Canaletto's broader epic views, these are taken from a lower, more human point of view, usually five to twenty feet above the water level. The virtue of this lower and frontal point of view is the sense of invitation and relative approachability it achieves. The two-dimensional character of an elevation view is a limitation particularly suited to Venetian architecture. Always more concerned with presentation and surface, Venetians expended great care and great fortunes on facades while the remaining envelope of the building, even when plainly visible, was often meanly treated. Even the Salute, less frontal and more versatile of facade than most structures because of its octagonal

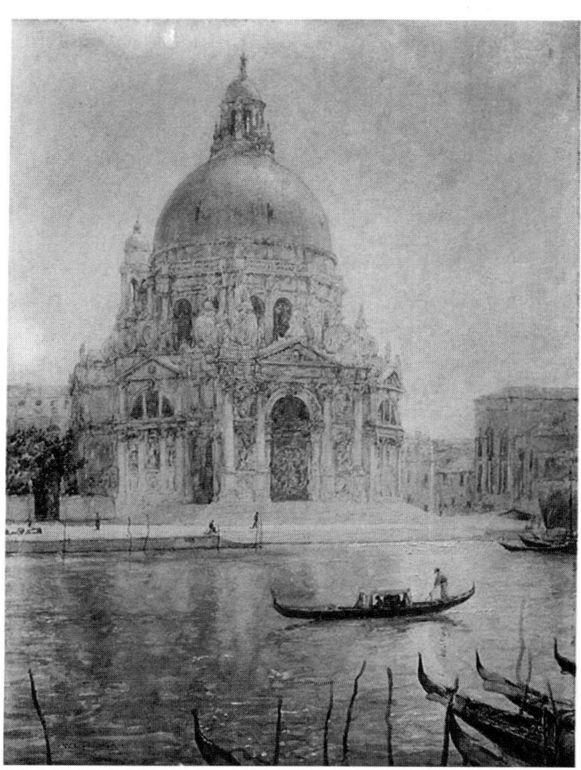

Fig. 29. Walter Launt Palmer, *The Salute at Noon*, ca. 1890–1900, watercolor, 23⅞″ × 18″, Metropolitan Museum of Art, Gift of Walter L. Palmer; see also fig. 37.

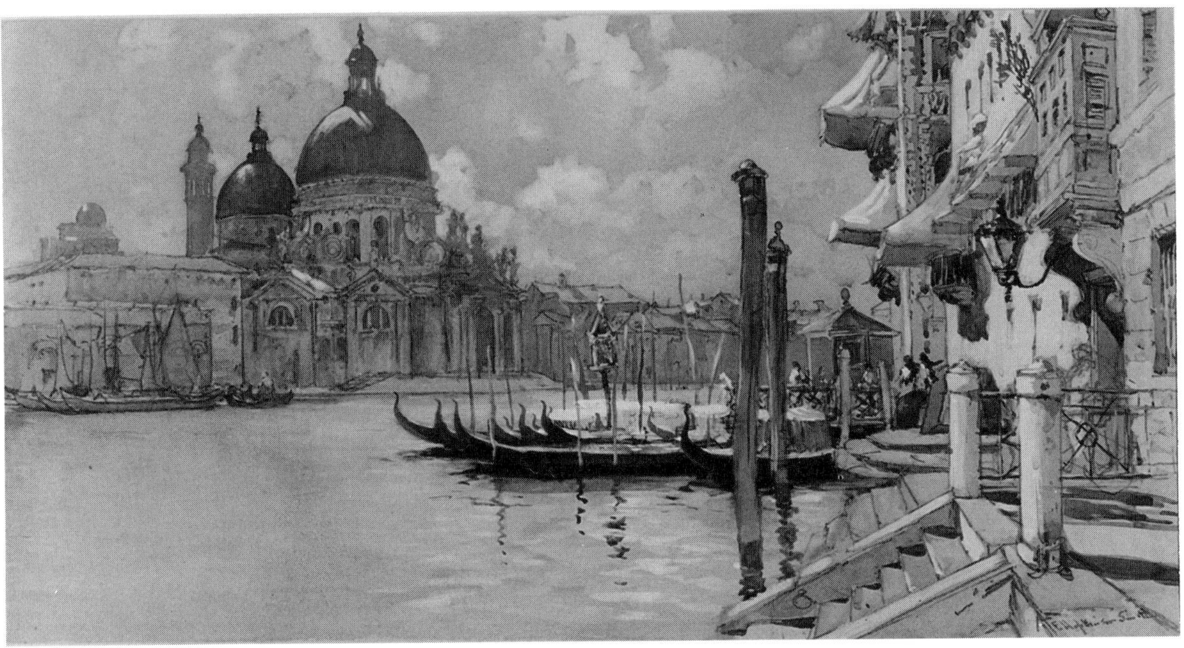

Fig. 30. Francis Hopkinson Smith, *Venice: The Grand Canal with Santa Maria della Salute*, before 1892, gouache and pencil on gray carton, 12¾″ × 23¼″, Isabella Stewart Gardner Museum, Boston.

shape and domed roof, wears the full vocabulary of ornament only on the three facets facing the Grand Canal—for the rest, it turns its bare haunches.

Palmer's Salute image is one of a large family of portraits of this celebrated baroque building. In fact there probably are more images of this church than of San Marco and the Doge's Palace combined, despite their greater intrinsic aesthetic and historic interest and their advantage of years. The reason for the popularity of this building lies in its felicitous combination of exuberance and overstatement with elegant and fine proportions (although Victorian painters such as George Loring Brown, as we have seen in his *On the Grand Canal* [fig. 24], often elongated the upper sections to bring it more in line with their proper idea of what a suitable termination for a public building ought to be—a tower/dome combination as on the Connecticut State House.)[26] Also significant in the Salute's visual reputation is the effect of the play of sun and shadow on its deeply sculptural surface against the blue of the sky and the azure of the Grand Canal. But most significant is the accident of its placement opposite that range of palaces which were destined to become some of the most-frequented hotels in Europe. This strip, comprised of the Hotel Royal Danieli, Grand Canal Hotel and Monaco (now Hotel Monaco e Gran Canale), Grand Hotel d'Italie-Bauer (now Hotel Bauer Grünwald), Hotel de l'Europe (now Hotel Europa e Britannia), and the Grand Hotel, line the opposite bank of the great waterway, their premiere rooms overlooking the church and beyond, the Giudecca, the Lido, and the blue Adriatic. *Venice: The Grand Canal with Santa Maria della Salute* (fig. 30) by Francis Hopkinson Smith points up this proximity with the facade of the Europa (the Palazzo Giustiniani), its pleasant awnings and waiting gondolas prominently in the foreground. The portal of the church is inflected slightly toward us, although the volute above is seen in profile. Here the monument is tamed, domesticated, taken on holiday. The whole image partakes of that mnemonic character that imprisons it within the point of view of the admiring tourist.

With a very different measure of success, the watercolors of Maurice Prendergast repossess and make contemporary the high mimetic visage of Venice's monuments. A visitor to Venice in 1898–99 and 1911, Prendergast is one of the few artists who worked extensively in all three modes, high mimetic, low mimetic, and ironic. Representative of the high mimetic are *Saint Mark's Square, Venice (The Clock Tower)* (fig. 31), *Venetian Palaces on the Grand Canal* (fig. 32), and *Square of San Marco, Venice (Splash of Sunshine and Rain)* (fig. 35).[27] Even more than in the Joseph Lindon Smith *Palazzo Dario* (fig. 8) or Palmer *Salute* (fig. 29), here the perimeter of the monument coincides with the perimeter of the painting. The format mimics the building, enclosing it and only it in its sacred space, like an icon deliberately abstracted from nonprecious reality. Paradoxically it is Prendergast more than any other artist who bestows upon his subject a tone of absolute contemporaneity. One breathes in these images the spirit of his own day, a tone given to his pictures as much by his inclusion and treatment of figures as by his oft-remarked "impressionistic" technique and palette. One is repeatedly struck with the avoidance most other artists felt for people in their pictures of Venice. When figures do appear, they are often disappointly overplayed, as in the cloyingly sweet tourists of Ralph W. Curtis (1854–1922, as in *The Gondola* at the Isabella Stewart Gardner Museum, Boston) and the cloyingly picturesque peasants of Frank Duveneck (1848–1919; see fig. 86). In Prendergast's images both Venetians and visitors possess an enviable grace and naturalness. Half of the magic of these pictures is to be found in the compatibility Prendergast contrives between these heroic structures and his fragile but ennobled humans, so well naturalized in this extraordinary habitat.

In the image of the clock tower (fig. 31), a multitude of parasoled women, hatted men, and children spill out of the archway that tunnels under the clock tower and links the Piazza to the Merceria dell' Orologio, one of the principal pedestrian thoroughfares between the Rialto and San Marco. We look at the scene from a slight eminence, about ten feet off the ground. As a result, the pavement spreads generously under our feet—the figures falling down the page in a much-remarked Japanese fashion—and the tower itself seems less lofty than its seventy feet. In fact, Prendergast has striven to portray the buildings as much as possible as a flat elevation, not as a towering structure looming over our heads. In a second version (1911, Stanford University), he shows the crowning balustrade and the great bronze bell ringers (here deleted) from a vantage point quite incompatible with the space defined on the pavement. For both images he has mounted, as it were, a fictitious scaffold to see the top half of the structure from about twenty-five feet off the ground, or he has backed down the Piazzetta about seventy feet. This combination, this synthesizing of views we have seen before in the Turner and other compositions, but here it is the vertical

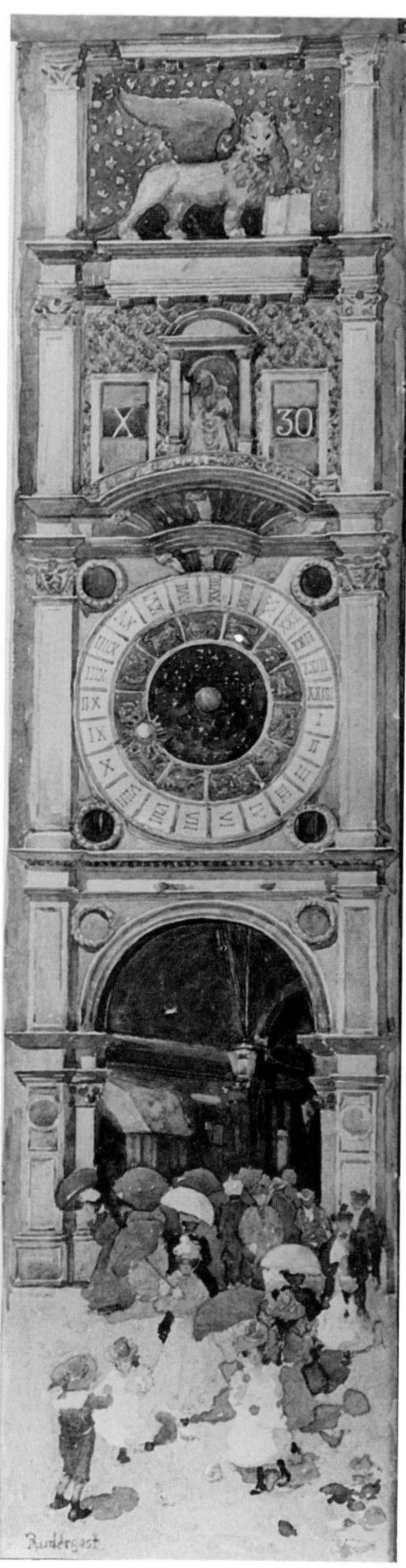

Fig. 31. Maurice Prendergast, *Saint Mark's Square, Venice (The Clock Tower)*, ca. 1898–99, watercolor, 23½" × 5¾", William A. Farnsworth Library and Art Museum, Rockland, Maine.

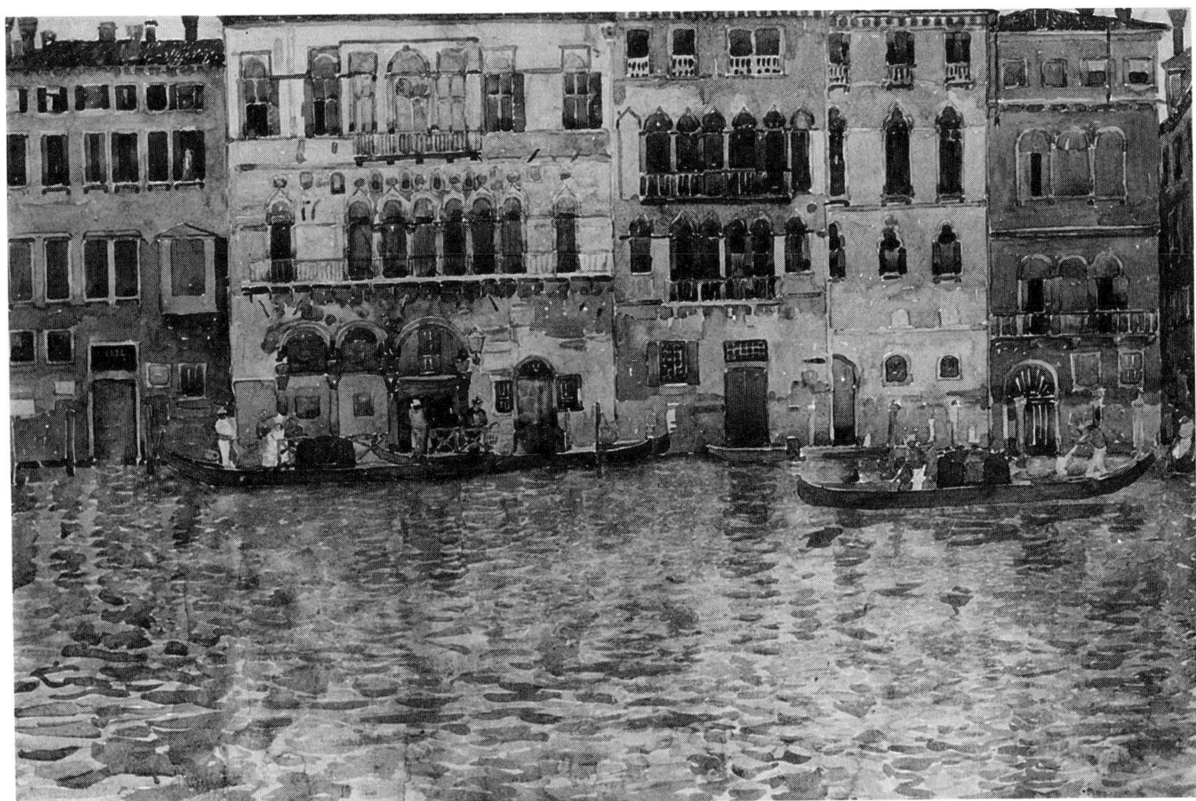

Fig. 32. Maurice Prendergast, *Venetian Palaces on the Grand Canal*, 1899, watercolor, 17¾″ × 14⅛″, collection of Mr. and Mrs. Arthur G. Altschul; see also fig. 37.

dimension which is being manipulated and synthesized from multiple vantage points. The result is a structure seen in its entirety, in its own calm, self-sufficient majesty. It is a heroic structure, not, as the modernity and informality of the figures might suggest, a mere building in a low mimetic scenario. It retains its stature and contrives to reflect this posture on the pedestrians as the presence of the Virgin and her heavenly companions elevated the doge and the terrestrial structures in Tintoretto's *Doge Pietro Loredan* (fig. 17).

The suprareality of this extraordinary tower is made clear by its heraldic and royal coloring. The zodiacal wheel, the quiet Madonna, and the great winged lion are all picked out in a lapis lazuli shade of blue and precious gold, simulating a page from a book of hours in which the value of the object portrayed is reflected in the materials portraying it. This conceit is further carried out in the frame on the later version, almost certainly the work of Maurice's frame-making brother, Charles, with its gilt gessowork on a rich blue ground.

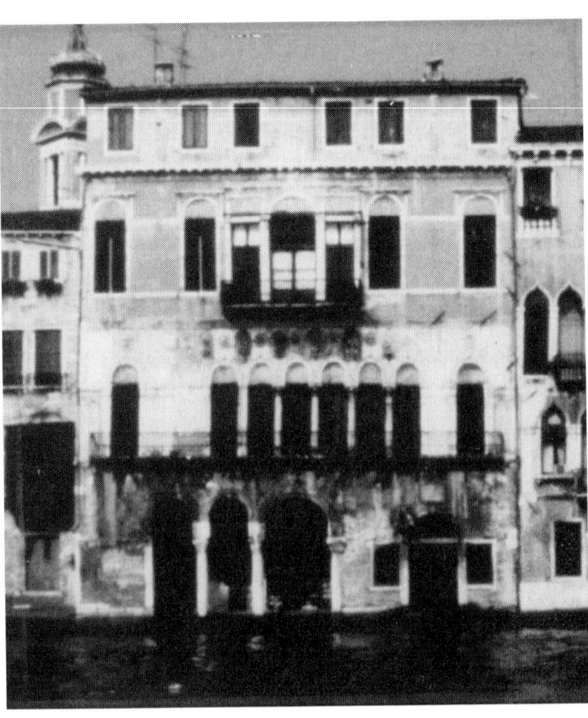

Fig. 34. Site of Maurice Prendergast, *Venetian Palaces on the Grand Canal* (fig. 32): Cà da Mosto, twelfth and thirteenth centuries; uppermost floor seventeenth century.

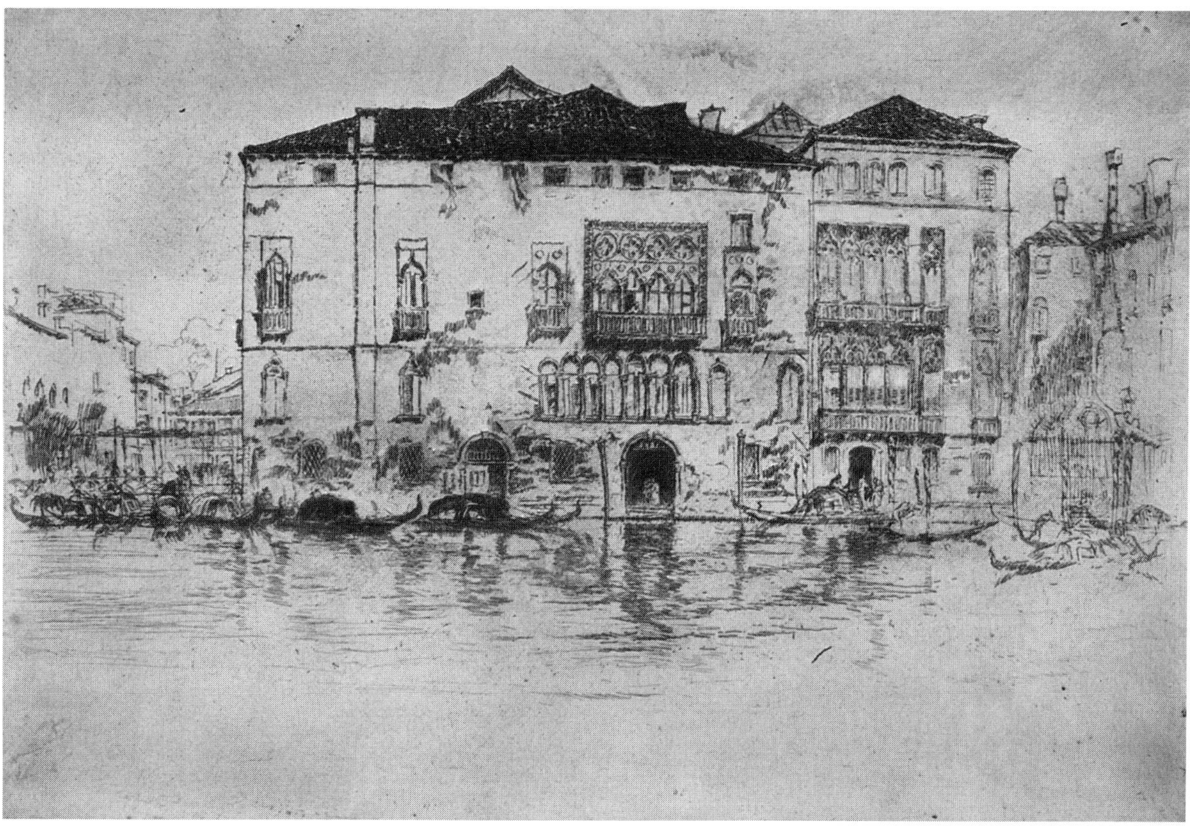

Fig. 33. James McNeill Whistler, *The Palaces*, 1880, etching and drypoint, 9⅞″ × 14⅛″, Los Angeles County Museum of Art, the Julius L. and Anita Zelman Collection; see also fig. 37.

That sense of mastery over an architectural object which Lévi-Strauss discusses as one of the results of creating an image of it ("Being smaller, the object as a whole seems less formidable. . . . [It] can be grasped, assessed and apprehended at a glance.") is clearly at work here and in other Prendergast views of tall structures. In this case the artist has relieved us of the discontinuity of tilting our eyes through an arc of ninety degrees to take in the prospect from the pavement to bell ringers. To make up, in a sense, for this diminution, to allow us to resee it as grand, he has emphasized the isolation, the amputation of the structure from its flanking fellows.

While Prendergast clearly does not read his buildings factually—for him as for all artists the monument is a live actor, interpreted, manipulated, and controlled by the artist, not simply recorded—he could be said to interpret them less historically and morally than some. *Venetian Palaces on the Grand Canal* (figs. 32, 37) impresses us more with its odd spatial arrangements than with any immediate sense of the pressure of centuries or the moral nature of the past or present inhabitants. A large palace with three arched openings at its waterline and two moored gondolas at its door occupies the principal space left of center. It is balanced on the right by a pair of thin buildings, and flanking on both sides are smaller, less elaborate houses, one pink and one brown, contrasting with the buff of the central structures. The whole is raised up uncomfortably high in the rectangle, pressing the upper limits of the paper with cornices and chimney pots. The water is full of life and variety but presents a barrier to the viewer and seems disproportionately treated at the expense of the sky. The ingenuously frank frontality, as in the anonymous *Venice* and the Joseph Lindon Smith *Palazzo Dario* images, puts off our questions about the third dimension.

By contrast, the superficially similar large-scale etching by James McNeill Whistler called *The Palaces* (figs. 33, 37) presents a very different interpretation of a similar subject.[28] Whistler's pair of palaces, like Prendergast's, are flatly perpendicular to the viewer's line of vision, but they are bilater-

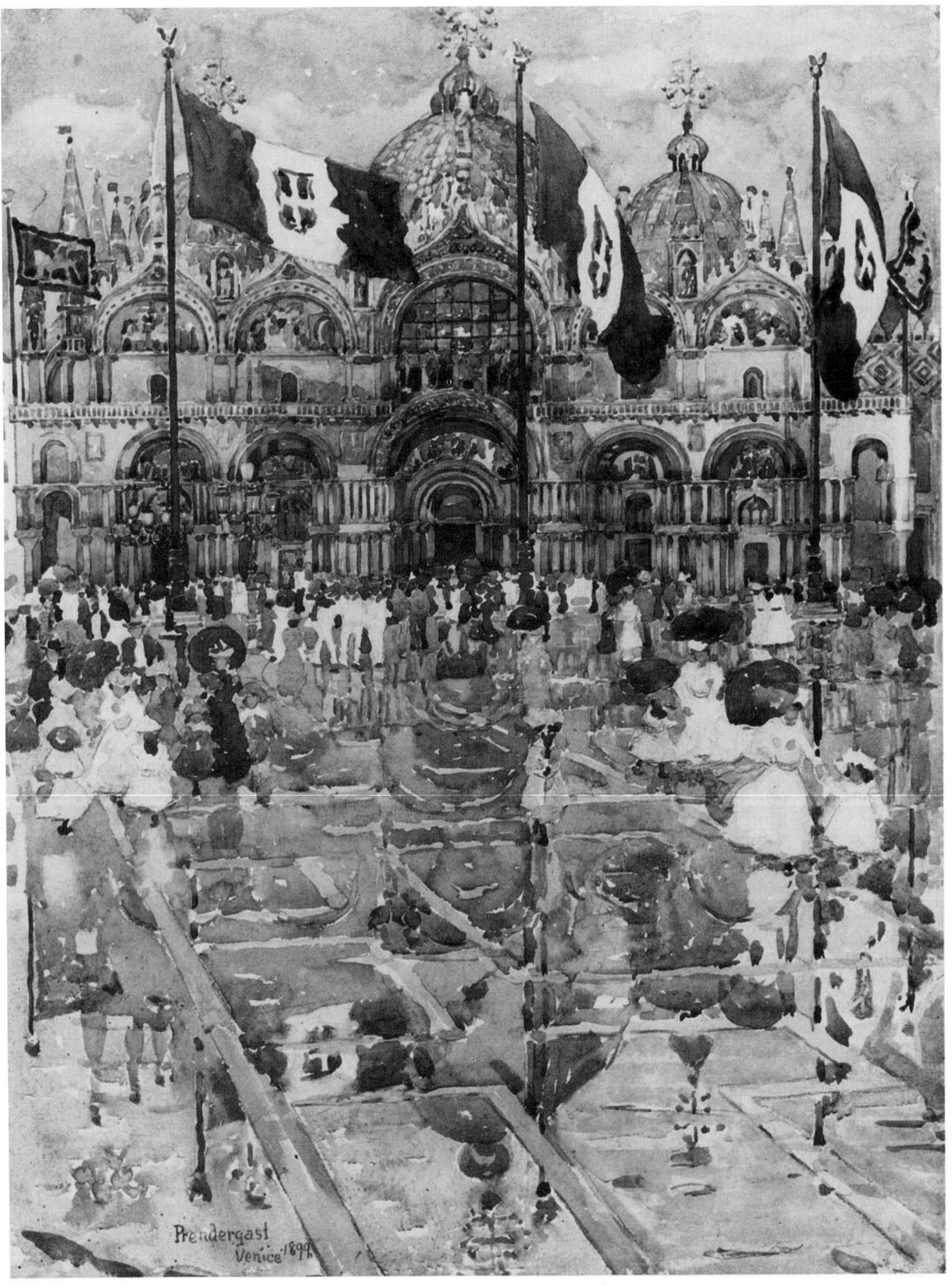

Fig. 35. Maurice Prendergast, *Square of San Marco, Venice (Splash of Sunshine and Rain)*, 1899, watercolor, 19⅜″ × 14¼″, collection of Alice M. Kaplan; see also fig. 37.

ally asymmetrical, well located within the fictive space defined by the plate, and suggest at every possible opportunity the third dimension. Intriguing vistas plunge deeply into space on either side; the rooflines suggest spatial volumes and multiple remodelings; and the entrances are deep apertures through which we glimpse tenebrous interiors. Curtains flutter from the servants' quarters under the roof, and deep bruises and shadowed irregularities mark the passage of time on the exterior. Pathos here points to the "relaxed charm" of the romantic mode. A deep long ripple on the water gestures us toward the axial portal, and the gondolas on the sides point out in our direction with a suggestive diagonal. Whistler has contrived to make the palace simultaneously historic, somewhat inhabitable, and very poetic. We sense here James's "we are divided . . . between liking to feel the past strange and liking to feel it familiar" and liking best of all an equal balance between the two sensations. Whistler has given his palaces a temporal dimension, suggesting both the long extent of time since construction and the small incident of today. Yet how lightly the hand of time (or the tone of pathos) intrudes on our imagination here when compared to that which Ruskin demands in his description of a slightly older palace: "It is a ghastly ruin; whatever is venerable or sad in its wreck being disguised by attempts to put it to present uses of the basest kind. It has been composed of arcades borne by marble shafts, and walls of brick faced with marble: but the covering stones have been torn away from it like the shroud from a corpse; and its walls, rent into a thousand chasms, are filled and refilled with fresh brickwork, and the seams and hollows are choked with clay and whitewash, oozing and trickling over the marble,—itself blanched into dusty decay by the frosts of centuries."[29] For Ruskin structure is humanoid, and nothing presses harder on his imagination than the sense of something architectural, live, and noble, murdered and violated in its grave. The sense of historic process arouses our pity and even our righteous indignation about "present uses of the basest kind." The reading is, above all, time oriented and moral. Prendergast's palace, the twelfth-century Cà da Mosto, is ancient, but his treatment—unlike that of Ruskin or Whistler—repudiates historic time. It is also amoral, emphasizing instead the absolute contemporariness of the structure and of his interpretation; he has willfully sheared off the seventeenth-century fourth story of the principal palace to maintain his symmetry (see fig. 34). He insists that we see it heroically, brightly in the light of 1899.

The most extraordinary of Prendergast's high mimetic paintings of Venice is the compressed and exuberant facade of San Marco in *Square of San Marco, Venice* (*Splash of Sunshine and Rain*) (figs. 35, 37). As in *Venetian Palaces,* the architectural structure is pushed to the upper half of the image, brushing its lightning rods on the frame, while in the lower half a wide expanse of watery reflection plays back the image. As in the clock tower paintings, the vertical limits of the building define the pictorial frame. Our vantage point is on the direct axis with the central portal and the domes, about twenty feet above the pavement. As the church's facade is not at right angles to the Piazza, the marble lines that follow the axis of the Piazza move through the picture plane on an oblique diagonal. The vantage point is, indeed, precisely that selected by Bellini for his primary point of view in the *Procession* (see figs. 12 and 13, 36 and 37),

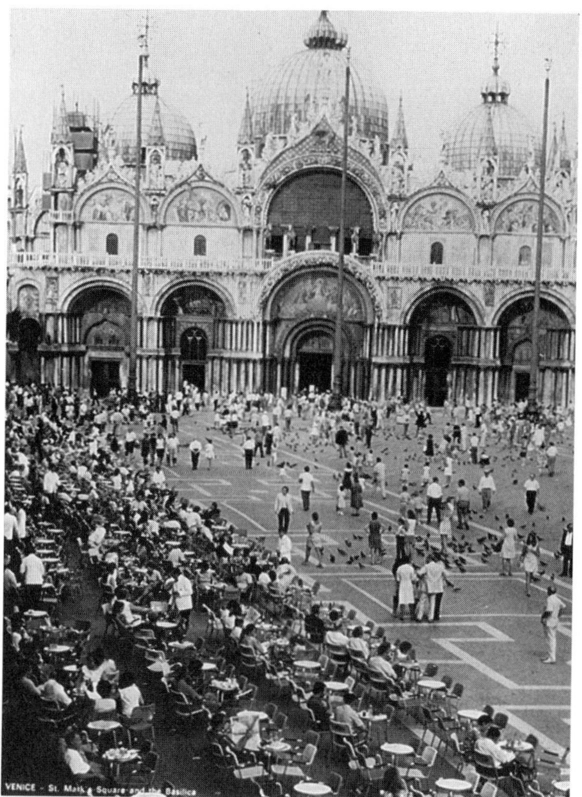

Fig. 36. San Marco from the vantage point indicated in fig. 37 (G), that of Maurice Prendergast, *Square of San Marco* (fig. 35).

trimmed vertically here to exclude the flanking buildings. Prendergast, however, unlike Bellini, preserves the incongruity of this topographical fact. One feels the white lines *ought* to converge at the portal, and it is eccentric and unsettling to watch them orient themselves so precisely to an unseen, unexplained system for which we have no clue within the picture frame and which clearly wars with the primary element in the painting. Capitalizing on these unsettling elements is one of the most notable characteristics of Prendergast's earlier style. A modern photograph (fig. 36) gives a clear sense of the site.

One of the remarkable aspects of this image is Prendergast's ability to sustain the high mimetic celebratory tone, yoking the great grave monument and mere humans together without bathos, pathos, or anticlimax. The scattered figures—often portrayed as negative spaces, mere bare paper defined by surrounding pigment—walk easily in this space and are ennobled by their association with the great building, as Bellini's processional figures are by the same device. Here the building makes no appeal to our pity for the ravages of time, it casts no ironic glance on the diminution of life since its era of grandeur; instead it is seen clearly and majestically as a great protagonist participating in contemporary life.

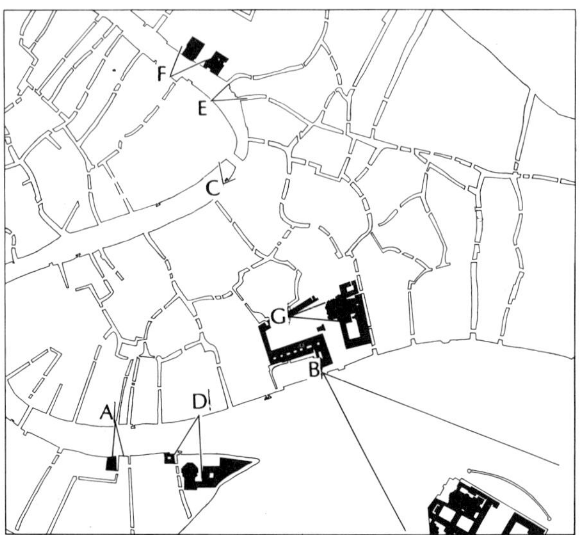

A. Smith, *Venetian Scene (Palazzo Dario)*, fig. 8
B. Colman, *San Giorgio Maggiore*, pl. 2
C. Unknown, *Venice (Rialto)*, fig. 28
D. Palmer, *The Salute at Noon*, fig. 29
E. Prendergast, *Venetian Palaces on the Grand Canal*, fig. 32
F. Whistler, *The Palaces*, fig. 33
G. Prendergast, *Square of San Marco, Venice*, fig. 35

Fig. 37. Map of sites of figs. 8, 28, 29, 32, 33, 35, and pl. 2.

This high mimetic celebratory tone is difficult to maintain in the light of late nineteenth-century reality, but like Prendergast in *Square of San Marco, Venetian Palaces,* and *Saint Mark's Square, Venice (The Clock Tower),* Henry James also uses it, equally adroitly, in *The Wings of the Dove* (1902). Although the action of the novel is also set in London, the most memorable, emblematic scenes take place in Venice—on the Piazza ("a great social saloon"), in the fictive Palazzo Leporelli (Milly's "great gilded shell," "the ark of her deluge"), and Merton Densher's rented rooms near the Rialto ("refined in their shabbiness, amiable in their decay").[30] As a setting Venice functions to support the tone of the novel and becomes an integral aspect of its final appeal. As is fitting for a Venetian setting, James gives us base conspiracy, illicit love, even murder in a sense, combined with a high heroic redemption. Milly Theale, like Venice, is a quantity of ascribed value; she is young, handsome, wealthy, dovelike, and fatally ill. Her harmony with the general atmosphere of the city and the specific setting of her rented palazzo is noted by Densher early in their "courtship"; he finds a spell of sorts in "her welcome, her frankness, sweetness, sadness, brightness, her disconcerting poetry, as he made shift at moments to call it, helped as it was by the beauty of her whole setting and by the perception, at the same time, on the observer's part, that this element gained from her, in a manner, for effect and harmony, as much as it gave" (2:202).

As one would expect, the death of Milly is attended by general mourning; with Ruskin's pathetic fallacy, storms lash the city, and in the Piazza "there were stretches of the gallery paved with squares of red marble, greasy now with the salt spray; and the whole place, in its huge elegance, the grace of its conception and the beauty of detail, was more than ever like a great drawing-room, the drawing-room of Europe, profaned and bewildered by some reverse of fortune" (2:285). James has alluded in his title not just to the beatific Biblical dove but also to the city of Venice and to Ruskin, its greatest nineteenth-century champion. The chapter on the Venetians (Veronese, Titian, and Tintoretto) in *Modern Painters* is entitled "The Wings of the Lion" (alluding to the lion of Venice's patron, Saint Mark), and it concludes with a resonant Ruskinian coda: "and swiftly, and utterly, as a rainbow vanishes, the radiance and strength faded from the wings of the Lion."[31] But the romantic, elegiac note Ruskin sounds is not James's. For James there is the possibility of education, in the broadest sense, and of redemption. Like Prendergast he sees Venice and its monuments as contemporary actors in the human drama. Much of value has utterly vanished and is invisible, but what remains is part of the present, is valued, and is, aesthetically speaking, useable.

A wide range of American artists worked in the high mimetic mode, and like Bellini, their interpretations offered recognizable monuments at ascribed value, seen from a vantage point often higher than normal human height and composed with a sense of symmetry or careful balance. Their works vary in tone, scale, period, and subject, but all, to some degree or other, cast Venice in the epic light. Some, like Colman, literalized a theory of order and hierarchy in a straightforward, uncomplex vision. Others, especially Prendergast, engaged the mode itself in a dialogue. His refusal to allow the customary fictive margin around and above the monument implies a probing, a questioning of the nature of artifice, especially high mimetic artifice. Not just a symptom of Prendergast's movement toward two-dimensional modern picture space, or of his knowledge of Japanese prints or avant-garde French painting, this restriction and constriction of the imaged building probes, teases, and confounds our expectations, especially our expectations about monuments. Enframed and symmetrical they are, but puzzles, he insists, they remain, images to jar us out of complacency, out of any usual form of monument watching. They have no space, we have no space but that tipsy gulf of water or pavement to measure them. His strategy, his conspiracy, seems to be to jar the mnemonic device into really entering itself, in its own right, at its own value, into our consciousness.

THREE

Belatedness in a Fallen World: The Low Mimetic Mode

During the period on which this study focuses, the dominant mode (literary and painterly) was low mimetic. Traces and strong memories of high mimetic and romance were present as we have seen, and hints of an ironic mode visible, but the bulk of work was low mimetic in character. In Frye's definition, the protagonist in this mode is "superior neither to other men nor to his environment, the hero is one of us: we respond to a sense of his common humanity, and demand from the poet the same canons of probability that we find in our own experience."[1] In painterly terms, the subject (in our case an architectural protagonist) and the point of view, the stance, and the scope of vision of the viewer are nonheroic. It is the posture of the low mimetic painter of Venice to appear to take life and incident more or less as he finds it, to avoid the principal monuments, and to appear to decline to interpret the scene he views. In high mimetic views we have noted that the artist concentrates on buildings of ascribed value, adopting a point of view and a tone that imply a collaboration and agreement on the part of the viewer, an understanding of the high value of the object portrayed and the acceptance of that evaluation at face value. In the low mimetic mode the artist declines to declaim, declines the role of omniscient narrator. He is less overtly a displayer or an active interpreter and more a discoverer, concentrating on small but "telling" visual incidents. The withdrawal from the role of active interpreter is attended by a greater self-consciousness of craftsmanship, of the art of portrayal per se. Thus it is common to read about such an artist as Sargent that his Venetian subjects are "random," "just problems of form and color, opportunities for the exercise of his supreme craftsmanship," "vehicles for statements about colour and light."[2] However, from an inspection of the works themselves it is clear that careful, nonrandom "rules" for site selection are operating and that craftsmanship is, as usual, a means to an end, to an achieved vision which includes and even focuses on subject.

In terms of technique, artists of low mimetic images often employed media that suggest spontaneity, in which the gestural stroke of the brush or pen or chalk or etching needle is visible and readable as mark as well as fictional form. While some low mimetic views are, of course, oil paintings, many are modestly scaled etchings, pastels, and watercolors, executed with an eye more for inference than description. While the high mimetic artist desired wholeness of form and clarity of vision, a quintessentially low mimetic artist like Whistler delighted in fragmentary form described entirely in inferential terms. But the "incompleteness" of form, the "spontaneity" of the strokes, and the "accidental" quality of subjects are equally part of a carefully, artfully planned and arranged posture toward art making and toward the world.

Casting themselves in the role of discoverers of unknown sites and truths rather than re-recorders of well-mapped sites and truths as in the high mimetic mode, artists of the low mimetic mode sought what Henry James has termed "the speck of truth, of beauty, of reality, scarce visible to the common eye"[3] for their subject. And having found this mote, this antithesis to the grand monument of ascribed value, they sought—by means of the isolation and concentration available to art—to elevate to value the intrinsically nonvaluable, to show the common eye that which is remark-able within its own common purview. The artistic product could be a gem even if the subject had no gemlike characteristics. For it was clear to them as it was to James that, if the art were well done, the big subject of the Doge's Palace was not necessary: "where a light lamp will carry all the flame I incline to look askance at a heavy."[4] These "light lamps" are, of course, only comparatively speaking mere motes. After all, the subject remained Venice and had, therefore, already a given modicum of magic and value. The avoidance of "heavy lamps" or at least the direct glare of heavy lamps was at least in part attributable to a sense of artistic and historic belatedness. The long shadows of predecessors—Byron and Turner, and before them the prodigious Shakespeare and Tintoretto—made a direct appropriation of their subjects, their tone, their mimetic stance impossible. Moreover the Victorians, trapped in de-Byronized prosaic modernity, responded necessarily to a different, a more modest sense of place. Their works can be read as symptoms of a world in which models of physical, psychological, and social reality were profoundly unlike those of their predecessors. Perhaps most significantly Venice itself could no longer maintain the brave posture of high mimetic (even in the elegiac romantic mode) after Ruskin's eloquent and popular chronicle of its fall in *The Stones of Venice* (1851–53). The sense of power and confidence inherent in the broad-sweeping, clear-eyed, monument-celebrating heroic mode was difficult to maintain, even naive, in the face of the oppressive Ruskinian sense of its postlapsarian physical and moral decay.

While for Ruskin architecture itself signaled a specific loss of nature, it could also express the inherent nobility or baseness of its makers.[5] An aesthetic achievement, it was also a touchstone, an eloquent record of moral fervor. By reading her stones he read the inner history—the moral and political as well as the aesthetic history—of the Venetian people: "For the evidence which I shall be able to deduce from the arts of Venice will be both frequent and irrefragable, that the decline of her political prosperity was exactly coincident with that of domestic and individual religion." These Venetians were, he deduces from their arts, "long disciplined by adversity, and compelled by . . . position either to live nobly or to perish;—for a thousand years they fought for life; for three hundred they invited death; their battle was rewarded, and their call was heard."[6] Although Ruskin seems to have intended the case of Venice to be in some measure a warning, a lesson for the present, some understood its message, its tone, less with pity and fear for the awfulness of Venice's fall and decay than with the pleasure of a languid charm. As William Dean Howells (1837–1920) put it in the chronicle of his sojourn in the city as consul, *Venetian Life* (1866), "for my own selfish pleasure, I should be sorry to have Venice in any way less fallen and forlorn that she is."[7]

"Fallen and forlorn" are not so much literal qualities seen in the low mimetic images as qualities felt in the several composing strategies that the artists devised. What these images have in common is their insistent avoidance of the heroic posture and, by implication, an understanding of the postlapsarian nature of their subject. The artists do not appropriate ascribed value but labor to construct, synthesize, discover value. The order and system of hierarchy within the image is not appropriated from the subject itself—as in the *Palazzo Dario* and similar images—but is framed and asserted, created by the artist afresh for each image. For part of the fiction of the low mimetic mode is to show us a familiar, a "common humanity" world but simultaneously to discover it and enlighten us on its nature. Each artist then, becomes a stout Cortez overlooking not the wonderful and the magnificent but the quotidian and the ordinary and, by the alchemy of his art, imparting some measure of value to the site so discovered.

The Slide off the Monument

As invention is not unlimited, low mimetic images of Venice seem to fall into families or types based on point of view, visual field, format, composition, and principally on subject and treatment of subject. The first of these types that I will consider involves a dodge, an incomplete repudiation of the monument and a complete repudiation of the monumental. The artist working in the low mimetic mode knows all about high mimetic and about our knowledge of it. He plays with our modal expectations and leans on our knowledge of topography, often carefully including heroic monuments from nonheroic vantage points. In this way the artist jolts his viewers with his unusual and eccentric interpretation, discovering and appropriating the monument anew for himself and for his audience.

Prendergast's image of the Rialto bridge (fig. 38) and Eugene Lawrence Vail's (1857–1934) *Jour de fête à Venise* (fig. 40), like the *Cà d'Oro* (fig. 9), are not portraits that confirm our knowledge of the monuments portrayed or of the conventions of monument portrayal in general. Like the earlier anonymous watercolor of the Rialto (fig. 28), the arc of Prendergast's bridge is distorted, emphasizing the upward leap of the two sides (see fig. 39).[8] Most significantly, the bridge is abruptly, arbitrarily truncated

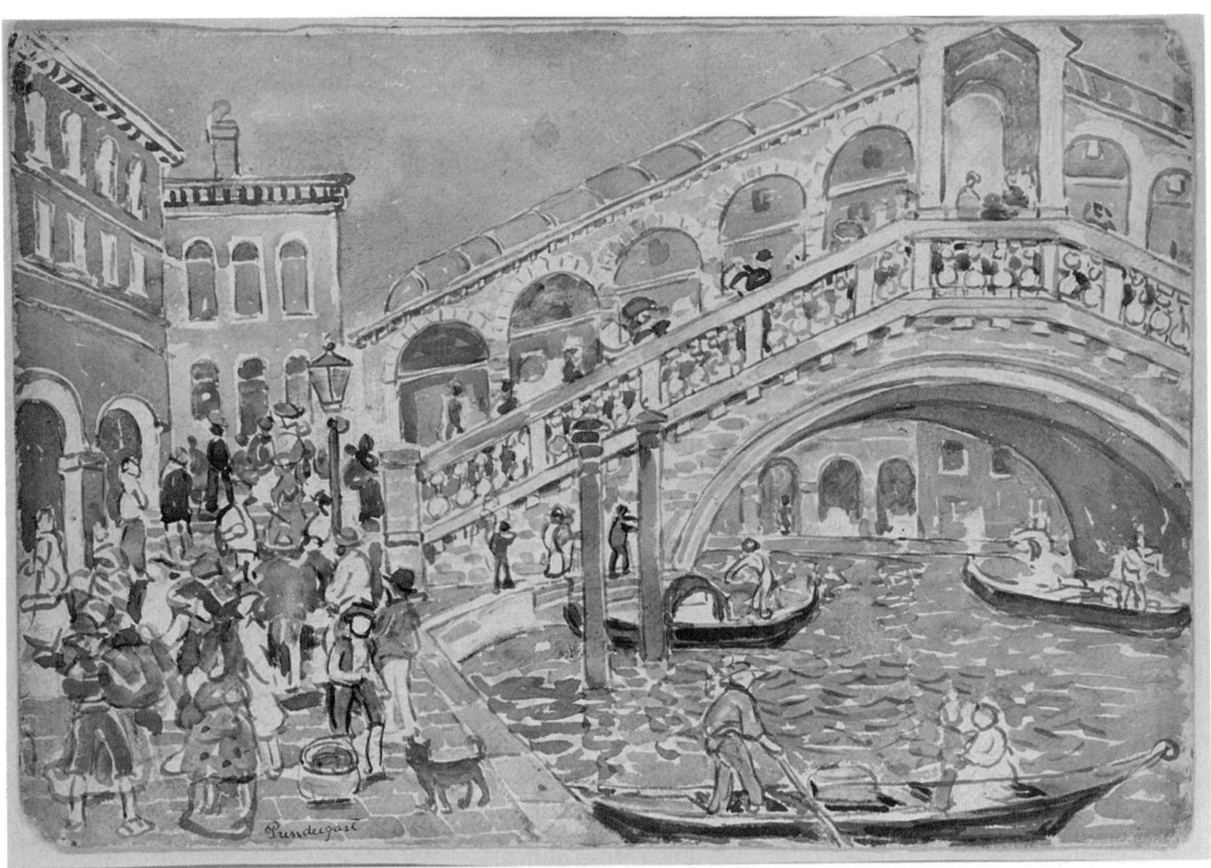

Fig. 38. Maurice Prendergast, *The Rialto Bridge, Venice*, ca. 1911–12, watercolor, 15¼″ × 22⅛″, Metropolitan Museum of Art, the Lesley and Emma Sheafer Collection, Bequest of Emma A. Sheafer, 1974.

on the right-hand side. We can complete the image only because we know the bridge and the rules of symmetry fundamental to its structure. Similarly, the Vail painting purports to be "about" enormous oversize flags, while two-thirds of the facade of San Marco uneasily and asymmetrically fills the background. In both cases the artists have departed from the symmetry and completeness that "explain" a building to a viewer. They have selected significant slices of recognizable portions of well-known elevations, but they have insisted that a merely human point of view—unfiltered, unheroicized, unorganized and therefore partial experience—be shown. The effect is unsettling and, taken to extremes, moves into the ironic mode.

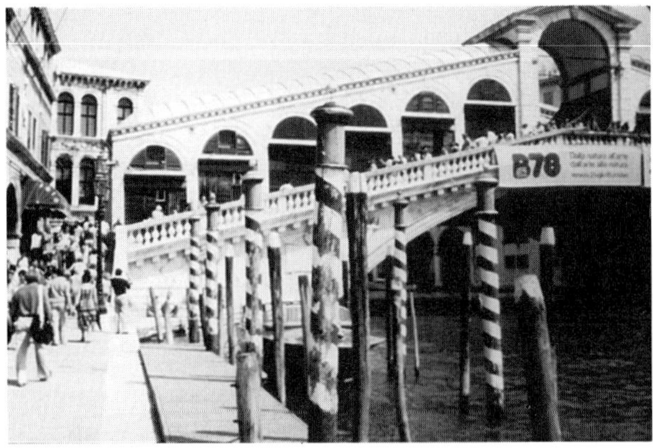

Fig. 39. Site of Maurice Prendergast, *The Rialto Bridge, Venice* (fig. 38).

An even more successful low mimetic strategy for incorporating yet repudiating high heroic monuments is not so much to see them in partial or sliced frontal views as to see them "backwards." In such images as *Venice: Off San Giorgio* (fig. 41) by Edward Darley Boit (1840–1915), *Rio Santa Croce e Santa Maria della Salute* (fig. 42) by Andrew Fisher Bunner (1841–97), and *In Venice* (fig. 43) by William Merritt Chase (1849–1916), the observer is offered nearly unrecognizable rear views of three time-honored churches: San Giorgio Maggiore (Boit), the Salute (Bunner), and Santa Maria del Rosario (Chase) (see fig. 44). All sense of symmetry, of

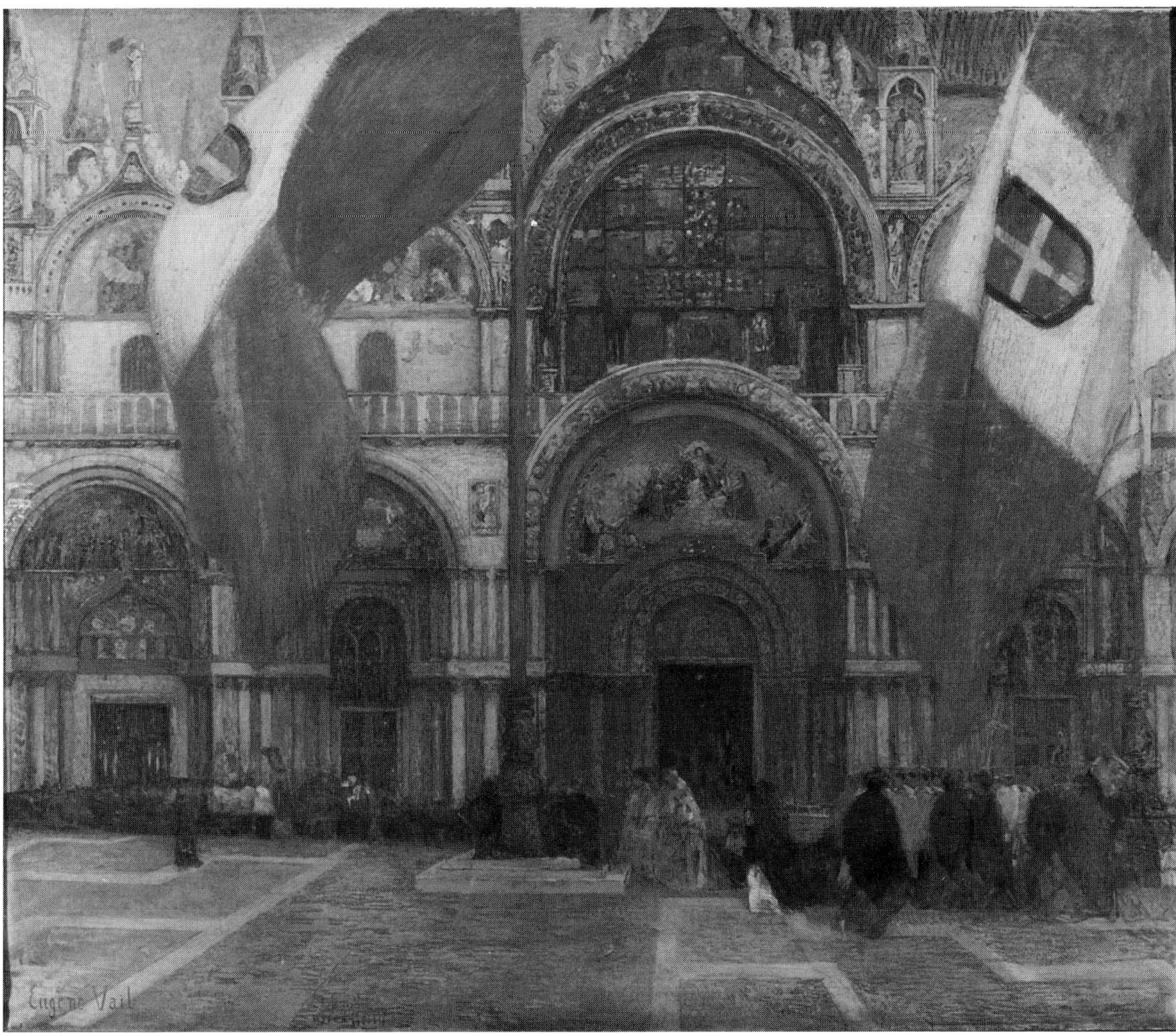

Fig. 40. Eugene Lawrence Vail, *Jour de fête à Venise*, ca. 1903, oil on canvas, 68″ × 78½″, Brooklyn Museum, Gift of Alfred W. Jenkins.

declamatory ecclesiastical statement are lost as the disoriented viewer struggles to recognize a familiar sense of place in the clusters of buildings portrayed. When compared to the Colman view of San Giorgio (pl. 2) or Canaletto's *Bacino* (fig. 3), Boit's interpretation of the church and its surrounding buildings represents a diminution, a distinctly more modest posture than his predecessors. He has chosen to work in small size and in watercolor to interpret an obscure, backwards view of one of Venice's primary architectural ornaments. Yet there is a sense of assertion in the "discovery" aspect of such a view. Boit has willfully ignored the architect's intentions, skirting around the builder's demands for scale, tone, and proper approach, and created his own hierarchy and order out of the given elements. Taking a water rat's view of the scene he has shrunk San Giorgio's campanile and dismissed the dome, enlarging a meager lighthouse to something like equal weight with the disconcerted church. In this way he repudiates the high mimetic pictorial structure and subject while still evoking its resonance.

Bunner's strategy is somewhat different—he undercuts the celebratory tone of the monument not by diminishing its parts but by placing them in a juxtaposition with time-worn vernacular forms. The point from which he observes the serene Salute is on the Giudecca near the Redentore (see fig. 44). From the narrow confines of the Rio Santa Croce he has a telescoped prospect across the wide Giudecca Canal to the shabby dwellings along the Zattere, the swelling domes of the Salute, and beyond, to the campanile of San Fantino across the Grand Canal. This extremely narrow and confined pros-

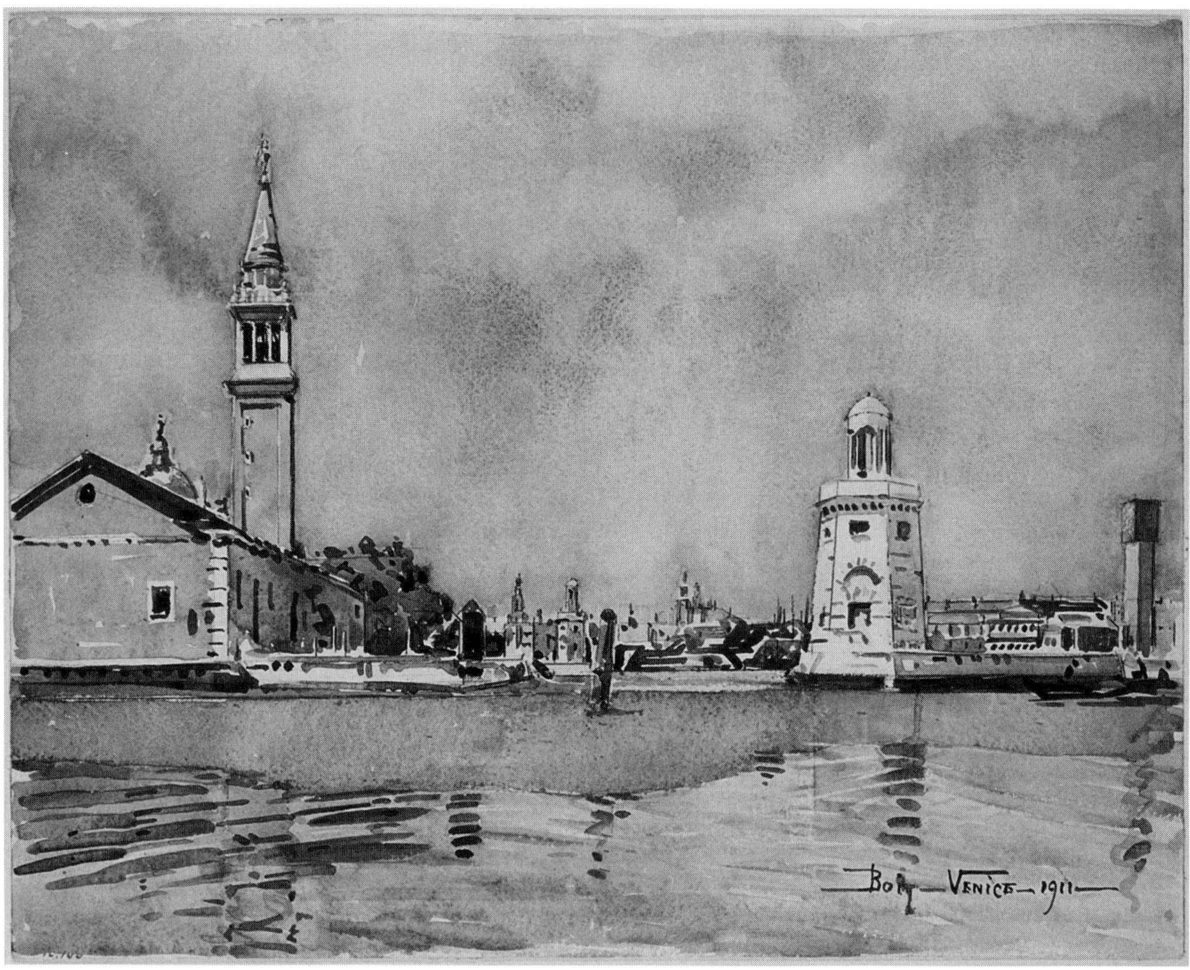

Fig. 41. Edward Darley Boit, *Venice: Off San Giorgio*, 1911, watercolor, 14¼″ × 19″, Museum of Fine Arts, Boston, purchased, Picture Fund; see also fig. 44.

pect is one which recurs often; in fact, it is one of the hallmarks of low mimetic images. This apse-on view gives us a clear inventory of the Salute's minor dome and twin towers, but the soaring volutes, the spacious steps, and the heroic portal are invisible. They are implied, in fact invoked, in the name of the image, and in that respect, these views generate an odd three-dimensionality which is usually absent in heroic images of the frontal facade-oriented architecture of Venice. The artist gives us the back, and from the name we supply the front elevation. These back elevations, being of little concern to the designer of structure or of civic space in Venice, present an odd jumble where, even if symmetry is present as in this case, the sense of scale and approach are oddly jolted by neighboring structures. Here Bunner has reorganized the view with his arbitrary but neat narrow axial point of view. However, we read the arch of the little bridge and the swelling volume of the dome as related forms, a yoking that is less flattering to the dome than to the bridge. The parapet is cracked and irregular, laundry hangs from neighboring windows, and shutters hang askew. That this is a fallen world with heroic memories is clearly part of Bunner's interpretation. This postlapsarian vision is one which had been seen in views of Italy, especially rural pastoral Italy, since the late seventeenth century. However, in these low mimetic Venetian images the scene has shifted to the city, and it takes on a different tone in these urban surroundings where no lush vegetable forms or grazing flocks suggest regeneration and life within a sense of loss.

One of the most notable aspects of all low mimetic oblique views of the Salute, of which Bunner's is a good example, is the visual divorce of the domes from supporting, preparatory structure underneath.[9] Above the tiled roofs of rather ordinary

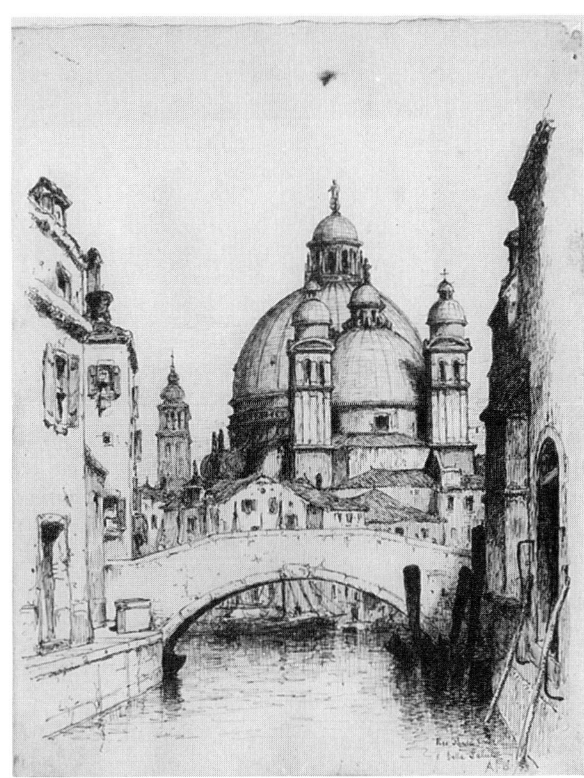

Fig. 42. Andrew Fisher Bunner, *Rio Santa Croce e Santa Maria della Salute*, ca. 1883, pen and ink, 13″ × 9⅜″, Metropolitan Museum of Art, Gift of Mrs. Andrew Fisher Bunner, 1899; see also fig. 44.

structures they partake (as Ruskin described the San Marco domes) "of a natural buoyancy, as if they floated in the air or on the surface of the sea."[10] Unlike their rectilinear weight-bearing neighbors these unreal bubbles suggest the fantastic while they assist the viewer in his search for spatial orientation and measure. The site of Chase's *In Venice* would be irretrievable, so ordinary is his prospect, if he had not included the dome and spires of Santa Maria del Rosario (dei Gesuati) and the long spine of its nave, in the upper right of his picture. The low mimetic character of this image is evident not

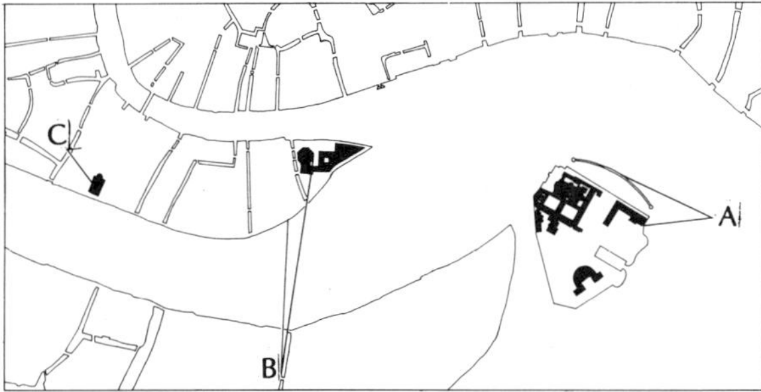

A. Boit, *Venice: Off San Giorgio*, fig. 41
B. Bunner, *Rio Santa Croce e della Salute*, fig. 42
C. Chase, *In Venice*, fig. 43

Fig. 44. Map of sites of figs. 41, 42, 43.

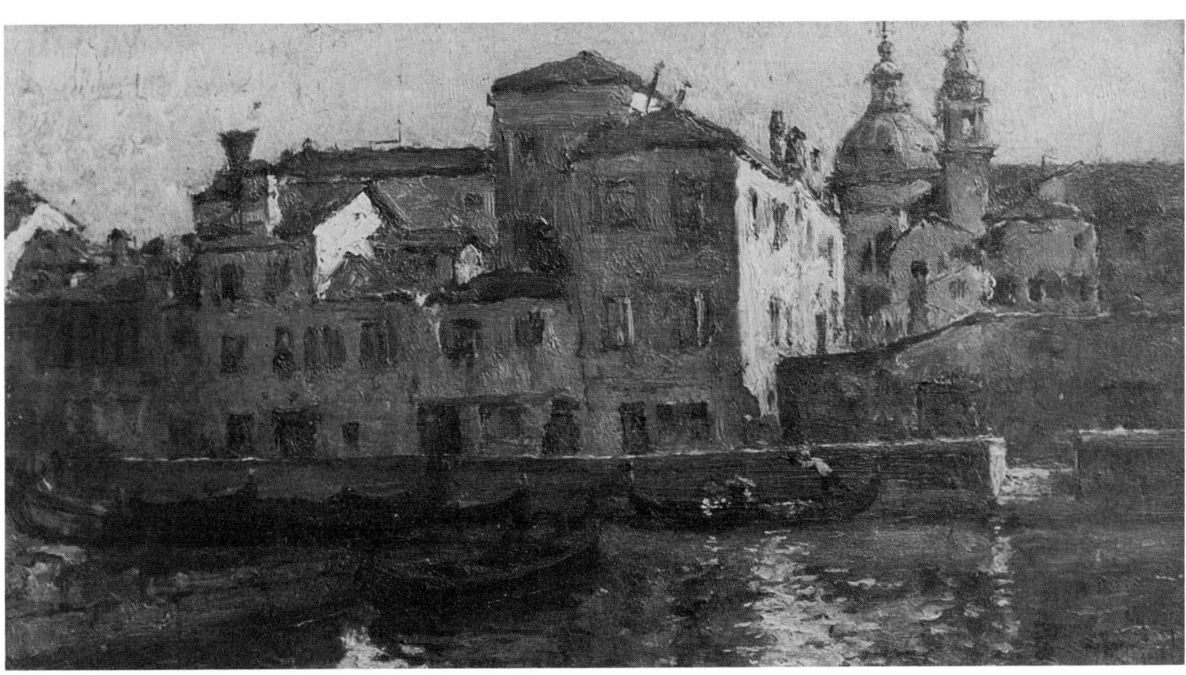

Fig. 43. William Merritt Chase, *In Venice*, ca. 1877, oil on wood panel, 6½″ × 11⅜″, Museum of Art, Rhode Island School of Design, Providence, Bequest of Isaac C. Bates; see also fig. 44.

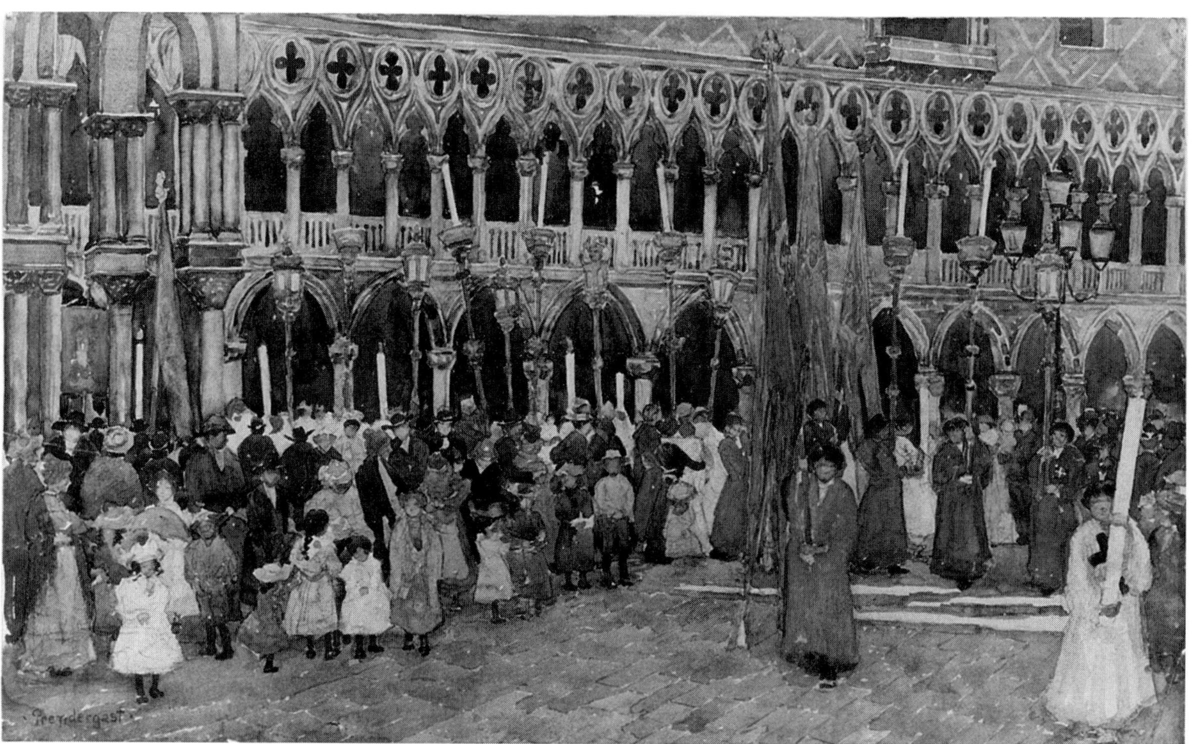

Fig. 45. Maurice Prendergast, *Festival Day, Venice*, ca. 1898–99, watercolor, 12⅝″ × 20″, Mount Holyoke College Art Museum Collection, South Hadley, Massachusetts; see also fig. 48.

only in the homely ill-lit structures and boats he includes, but also in his decision to stand on the Campo San Trovaso and turn his back to that church (see fig. 44). This partial inclusion of the Gesuati, a church famous for its superb Tiepolos, a Tintoretto Crucifixion, and a robust eighteenth-century facade, is a quiet gesture of acknowledgement to the tradition in which he sees himself but with which he declines to compete.

The Chase view is an oil painting, but it is a scant six inches high. Its modesty of scale and subject has a parallel in Bunner's insistent pen-and-ink, Boit's watercolors, and the pastels and etchings repeatedly preferred by other artists of Venetian scenes during this period. These had been traditionally regarded as secondary media, either preparatory (watercolor and pen drawing) or reproductive (etchings). They were less expensive to make and to purchase, and consumed less time in production than oils (a pastel work, for instance, often being accomplished in a single sitting). In comparison with oil painting, expecially the oversized heroic compositions of the first half of the century, the reputation of these media, so to speak, was for physical smallness, modest aesthetic ambition, and speed. Not by any means new on the artistic scene (pastels, for instance, were widely used in eighteenth-century France and watercolor in eighteenth-century England), in the late nineteenth-century they take on new uses, permit the artists new freedoms. It was not illogical for low mimetic artists approaching the subject of Venice (home of the great colorists Titian, Tintoretto, and the master of large-scale complex composition, Veronese) to seek a different means of expression. Works in these minor media did not, of course, necessarily take less time to create than an equivalent subject in oils, but they retained their reputation for instantaneousness and impulsiveness which seemed to free the artist from that oppressive nineteenth-century critique: "lack of finish." So by adopting a posture of modesty in subject and medium, the artist could also obtain tolerance for a certain license in technique and handling.[11] The use of these media is, of course, most appropriate for these "backwards" images which seek to privatize and domesticate the public and the monumental.

Curiously the artist who consistently showed himself most fearless of the presence of his predecessors, least oppressed by his belatedness, is Maurice Prendergast. In his high mimetic watercolors

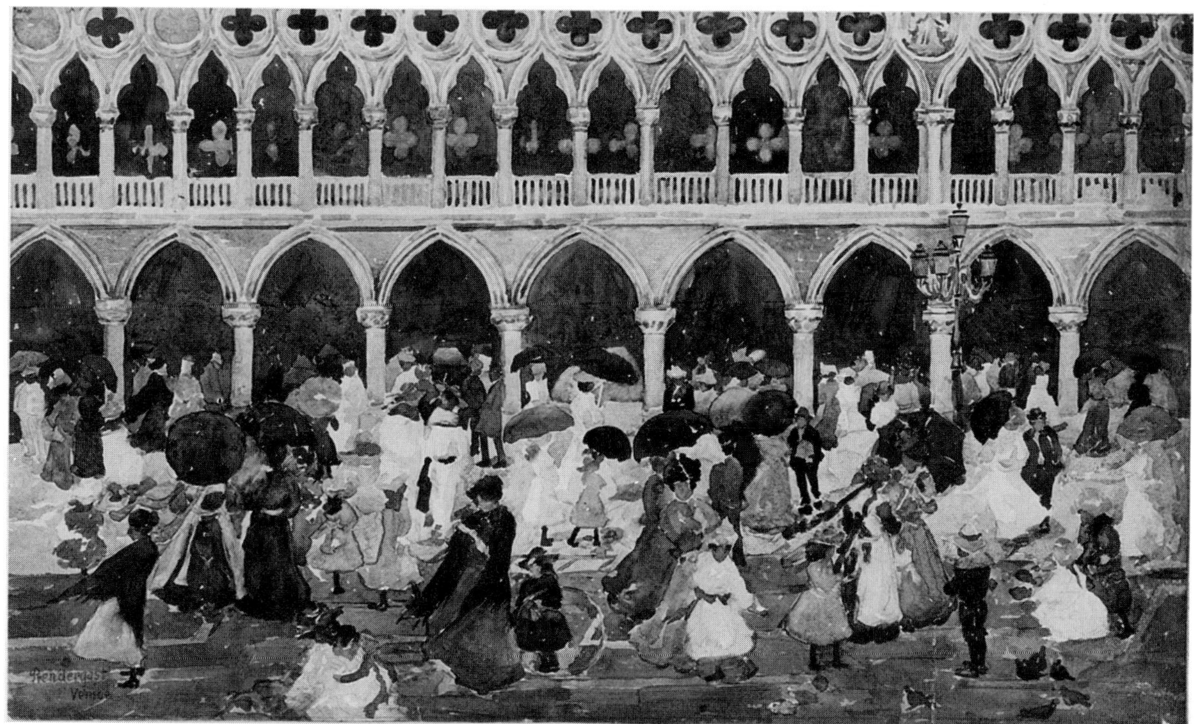

Fig. 46. Maurice Prendergast, *Sunlight on the Piazzetta, Venice*, ca. 1898–99, watercolor, 12½" × 20⅝", Museum of Fine Arts, Boston, Gift of Mr. and Mrs. William T. Aldrich; see also fig. 48.

that were considered in chapter 2, he seized upon the conventions of monument viewing and, with a dramatic constriction of format, insisted on the artifice of his realism. In his low mimetic images he often included a monument, but not as in *Saint Mark's Square, Venice (The Clock Tower)* (fig. 31), enframed and celebrated, nor as in the Boit and Chase pictures, slyly portraited from behind. In such images as *Festival Day Venice* (fig. 45), *Sunlight on the Piazzetta, Venice* (fig. 46), and *Umbrellas in the Rain, Venice* (fig. 47), he includes partial slices of the Gothic facades of the Doge's Palace—a structure Ruskin referred to as "the central building of the world"—frontally but as if by accident, a mere backdrop for scenes of public life.[12] The focus is on the figures—their movement, color, and relationships. The monument is not centered, not explained, not catechized. Our eye slides off its buff-colored repetitive arches after a moment's hesitation to confirm our place, and then loses itself in the bright blues and reds of figures and reflective pavement, full of incident and variety. Here the monument is not the overt reason or cause for the picture—it is a foil and support for the central action.

In high mimetic views the artist consistently preserved the vertical integrity of the building portrayed: campaniles are shortened (as in Tintoretto's *Doge Pietro Loredan*, fig. 17) or omitted altogether if their inclusion would be vertically partial (as in Tintoretto's *Doge Alvise Mocenigo*, fig. 15). Cupolas and roof peaks often brush the top of the frame, but the picture's vertical dimension has been calculated for and determined by their inclusion (see, for instance, figs. 8, 19, and 29). Prendergast presses this organizational principle in his high mimetic images, as we have seen, and abandons it altogether in some of his low mimetic views. In these three pictures (figs. 45, 46, and 47) he has excluded the solid wall of the upper half of the Doge's Palace, giving us only the lacy negative voids of the arcades, rhythmic and stable but not weight-bearing and substantial. Only corners of the building that are closely butted by neighboring structures are included; the Adam and Eve corner is carefully avoided (see fig. 48). The effect is one of closure and confinement; no sky or vista into deep space beyond the truncated building is permitted. The palace is in no way described as a volume or established in spatial relationship with other structures. Moreover, Prendergast's horizon

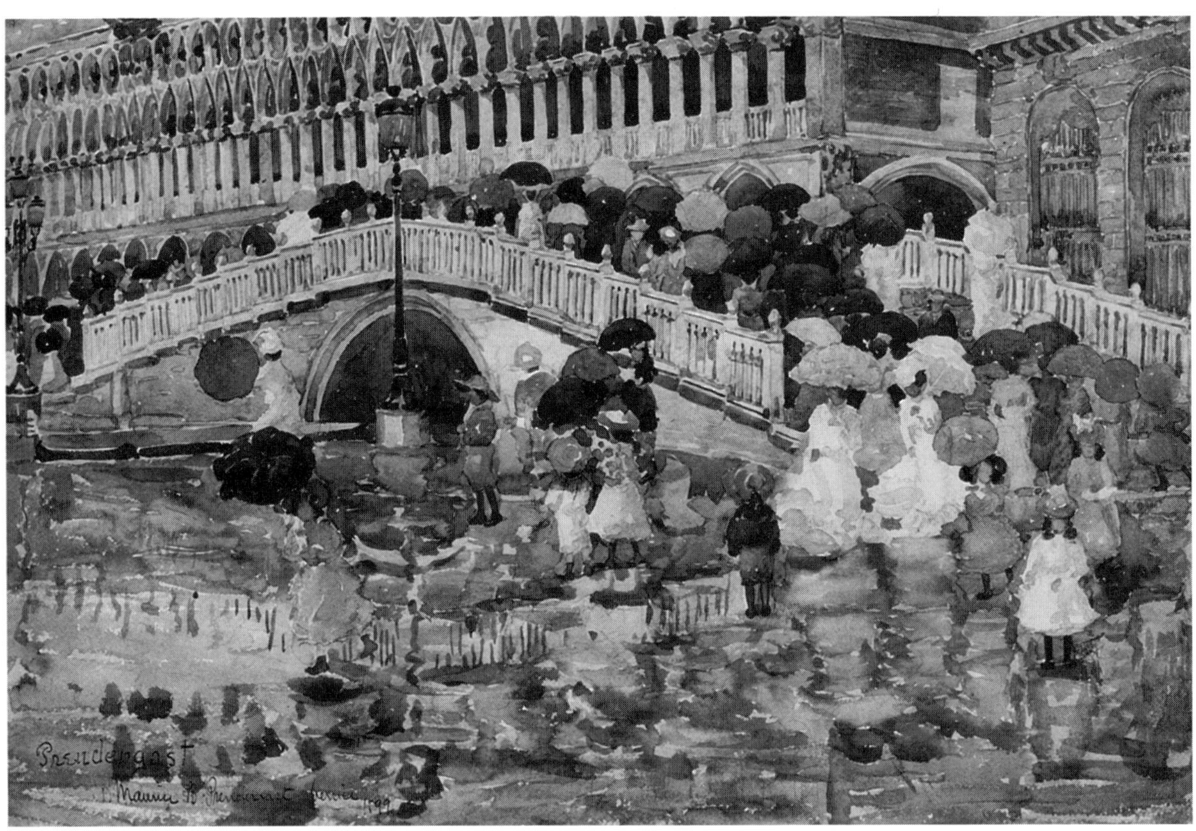

Fig. 47. Maurice Prendergast, *Umbrellas in the Rain, Venice,* (Ponte della Paglia), 1899, watercolor, 13⅝″ × 20½″, Museum of Fine Arts, Boston, Charles Henry Hayden Fund; see also fig. 48.

line is high—about half-way up the rectangle in these scenes—a structuring device that departs from the stable 1:2 ratio of most landscape and genre views, which places a third of the picture content below the horizon and two thirds above. By this eccentricity of arrangement, Prendergast permits the subject to press uncomfortably against the top of the frame, reminding us of the artificial, arbitrary nature of the artist's sense of closure. This is especially true of *Umbrellas in the Rain* in which the figures mount the Ponte della Paglia, placing the human content of the picture above the horizon line and leaving the bottom half to wet pavement. Also mildly discomforting is the slicing of the building, both vertically and horizontally. It seems not merely incomplete but also ungraspable.

If there is truth in Lévi-Strauss's observation about the nature of miniaturization as a means by which an object may be "grasped, assessed and apprehended at a glance," then the miniature that is incomplete fails to give us this satisfying power (see p. 27). Hence we are as baffled as "when we try to understand an object or living creature of real di-

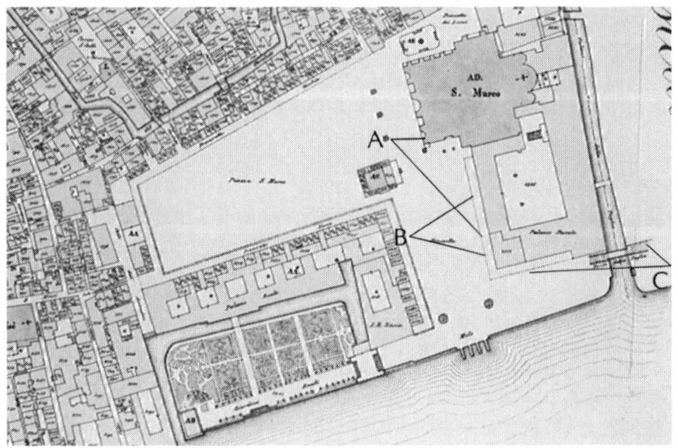

Fig. 48. Map of sites of figs. 45, 46, 47.

mension" because knowledge of the whole cannot precede knowledge of the parts. In fact we are at a greater disadvantage than when confronted by the real object, for the homologue has been sliced, and we can never know the excised parts (except by conjecture, extending the rules that govern the structure as we see it, or by memory of the object if recognizable, as in this case). The use of and toleration for "sliced" views, especially those truncated vertically, implies, then, a toleration for unresolved bafflement. This seems to be a characteristic of some low mimetic views and, as we shall see, of most ironic images. It is a fundamental point of distinction between these images and those in the heroic mode where all effort is bent on stability, wholeness, and comprehensibility.

Although the Ducal Palace is not the major element in these three images, the selection of fragments of its facade and the handling of those fragments dictates in large part how we interpret the human content of the pictures. Comparison with a contemporary (high mimetic) photograph of this site (fig. 49) suggests the degree to which Prendergast endows this very public site with the interesting accidents of private experience. That the whole image is carefully plotted from the outset and that the architectural portions were painted first is clear from such surviving unfinished works as a second version of *Umbrellas in the Rain, Venice* (ca. 1899, Metropolitan Museum of Art).[13]

Prendergast's ability to specify time and weather is extraordinary—rain and damp, twilight, wind, sun, and deep afternoon shadow. But unlike the romantic emphasis on time, this temporality is not overtly emblematic. It is more descriptive of time present than nostalgic of time past, and it finds expression in reflections and shadows—objects in human scale, not grand expanses of sky. He gives us a broad spectrum of figures, gondoliers, nursemaids, people of fashion, picturesque women in dark shawls, and dozens of children, all faceless but each distinct and plausible in posture and gesture. These are Henry James's "light lamps," the "specks of truth, of beauty, of reality,—scarce visible to the common eye," the raw material of low mimetic fictions, common humanity. The Ducal Palace is not common architecture, but it is treated here as a low mimetic, seemingly accidental stage set for random human action. It is, as it were, almost incognito, recognizable but treated without ceremony or celebration. As in the Blum *Cà d'Oro* (fig. 9) and the Boit *San Giorgio* (fig. 41) the center of interest slides off the heroic nature of the structure. The artist's arrangement of his elements deliberately undercuts the monument's given ascribed value and bestows dignity and value on elements not intrinsically precious, consecrated by history or by common recognition. And more than anything, he appropriates to himself the ability and prerogative to confer value.

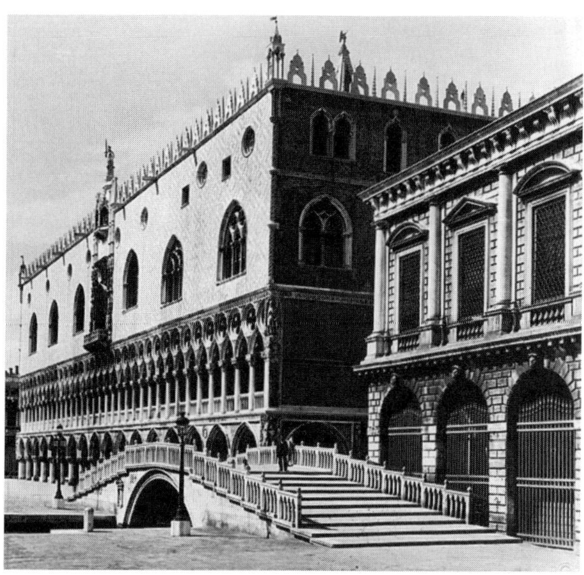

Fig. 49. *The Doge's Palace*, ca. 1890, photograph, Alinari/ Art Resource.

The ingredients, then, that make these low mimetic views are three: the emphasis on ordinary human figures, the inclusion of recognizable monuments only if treated unmonumentally, and, most important, the limited, merely human, incomplete frame of experience (for the low mimetic protagonist is superior to other men neither in power nor in knowledge or ability to comprehend). The ingredients that make these works of art are to be found in the artists' ability to arrange these elements in such a way—to borrow Henry James's terminology—as to resee and revalue them.

A Ghost upon the Sands of the Sea

A second type of low mimetic image is, like the previous group, closely related to the high mimetic mode. Images of the Riva curving off into space and images of the entire city from a distant point in the lagoon often have a high vantage point and include recognizable monuments. However, the difference between these images and Colman's *San Giorgio Maggiore* (pl. 2), for instance, is to be found in the relative attention or inattention given to the heroic structures, and in the tone of the interpretation.

The Riva degli Schiavoni links the Molo to the Riva di Cà di Dio, the Riva San Biagio, and the Riva dei Sette Martiri, a broad continuous walkway

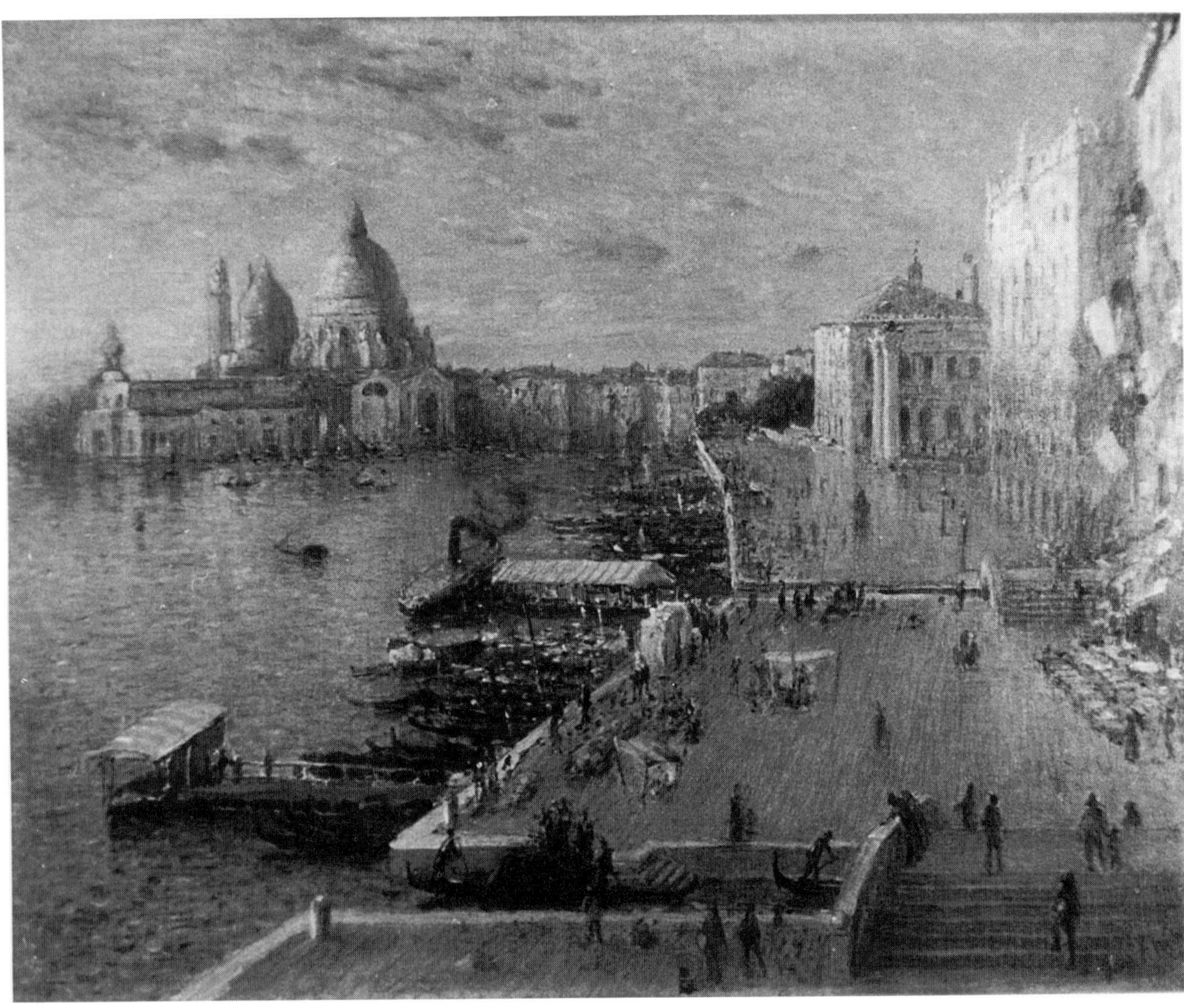

Fig. 50. John Ferguson Weir, *Venice*, ca. 1890, oil on canvas, 20″ × 24″, Mattatuck Historical Society, Waterbury, Connecticut.

which terminates at the Public Gardens (see fig. 53). It is the only place in the city where the nineteenth-century enjoyment of a promenade could really be indulged. Bounded on one side by the Bacino and on the other by palaces, churches, and a full complement of Venetian vernacular architecture, it offered not only physical exercise and social opportunity but also, uniquely, a good view of large sections of the city from dry land. Its long curve into space gave the artist an easily appropriatable composition—foreground events connected by a clear diagonal pathway to an eventful distant background. Moreover, the architectural elements were full of variety and significance. Curiously, most artists who portrayed the Riva avoided or understated the landmarks that John Ferguson Weir (1841–1926) concentrated on in his high mimetic *Venice* (fig. 50), with its panoramic view of the mouth of the Grand Canal, framed by the Salute on the left and on the right by the Libreria, the saints' pillars, the Doge's Palace, and the Danieli Hotel. This, like almost all Riva views, has a high vantage point. What this elevated prospect does for the artist is to prevent the scene from becoming bogged down in multiplied, layered, confused visual incident. But it has the disadvantage (to an artist operating with a low mimetic vision of his subject) of seeming grandiloquent, too full of tall and imposing landmarks, too high mimetic in posture. To preserve a clear sweep into the distance on the one hand and a nonheroic posture on the other, artists hit on differing strategies. Whistler, looking at the scene from a point about halfway between the Piazza San Marco and the Public Gar-

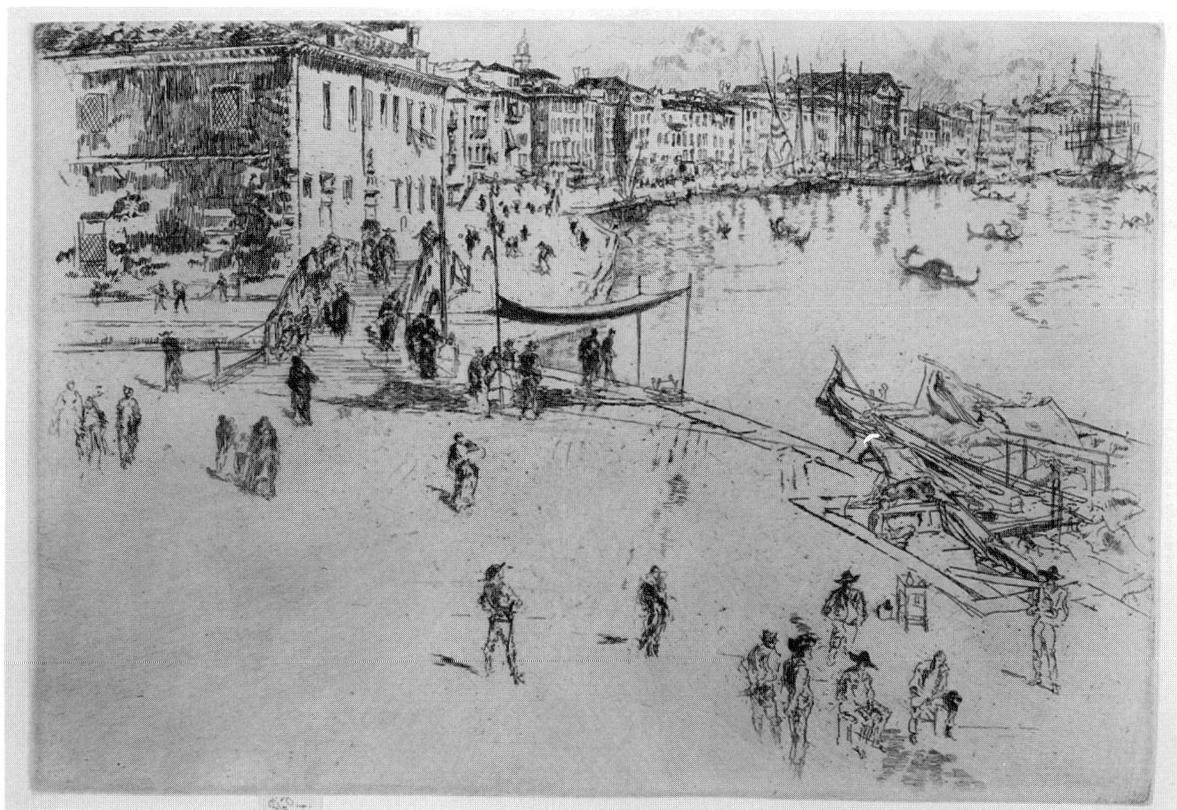

Fig. 51. James McNeill Whistler, *The Riva, No. 2*, 1880, etching and drypoint, 8³⁄₁₆" × 11¹⁵⁄₁₆", Freer Gallery of Art, Smithsonian Institution, Washington, D.C. (Acc. no. 87.16); see also fig. 53.

dens in *The Riva, No. 2* (fig. 51; see also fig. 53), fills the scene with incident. He concentrates foreground interest on a cluster of gondoliers, sweeps cleanly into the middle ground with roughly described vernacular buildings, and deliberately confuses the heroic elements in the background—the Campanile, and domes of San Marco—with masts and spars (the etching is a mirror image of the topographical features because of the reversal inherent in the printing process).

Prendergast's two complementary views of the curving Riva, *The Quai, Venice* (fig. 52), looking west from the Ponte di Veneta toward the Ducal Palace (just visible in the extreme upper left), and *Ponte della Paglia* (fig. 54), looking east from the second-story arcade of the Ducal Palace, employ another strategy for preserving a low mimetic character.[14] Prendergast tilts his cone of vision down and compresses it. The lower half of both images focuses on colorful crowds mounting and descending broad pedestrian bridges. An abbreviated middle ground leads to a long horizontal row of buildings in the background, pressing the upper edge of the frame. More than in other Riva views (despite the assurance of a lamppost and awnings), in *The Quai* we feel the perilousness of our aerial state. This effect probably arises from the extreme proximity of the near figures and the lack both of a clearly established footing and of the bridge's place and trajectory in space. What we might call Prendergast's low mimetic structure includes the precariousness of this point of view, the location of the foreground boat pointing directly away from the direction one's eye is invited to travel, the slicing of the frame on the right-hand side, which interrupts the sweep of the Riva back into space, and a vertical truncation of the whole image, which squeezes the Ducal Palace and slices across the Campanile. Compared with Weir's image of the Riva, *Venice* (fig. 50), which gives us an ordered sweep terminating in monumental structures, Prendergast's *Quai* completely denies that sense of spatial order, structural hierarchy, and visual procedure which are characteristic of high mimetic images; he has made something different out of exactly the same material.

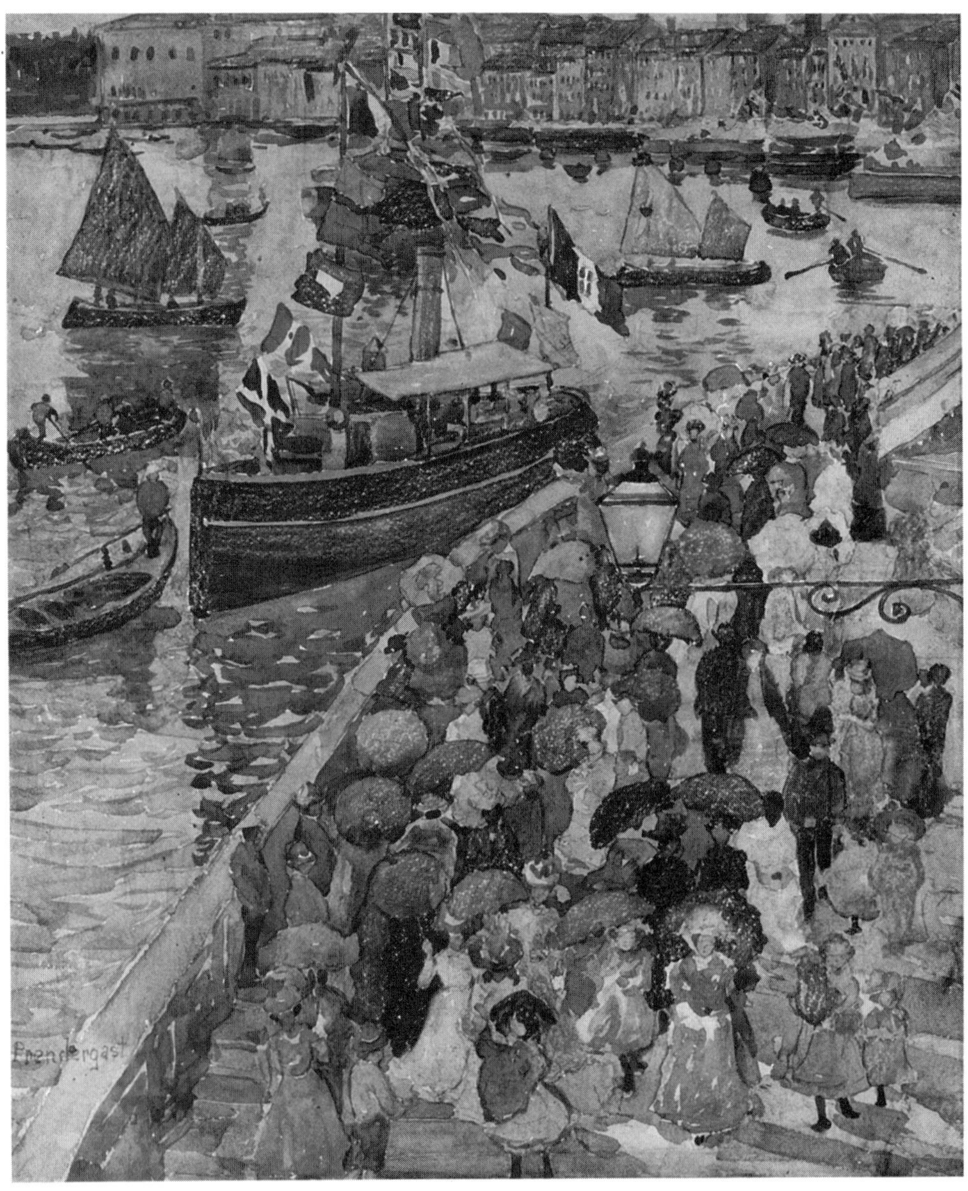

Fig. 52. Maurice Prendergast, *The Quai, Venice*, ca. 1899, watercolor, 15¾″ × 12³⁄₁₆″, Collection of Mr. and Mrs. Arthur G. Altschul; see also fig. 53.

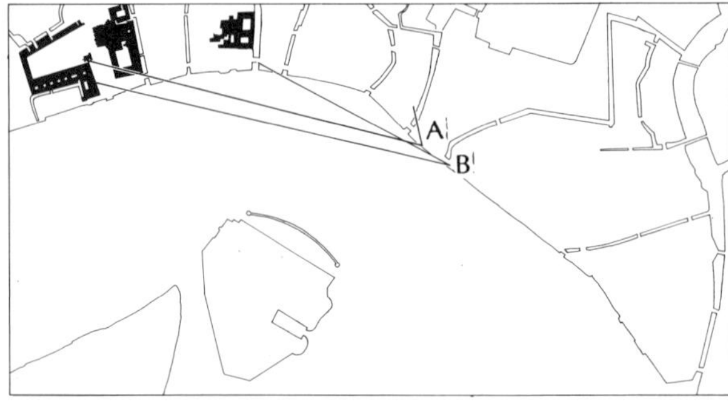

A. Whistler, *The Riva, No. 2*, fig. 51
B. Prendergast, *The Quai, Venice*, fig. 52

Fig. 53. Map of sites of figs. 51, 52.

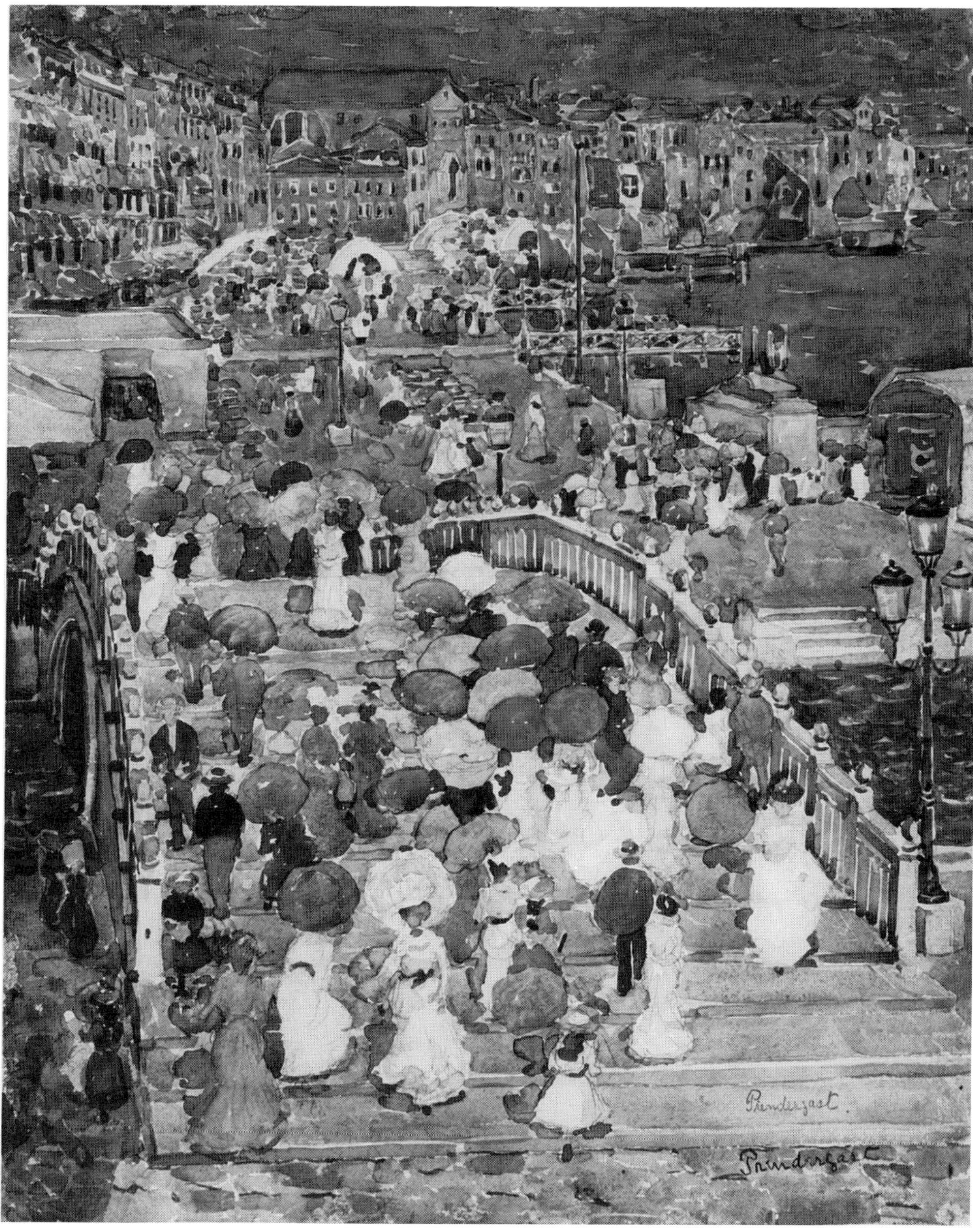

Fig. 54. Maurice Prendergast, *Ponte della Paglia (Marble Bridge)*, ca. 1898–99, watercolor, 17¾″ × 14⅛″, Collection of Mr. and Mrs. Arthur G. Altschul.

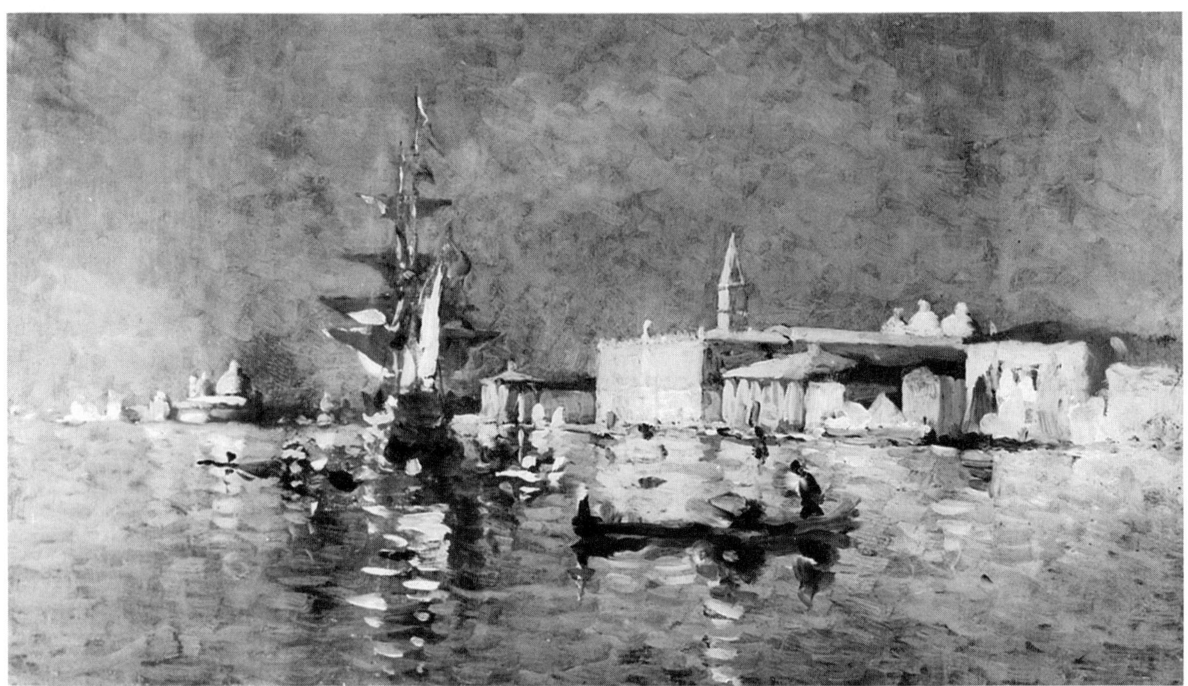

Fig. 55. Charles Gifford Dyer, *Venice, Grand Canal*, 1888, oil on panel, 9½″ × 17″, Elvehjem Museum of Art, University of Wisconsin, Madison, Gift of John C. Hawley in memory of Mary Oakley Hawley.

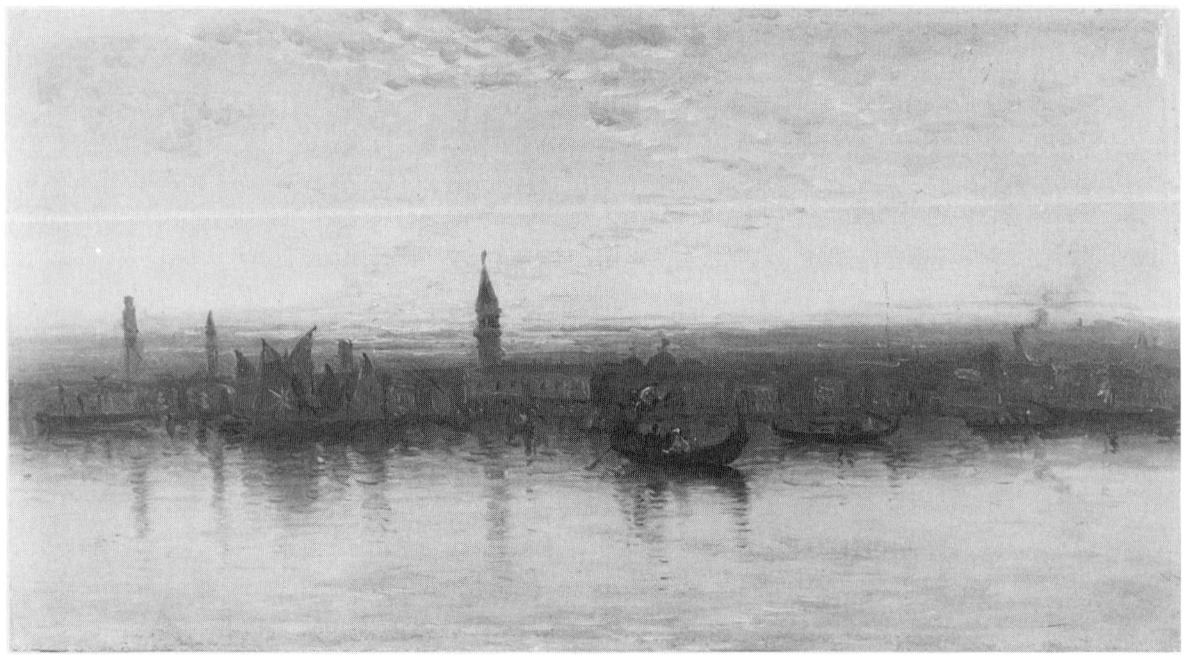

Fig. 56. Sanford R. Gifford, *A Twilight Sketch in Venice*, ca. 1875, oil on canvas, 6½″ × 11¾″, Ball State University Art Gallery, Muncie, Indiana, Gift of Mrs. F. J. Petty.

From the far end of the Riva, at the edge of the Public Gardens, the principal monuments of the city spread themselves out in a long thin line on the horizon. Views from this vantage point, such as *Venice, Grand Canal* (fig. 55) by Charles Gifford Dyer (1846–1912), and from far out in the lagoon, such as *A Twilight Sketch in Venice* (fig. 56) by Sanford R. Gifford (1823–80), portray a city that hov-

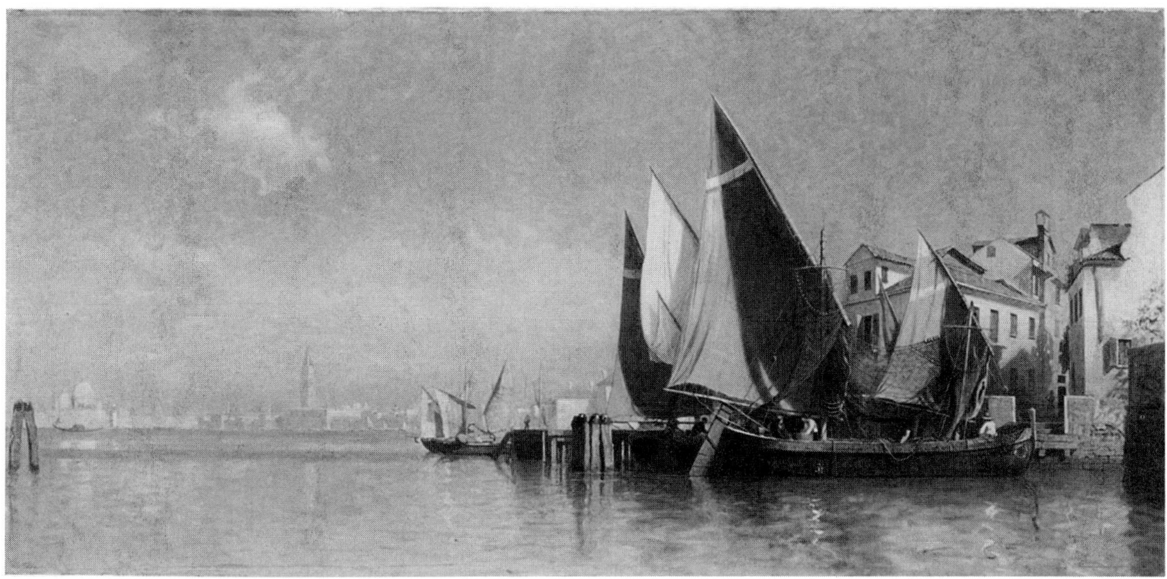

Fig. 57. William Stanley Haseltine, *Venice, I*, ca. 1875, oil on canvas, 23½″ × 48½″, Detroit Institute of Arts, Gift of Mrs. Roger H. Plowden.

ers quietly on the surface of a reflective lagoon. The architectural elements occupy relatively little of the picture surface, their ranged rectangular forms often interrupted by and juxtaposed to moored sailing ships and gliding gondolas in the foreground. Again, like the images considered earlier in this chapter, landmarks are included, but the character of the monuments is not stressed, is not the subject of the picture. The tone is usually one of heightened nostalgia perhaps best expressed by Ruskin in his preface to *The Stones of Venice:* "[Venice] is still left for our beholding in the final period of her decline: a ghost upon the sands of the sea, so weak—so quiet—so bereft of all but her loveliness, that we might well doubt, as we watched her faint reflection in the mirage of the lagoon, which was the City, and which the shadow."[15]

Modestly poetic, these images are usually small in size and quiet in tone. They view the city from the south or southeast, the Doge's Palace and Campanile often central in the composition and the island of San Giorgio usually eliminated. The architecture is often very indistinct, pale pink or buff generalized forms stretching from horizon to horizon. With the city reduced to a thin line with bumps (domes) and shafts (campanili), one's sense of place is established only by previous knowledge of the topography. In contrast to the tentative sense of structure, pale and ghostly on the distant horizon, the foreground is often full of large fishing boats, their sails saturated reds, yellows, and oranges, picked out in careful detail. In *Venice 1* (fig. 57), by William Stanley Haseltine (1835–1900) the foreground includes a cluster of outlying vernacular structures establishing our viewpoint and suggesting an excuse for a cluster of fully rigged sailboats.[16] These are not the massive steamships or noble square-rigged ocean sailers of high commerce but the heavy lateen-rigged boats of fishermen and small coastal ventures. Under their bright patterned sails and around their dark hulls, figures go about the daily business of living, equally oblivious of their extraordinary setting and of the observing, recording artist. The juxtaposition of these figures and their boats with the distant prospect is underlined by emphatic contrasts: large and small, distinct and indistinct, deeply hued and palely ghostly. The modest picturesqueness of these poor but colorful peasant folk contrasts markedly with the pale heroic scene portrayed on the horizon. Clearly there has been a diminution; a lapse of time seems to be traversed in the spatial distance between background and foreground. Visually the past and the present have been telescoped, and the effect is more one of poignancy and "quiet charm" than of tragedy. The loss, after all, is mitigated by the survival of the stones, architectural ghosts "upon the sands of the sea."

Some artists, such as William Gedney Bunce (1840–1916), made a career of these "thin line"

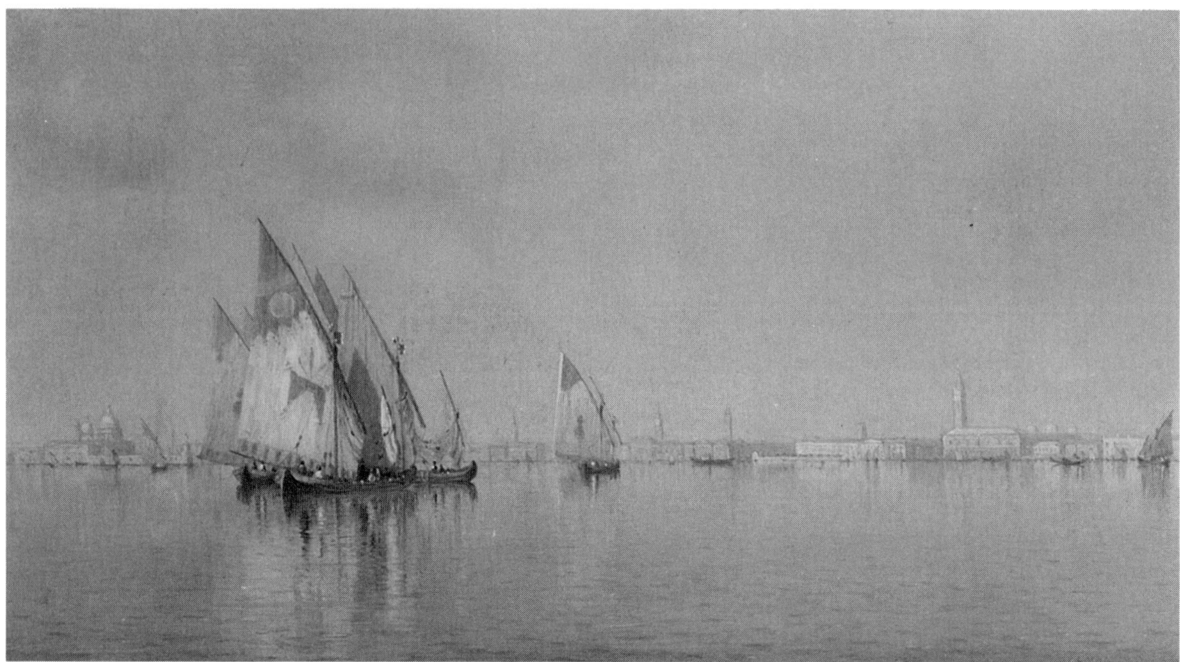

Fig. 58. Sanford R. Gifford, *Venetian Sails: A Study*, 1873, oil on canvas, 13¼″ × 23¼″, Washington University Gallery of Art, St. Louis.

images, concentrating their energy on flocks of colorful foreground boats and only suggesting the city with the briefest of delineations. More than any other type of Venetian picture, these distant views lent themselves to studio production. As the significant features were the word "Venice" in the title and large expanses of water and sky, the marine and architectural sections of the image were subject to much poetic license and painterly manipulation. In point of fact, these are the least topographically accurate accounts of all the views of Venice. A common alteration of topographic reality is one which we see in Sanford R. Gifford's *Venetian Sails: A Study* (fig. 58).[17] Here the familiar prospect from the Riva (see fig. 59) has been shifted in three ways: the distance between the Salute and the Doge's Palace has been wildly exaggerated to suit the long horizontal composition favored for these views, and the facade of the Doge's Palace has been inflected toward us, to face us fully even in its foggy indistinctness. And thirdly, the Campanile has been elongated to mimic the masts of the boats and to signal our eye to that part of the composition that impresses our memory here much more than our eye. Because the painters of these views were more concerned with the idea of Venice than with its actuality, more interested in its shadow than in its

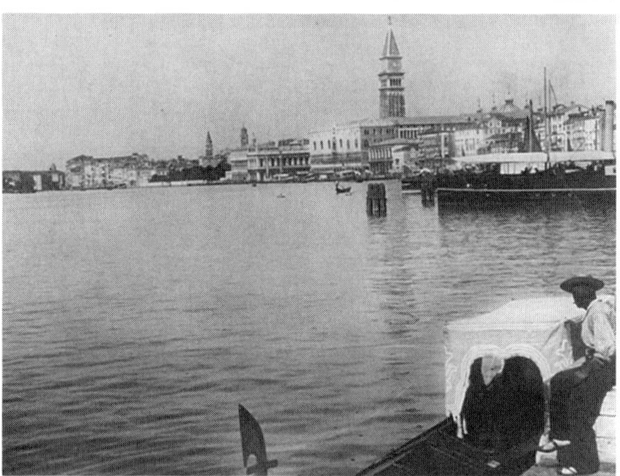

Fig. 59. *Venice from Riva San Biagio*, ca. 1900, photograph, Photograph Collection, Yale University Art and Architecture Library, New Haven, Connecticut.

substance, the visual clues need only be recognizable in a general sense. Such interpretive license operates positively only where the artist wishes to evoke a tone, where he declines to clarify, describe, or portrait any aspect of the city in favor of a general evocative resonance.

Of all the "thin line" views of Venice, Whistler's are among the most numerous and most extraordinary. They are notable not so much for the novelty of their point of view or for inventive structuring principles, but rather for the elegance of their technique. Commencing with a heroic prospect, Whistler first denies the heroic stature of his subject (by extreme miniaturization, by indistinctness, and by

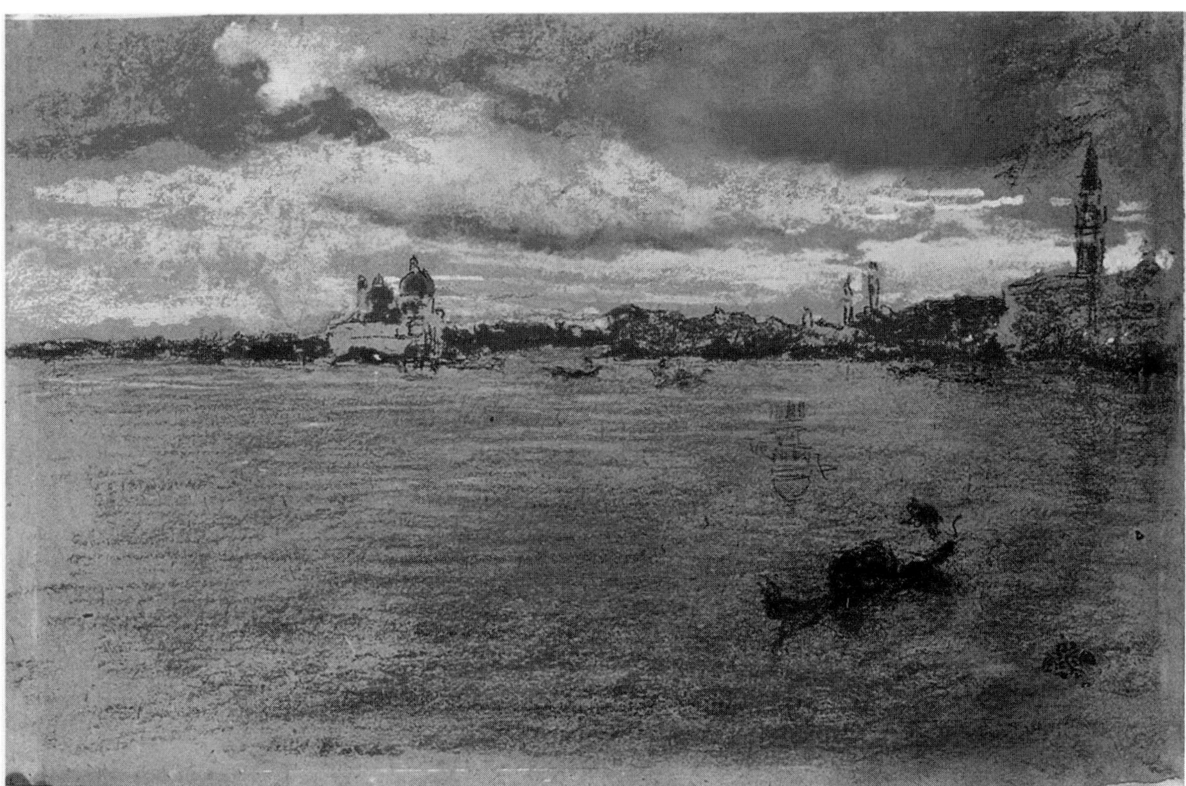

Fig. 60. James McNeill Whistler, *Stormy Sunset*, ca. 1880, pastel and charcoal on brown paper, 7¼″ × 11⅛″, Fogg Museum, Harvard University, Cambridge, Bequest of Grenville L. Winthrop.

confusion of the principal elements with spars, clouds, shadows, and their own reflections) and reelevates the view to value by purely artistic means. *Stormy Sunset* (fig. 60), *Venetian Scene* (pl. 3), *Long Venice* (fig. 61), and *Upright Venice* (fig. 62) are all seen from the same Riva prospect as the Dyer and Gifford views discussed above (see figs. 55, 58, and 59). Whistler's self-conscious manipulation of format is more extreme than that of many artists, moving from the long panoramic horizontal of *Long Venice* to the clipped vertical of *Upright Venice*. The scene shifts with his format, with his alteration of the horizon line, and with his inclusion or exclusion of architectural and marine features. As is customary with Whistler, the horizon is high in these images and no large boats with masts and spars occupy the foreground. Consequently, in both the etchings and pastels, a wide expanse of undescribed, inarticulated water intervenes between our vantage point and the distant Salute. The movement back into space and the architectural nature of the forms so scantily described are alike left to the imagination. More than any other quality or tone, this appeal to the imagination is the note struck by Whistler—we read the bulbous forms as domes and the shafts as campanili only because we are willing to do so; to us the sky is electric with sunset, the water pellucid with afternoon heat only if we expand the information given us. We grant to the author of any fiction the willing suspension of our disbelief, but Whistler asks an inordinate share.

In reducing Venice to a thin line with tall bumps and shafts Whistler is appealing to a distinct aspect of Victorian popular (and visual) psychology. Andrew Jackson Downing in *The Architecture of Country Houses* (1850) has an extended discussion of the suitability of specific architectural features for specific types of people. Of architectural patrons he sees three kinds: the rational men, best suited to the classical idiom and symmetrical forms; the men of sentiment or feeling whose instinctive sense of poetry requires asymmetry and shadowy corners; "and, lastly, there are the men of imagination—men whose aspirations never leave them at rest—men whose ambition and energy will give them no peace within the mere bounds of rationality. . . . It is for such that the architect may safely

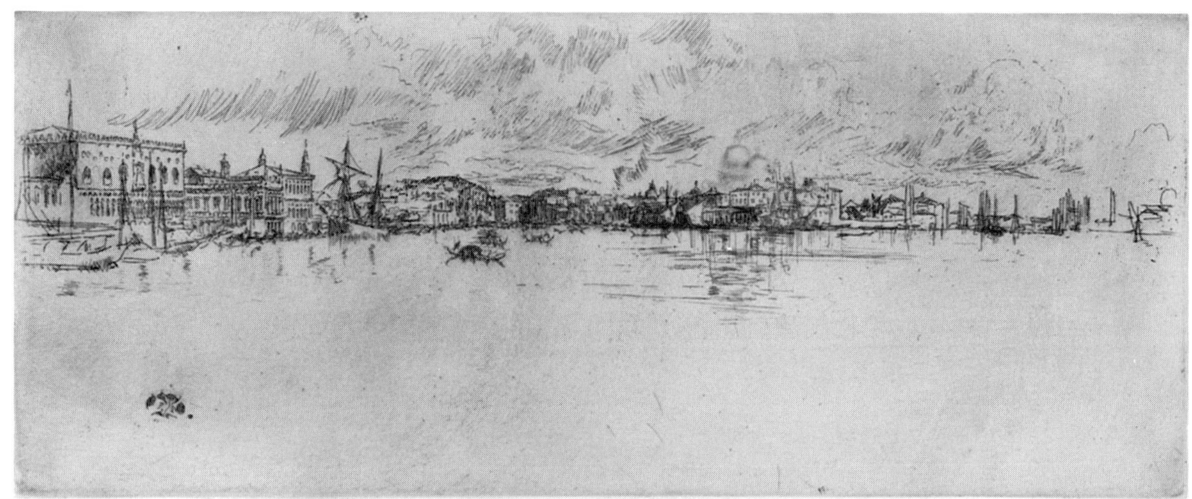

Fig. 61. James McNeill Whistler, *Long Venice*, 1880, etching, 5″ × 12$\frac{1}{16}$″, Freer Gallery of Art, Smithsonian Institution, Washington, D.C. (Acc. no. 87.23).

introduce the tower and the campanile—any and every feature that indicates originality, boldness, energy, and variety of character."[18] These select individuals, "eagles" Downing calls them, are particularly constituted to appropriate and understand towers. Downing here glosses these puncturers of the horizon as indicators of boldness and energy. Towers, of course, had a long military and literary history, but their vogue in structure and image during the nineteenth century suggests a distinct cluster of symbolic meanings that reached far beyond the realm of literary reference and deep into popular culture. Albeit useless for all practical modern purposes, they seemed to offer the insightful viewer not just an opportunity for recognition of his topographical orientation but also for imaginative aspiration through their pure symbolic power.[19] Within the specific context of Whistler's views, then, an imaginative person could generate a world of history and value—implicit here rather than explicit as in the high mimetic images—as well as pure artistic experience from abbreviated notations of architectural irregularities on the distant horizon.

When one speculates on the recurrence of nineteenth-century images of this type—the wide expanse of reflective still water spreading itself horizontally below a tall tower or looming mountain—it seems clear that this pairing of opposing elements had an emblematic potency beyond the physical actuality represented. Downing gives us some insight into the nature of this visual convention in

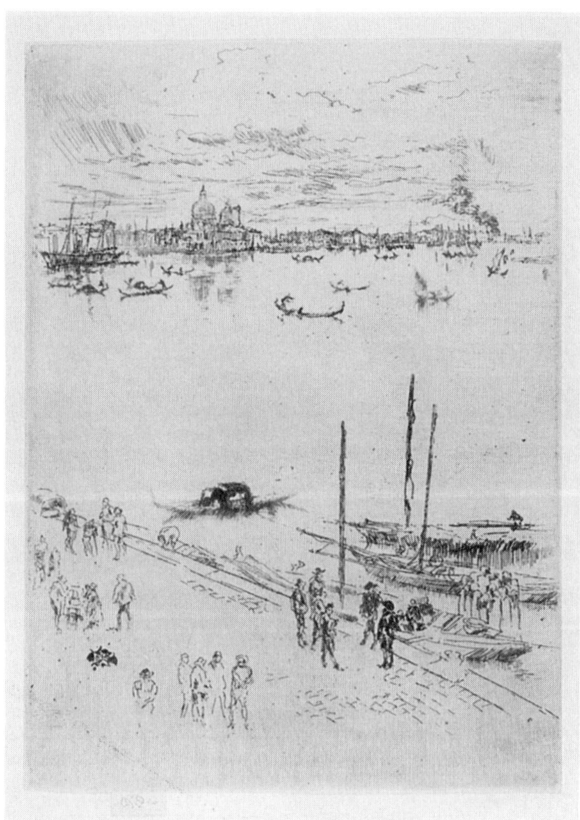

Fig. 62. James McNeill Whistler, *Upright Venice*, 1880, etching, 10″ × 7″, National Gallery of Art, Washington, D.C., Rosenwald Collection.

his discussion of a "Lake or River Villa for a Picturesque Site," a dwelling suggested for a man of imagination: "It is in this mental delight awakened by the contrast of symbols, of repose and action, of beauty and power, in the lake that slumbers peacefully, and the hills that lift themselves boldly or grandly above it, that we find the explanation of part of the peculiar charm which belongs to those picturesque towers and campaniles of the edifices . . . of . . . the Italian lakes." These paired forms become symbols—the horizontal one of repose and beauty, the vertical of action and power. He goes on to describe the specific design: "We must call the attention of the reader to the combination of power and domestic feeling in this villa—power in the high roofs and gables, and especially in the lofty heavenward-pointing tower, and domesticity in the peculiarly homelike look of the [long, low, horizontal] wing on the right."[20] Clearly these forms seem expressive to him of feminine domesticity and repose on the one hand and of masculinity and action on the other. The most perfect house or natural scene will, for the most perceptive viewer, or owner, be composed of these two contrasting, complementary gendered elements. That Downing's explicit perception was an instance of a generally understood "truth" is suggested by the extraordinary nineteenth-century vogue for structures that combine exaggerated but balanced horizontal and vertical elements and paintings in which a still body of water reposes beneath a mountain or a tower. In fact, the enthusiasm for Venetian views in general, so rich in tower/lagoon material, might be seen as a particular instance of this general enthusiasm. In many of these views, such as Whistler's *Lagoon, Venice: Nocturne in Blue and Silver* (fig. 63) and his etching, *Nocturne* (fig. 64), we might see, as Ruskin does, Venice's "faint reflection in the mirage of the lagoon [and wonder] which was the City, and which the shadow."[21] The scene, however enveloped in fog or twilight or shadow, clearly shows the tower forms reflected in the quiet water, and in this reflection the two are—however insubstantially—united. The complementary harmony of these two implicitly sexual elements (in the case of these two images, the recumbent Bacino and the

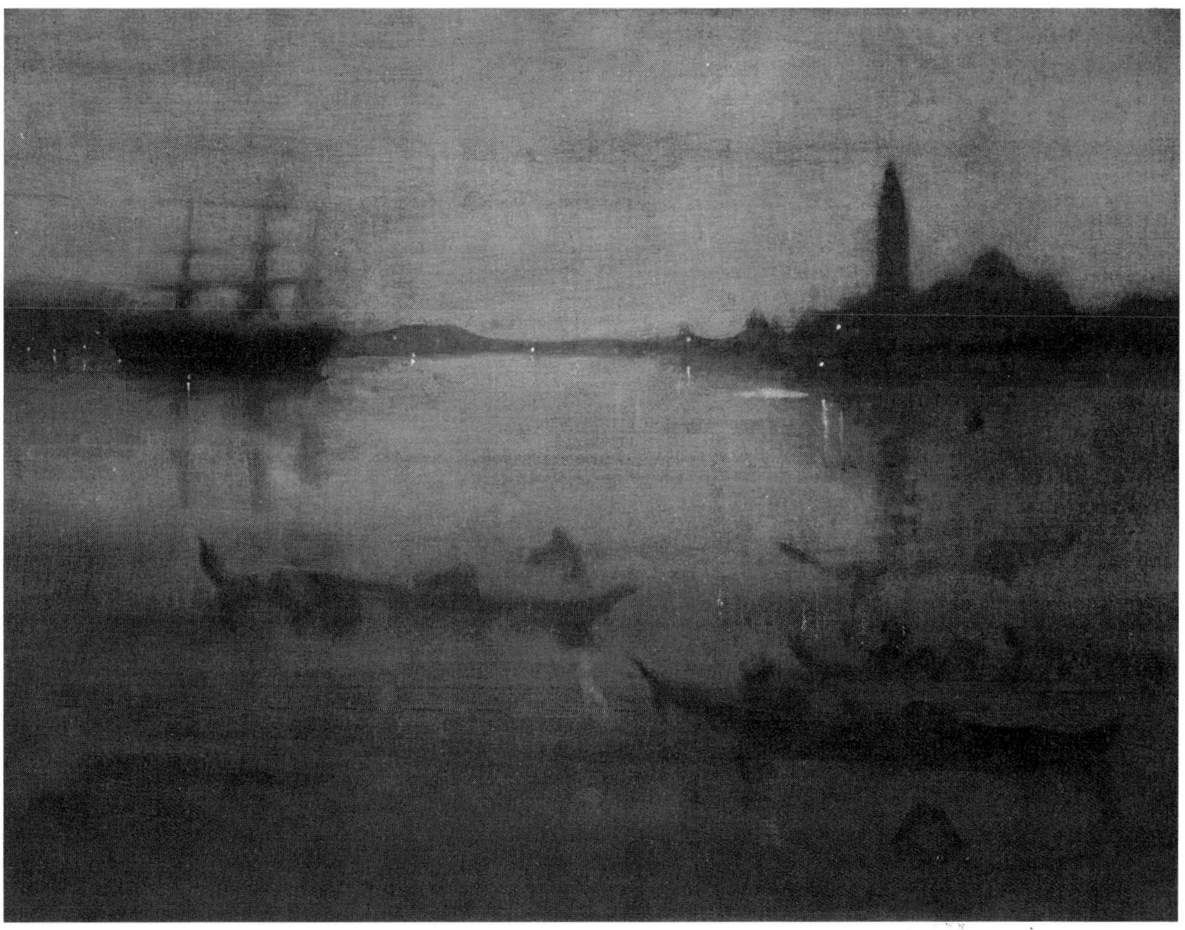

Fig. 63. James McNeill Whistler, *The Lagoon, Venice: Nocturne in Blue and Silver*, ca. 1879–80, oil on canvas, 20″ × 25¾″, Museum of Fine Arts, Boston, Emily L. Ainsley Fund.

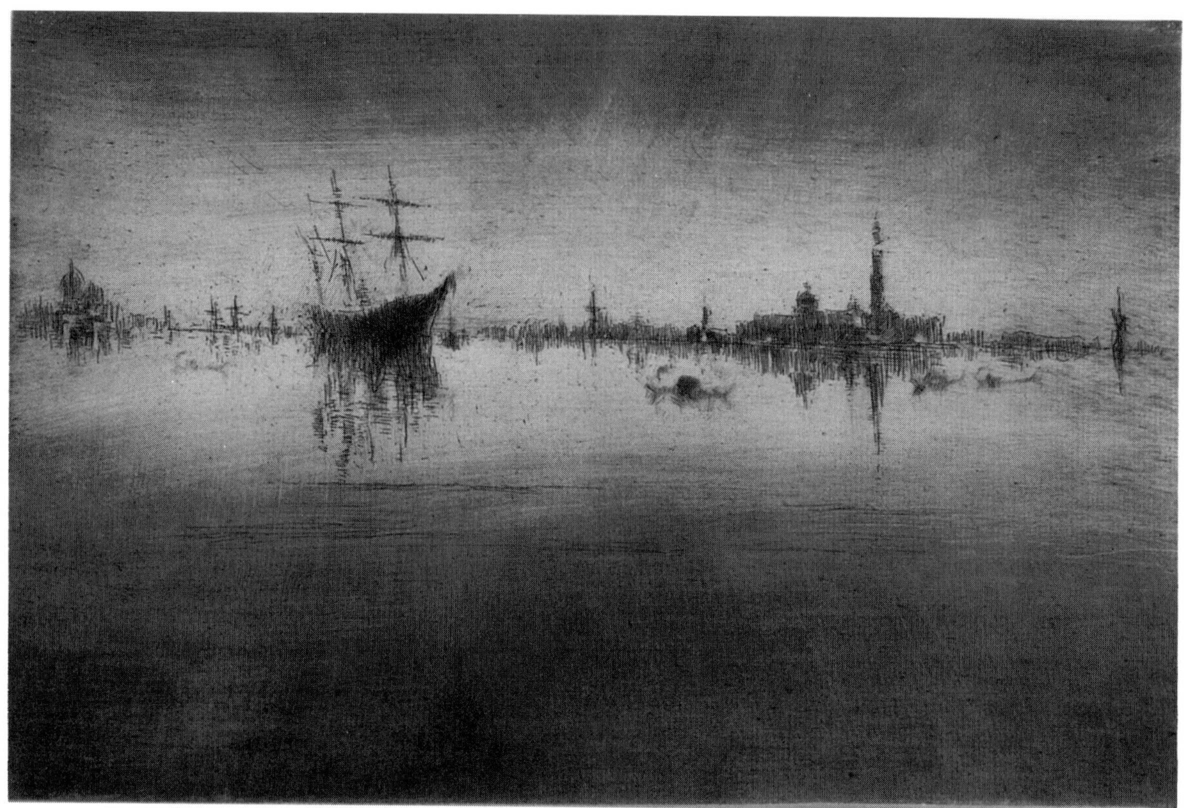

Fig. 64. James McNeill Whistler, *Nocturne*, 1880, etching, 7¼″ × 10⅜″, National Gallery of Art, Washington, D.C., Rosenwald Collection.

lofty tower of San Giorgio Maggiore) becomes a twilight shadow through which men of imagination can see an inner as well as a palpable reality, one based on the empathy of inert forms (natural and architectural) for human attributes and emotions.

Whistler's view is poetic, cloaked in darkness and artistic indirection. Its appeal is to the viewer's own conjuring powers, and it can operate on other scenes to evoke Venice as it can in Venice to evoke the process of time and of the imagination. In the "Ten O'Clock" lecture Whistler speaks with evocative fervor of London twilight moments, "when the evening mist clothes the riverside with poetry, as with a veil, and the poor buildings lose themselves in the dim sky, and the tall chimneys become campanili, and the warehouses are palaces in the night."[22]

Canals and Campi: The Unimportant and the Unrecognizable

As attentive to Venice's present as to the testaments of her terrible and splendid past, many visitors, such as William Dean Howells, wandered off the beaten path, away from the great and long-appreciated monuments into obscure byways of the city in search of discovery and experience. An explorer-researcher as keen-eyed as any geologist or naturalist in the Rockies, Howells records the nature and quarry of his disorganized quest:

> Dark and secret little courts lay in wait for my blundering steps, and I was incessantly surprised and brought to surrender by paths that beguiled me up to dead walls, or the sudden brinks of canals. The wide and open squares before the innumerable churches of the city were equally victorious, and continually took me prisoner. But all places had something rare and worthy to be seen: if not loveliness of sculpture or architecture, at least interesting squalor and picturesque wretchedness; and I believe I had less delight in proper Objects of Interest than in the dirty neighborhoods that reeked with unwholesome winter damps below, and peered curiously out with frowzy heads and beautiful eyes from the high, heavy-shuttered casements above.[23]

Pathways to the Objects of Interest which Howells strives to avoid (and notes about why they are of Interest) were to be found in small red Baedeker guides. One could follow the routes indicated and observe the observable and be sure of neither disappointment nor originality in one's Venetian experience. Howells, on the other hand, sets off in an un-Baedekerian search, a search full of bafflement, discovery, and pleasure for him. The experience he seeks is definitely low mimetic, and he records for us dozens of vivid vignettes—exchanges overheard, scenes of animosity and of beauty glimpsed. The world he walks through is labyrinthine, foreign, and in many ways inscrutable; what gives it poignancy and piquancy is its postlapsarian state: "I grew early into sympathy and friendship with Venice, and being newly from a land where every thing, morally and materially, was in good repair, I rioted sentimentally on the picturesque ruin, the pleasant discomfort and hopelessness of every thing about me here."[24] It was, in other words, the antithesis—morally and materially—to his sense of America and, as such, was an extraordinary object of interest in all its symptoms, physical and social.

When the artists searched these same byways for discoveries, seeking the telling vignette of interest, they relied more on architecture than on figures for material. Even seen at close range, Venice's buildings, rather than live Venetians, stood in, as we have so often seen, for the historic, moral, and social condition of the city.

By far the great majority of low mimetic images of Venice fall into a single subject type—the narrow canal hedged by buildings on both sides and receding to a bridge in the middle distance. *San Barnaba, Venice* (fig. 65) by Charles Herbert Moore (1840–1930) and *Venetian Canal* (fig. 66) by John Singer Sargent, showing opposite ends of the same canal (see fig. 80), are typical.[25] The one has a vertical format, tightening the composition and speeding the visual plunge into distant space. The other is broad, spreading itself more generously in the foreground. The one is seen in cool morning light while the other is pictured in the full glare of the late afternoon sun. In both cases, however, the lateral structures are unrecognizable and, for the most part, of no great distinction. A bridge reaches over the water, uniting the two ranges of buildings. Prominent in both these views is the high brick tower of San Barnaba, rising boldly above the canal and reflected in the rippling water. Not a point of visitation, unmentioned in Baedekers of these years, it is, nevertheless, a point of orientation. Sargent seems to prefer that it *not* orient us precisely, for he names the view *Venetian Canal* rather than specifying the site.[26] The low mimetic structure of these views is evident in the relatively narrow cone of vision, the lowness of the point of view, and the evident desire to avoid Baedekerized Venice. Moore's view is taken from just above water level—he is evidently in a gondola—with his back to the Grand Canal. The building in the right foreground is the Palazzo Rezzonico, one of the grandest structures on that grand waterway and the home of Robert Browning during much of the decade of the 1880s. Moore, however, pictures not the Grand Canal or the majestic Rezzonico; he slights the celebrated in favor of a narrow, modest, and relatively unknown waterway. Sargent's point of view is also low, but as the surface of the *fondamenta* (canal-side walkway) is visible, he is above ordinary boat level. In fact he is sitting on dry land at a sharp bend in the canal, but he prefers we not realize that; avoiding the parapet he sets our footing, so to speak, in the canal. In other Sargent images of this general type, he assures us of his water-borne vantage point by including his gondola prow, as in *Rio di San Salvatore* (ca. 1903–13, Isabella Stewart Gardner Museum, Boston) or by his knuckle-bruising view of the lower portions of a marble dado as in *Ponte della Canonica, Venice* (fig. 67).

Towers, being perhaps too recognizable, too near-heroic if detailed at all, are absent from most of these views. Instead, the towerlike function of antithesis to the horizontal expanse of water is taken over by the steeply vertical walls of buildings that line the waterways. Unlike high mimetic views in which the "rules" insist on the vertical completeness of architectural forms, here truncation of the lateral stuctures is omnipresent. These are, after all, mere slices, partial, accidental views blundered upon by those intent on avoiding Objects of Interest. The point of view is distinctly merely human—taking in what can be only partially compassed, seen, and understood from a single pedestrian or aquatic vantage point. The conceit is that these sites are not preknown, are "candid" discoveries and are, therefore, more appropriatable by the belated artist-viewer. What this compassless explorer can know is limited and nameless, but it

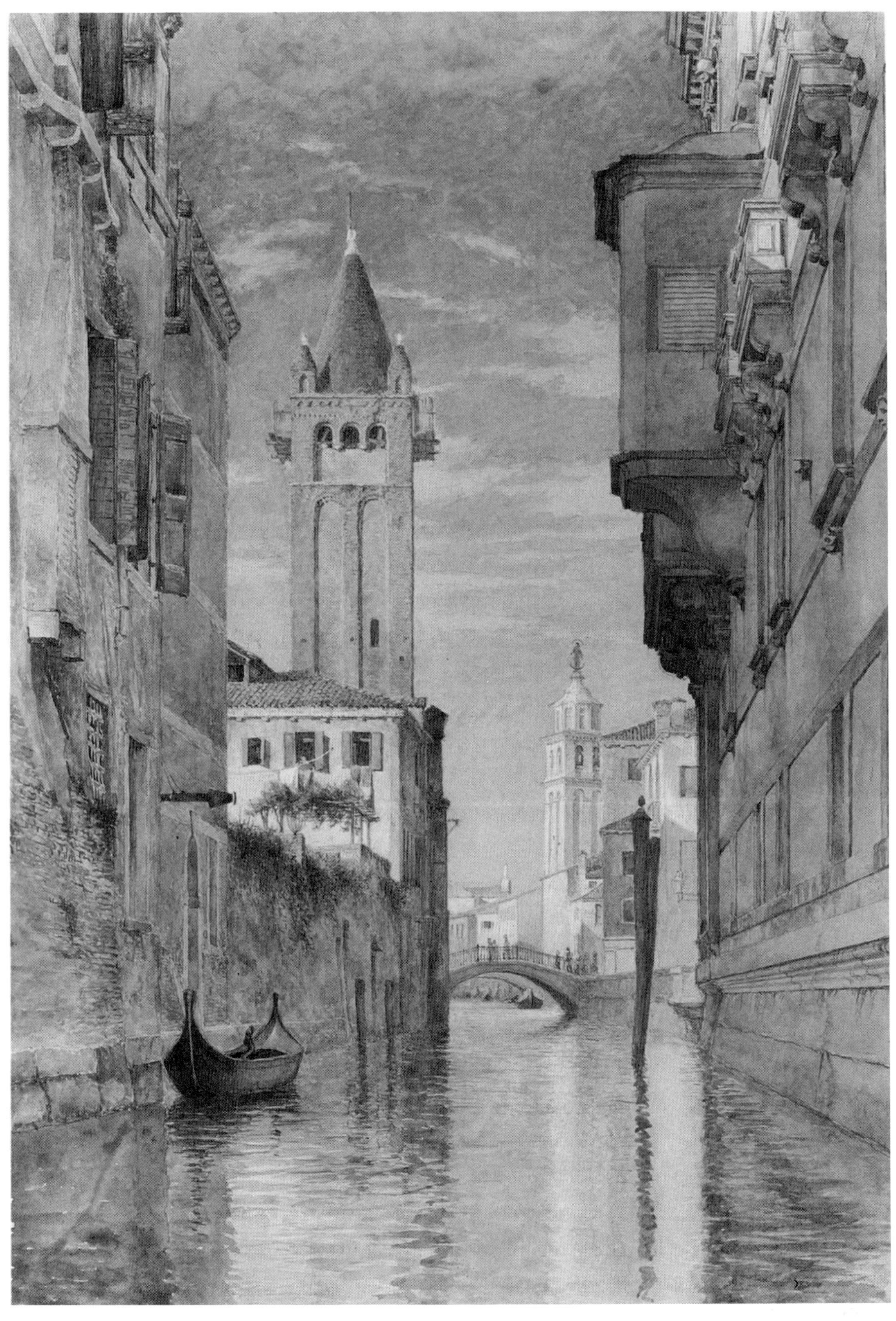

Fig. 65. Charles Herbert Moore, *San Barnaba, Venice*, ca. 1876–77, watercolor, 10¾″ × 7½″, Fogg Art Museum, Harvard University, Cambridge, Gift of Dr. Denman W. Ross; see also fig. 80.

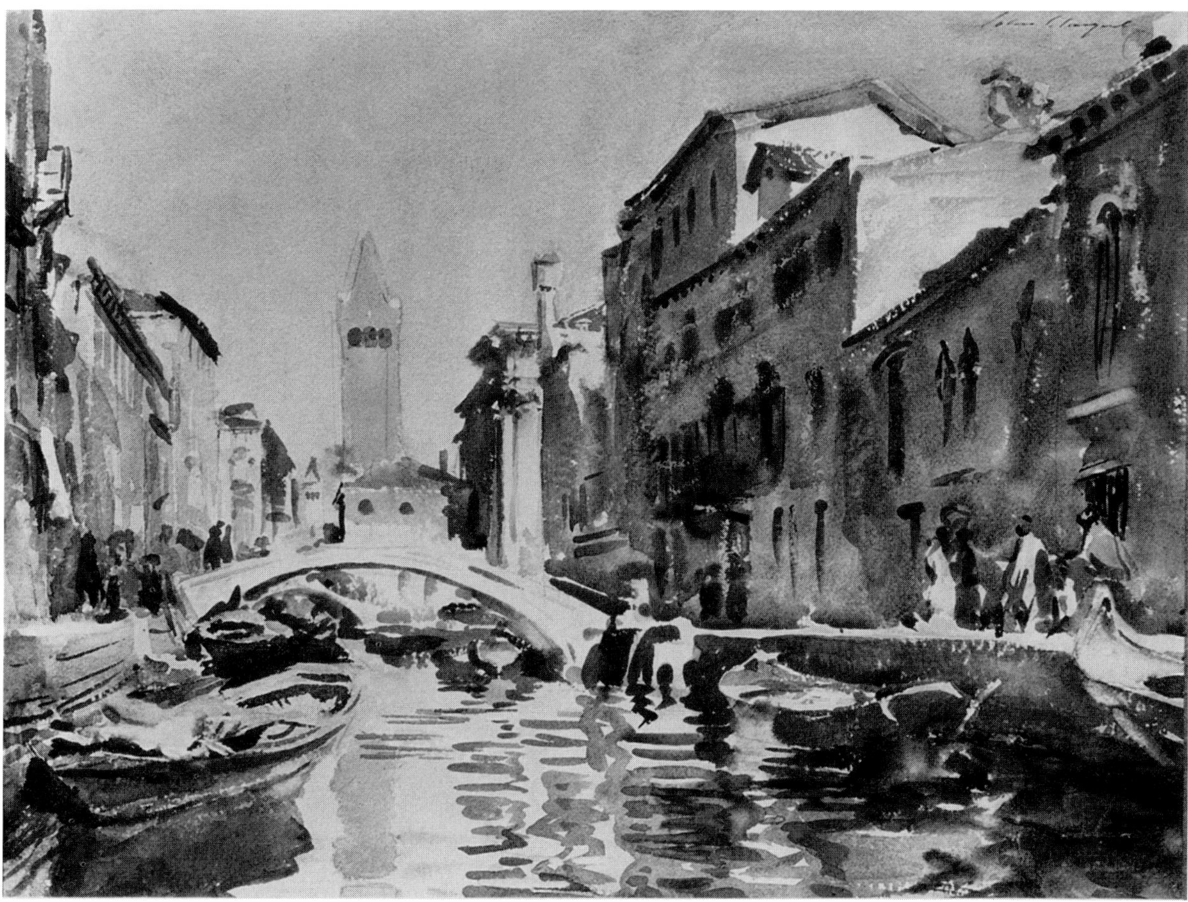

Fig. 66. John Singer Sargent, *Venetian Canal*, ca. 1904, watercolor, 15½″ × 20⅞″, Metropolitan Museum of Art, Purchase, Joseph Pulitzer Bequest, 1915; see also fig. 80.

is possessable from a personal, even intimate, and certainly comfortable point of view. That so many "discovered" this same visual structure, this way of knowing and capturing their Venetian experience, suggests the power of the mode, the naturalness of its laws to its users. Views by Charles S. Forbes (1856–1926; *Scene in Venice, Bridge over Canal*, fig. 68), George Washington Stevens (1866–1926; *A Canal in Venice*, fig. 69), Robert F. Blum (*Canal in Venice, San Trovaso Quarter*, fig. 70), as well as those by Whistler (*The Bridge*, ca. 1880, from the Twenty-six Etchings set) and Prendergast (*A Bridge in Venice*, 1898, Cleveland Museum, and *Venice*, fig. 71), reiterate this basic syntax of forms and organization.[27] In addition to the quiet canal and glimpses of looming, only partially perceived structures, these views usually include a bridge in a position of prominence. Individualized but anonymous, these footbridges offer the perfect solution to the problem of middle-ground vacuity. Bridging both the actual and metaphorical expanse between level canal and perpendicular facade, these taut and graceful forms with their single-span arches lead the eye through all the degrees between the flat horizontal of the water to the erect vertical of the walls. Visually pliant and somewhat magical in their defiance of gravity, these aerial protagonists become stable equal signs between the two pressing ranks of facades, as well as mediators between them and the watery expanse below.

For variety and interest, some artists threw the equation out of balance and constructed one with more tension or dynamism. One of the most striking is Whistler's *A Side Canal in Venice* (pl. 4), a pastel of the most eloquent suggestiveness; it portrays a bridge (from the perspective of a second, unseen span) whose steep diagonal recession violates both the norm of Venice picturing and also the spatial expectations of the axial calle to which it gives access. The tension of this oblique geometric eccentricity presents us with the kind of spatial ambiguity Whistler cherishes, but violates no sense of the

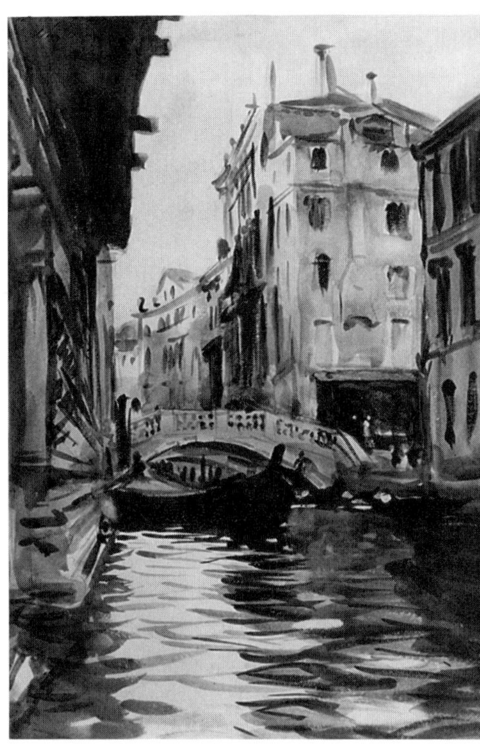

Fig. 67. John Singer Sargent, *Ponte della Canonica, Venice*, ca. 1903–13, watercolor, 18″ × 12″, Isabella Stewart Gardner Museum, Boston.

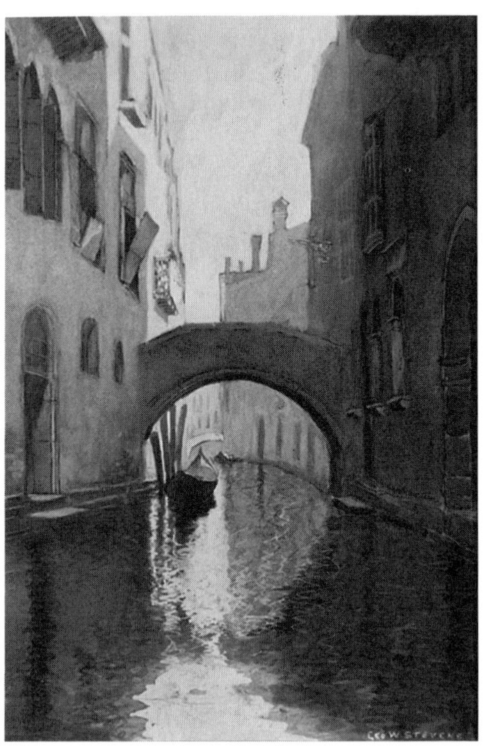

Fig. 69. George Washington Stevens, *A Canal in Venice*, ca. 1902, watercolor, 18⅞″ × 12⅛″, Toledo Museum of Art, Toldeo, Ohio, Bequest of Carl B. Spitzer.

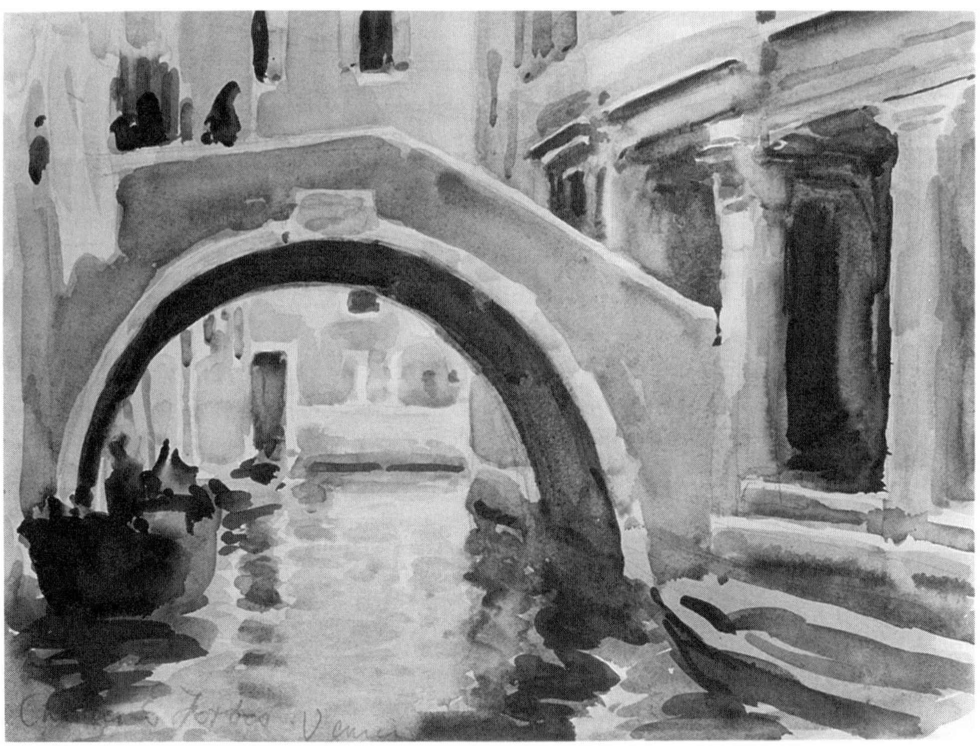

Fig. 68. Charles S. Forbes, *Scene in Venice, Bridge over Canal*, ca. 1905, watercolor, 19″ × 21½″, Fogg Art Museum, Harvard University, Cambridge, Gift of Paul R. Forbes.

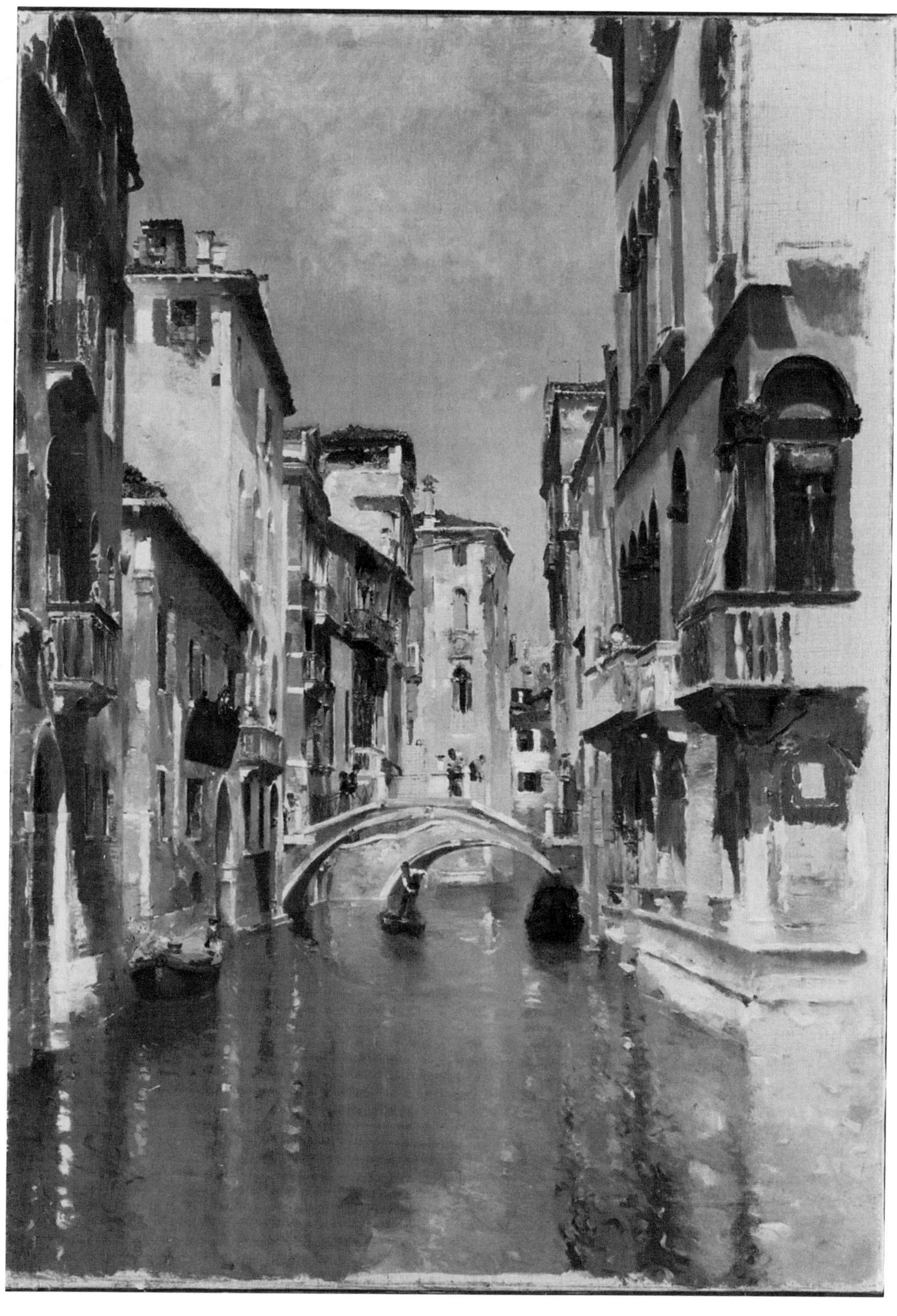

Fig. 70. Robert F. Blum, *Canal in Venice, San Trovaso Quarter*, 1885, oil on canvas, 34⅛″ × 23⅛″, National Museum of American Art, Smithsonian Institution, Gift of William T. Evans.

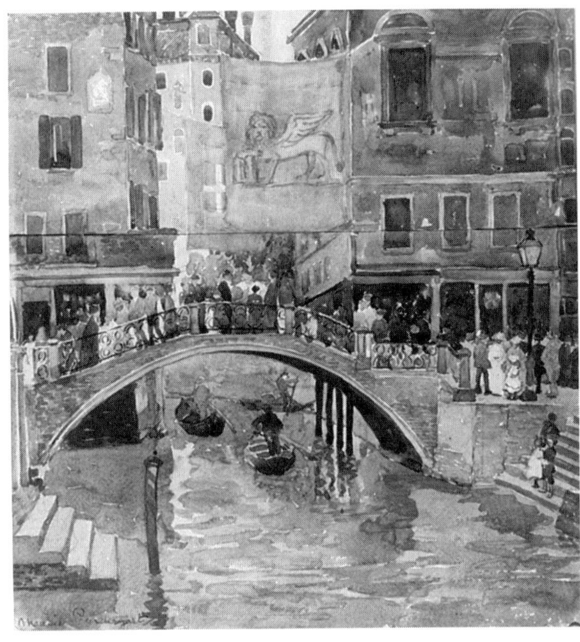

Fig. 71. Maurice Prendergast, *Venice*, 1898, watercolor, 17¼″ × 15⁹⁄₁₆″, Collection Addison Gallery of American Art, Phillips Academy, Andover, Massachusetts.

probable in terms of Venetian topography. In fact the question could easily become, why do so few artists picture these frequent irregularities in the geometry of the city, preferring instead the tidy perpendiculars of water, wall, bridge, and picture plane. Less eccentric are Francis Hopkinson Smith's *Venice: Canal Scene, II* (fig. 72) and Prendergast's *Venice* (fig. 73). Here the bridge, still flatly parallel to the picture plane, is thrust over to one side, linking two unequal quantities. Our footing is, visually, aquatic, although many canal views, including Prendergast's *Venice*, were done from dry land—this from behind a railing that the artist has chosen to exclude (see fig. 74)—to allow us more precipitously, more spontaneously, to enter the scene. It is in these "unbalanced" modifications of the convention that we realize how strong the convention is. Although Howells asserts that "there is a perfect democracy in the realm of the beautiful, and whatsoever pleases is equal to any other thing there, no matter how low its origin or humble its composition,"[28] it is clear that some low and humble scenes are more equal than others, are repeatedly chosen, recorded, and interpreted. Artists did not just "do" anything; even their democratic eye saw, selected, and helped portray those images that suited certain unstated conditions which, in fact, in this case were not very complex.

Departing from the classic syntax of narrow canal-with-bridge, several artists executed low mi-

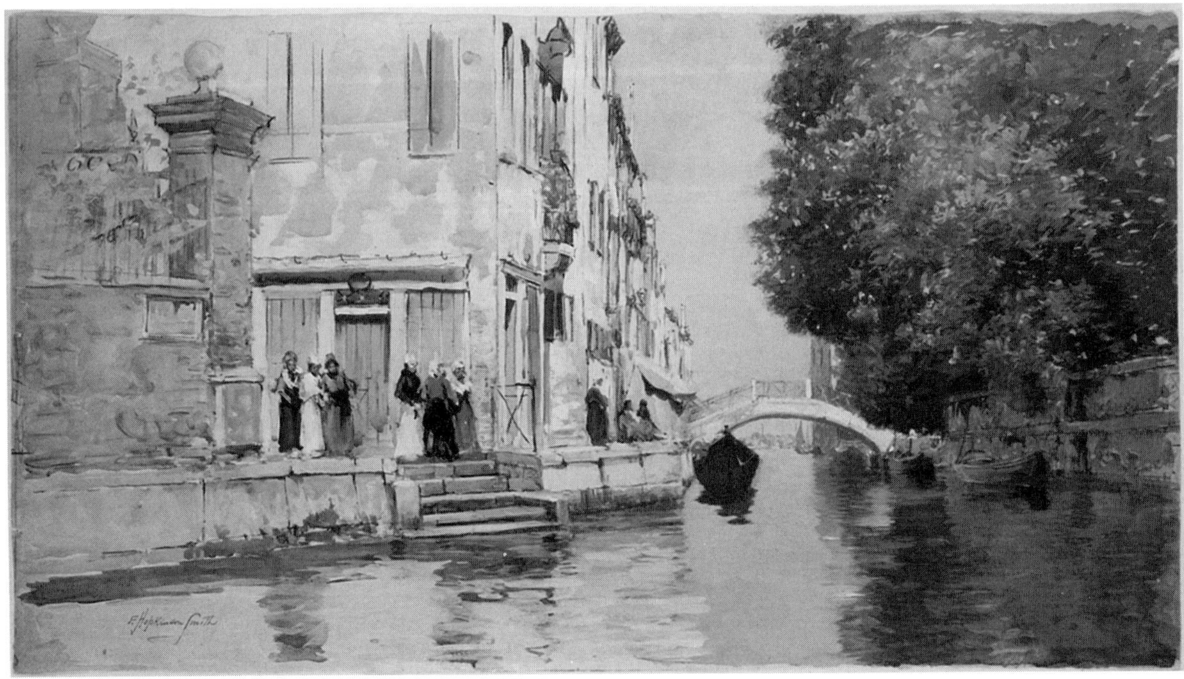

Fig 72. Francis Hopkinson Smith, *Venice: Canal Scene, II*, before 1895, watercolor, 13″ × 24¼″, Museum of Fine Arts, Boston, Gift of Estate of Nellie P. Carter, 1935.

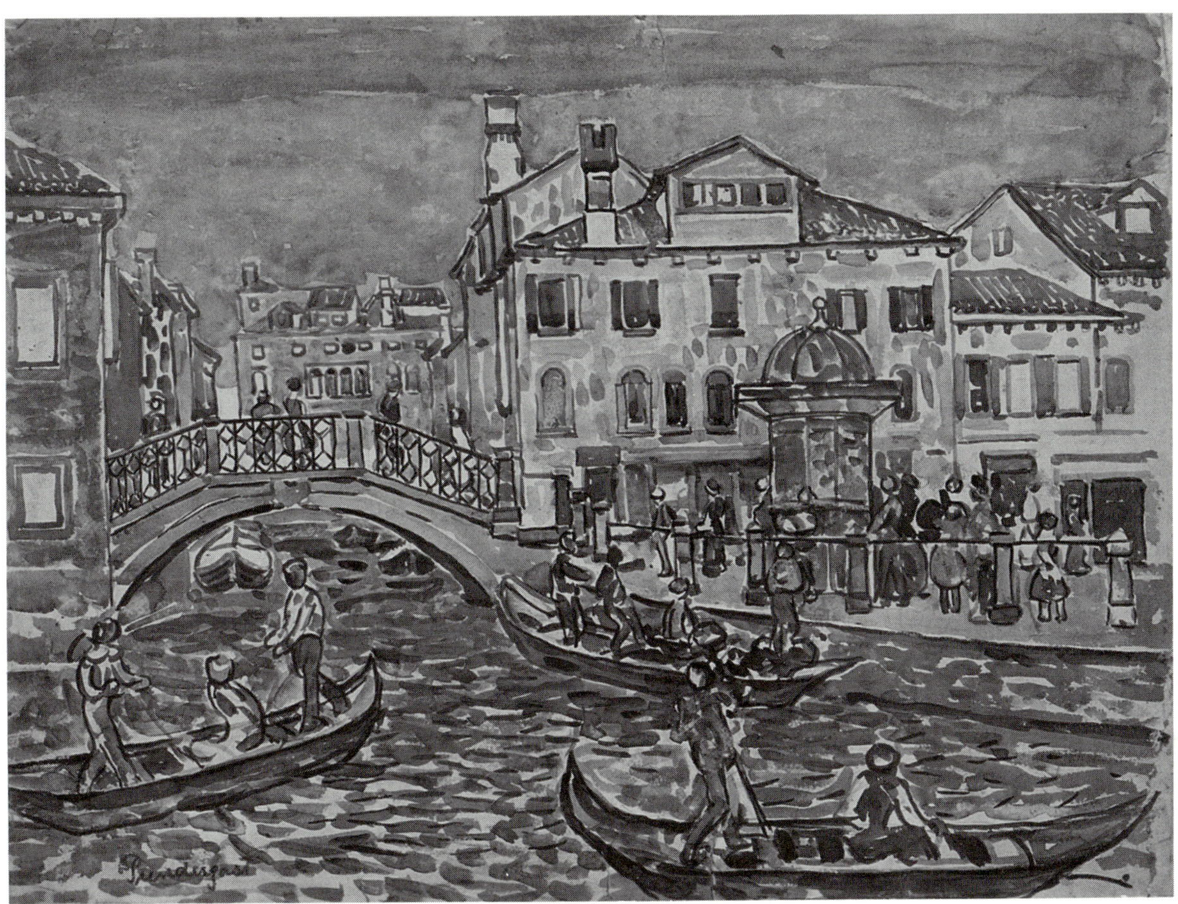

Fig. 73. Maurice Prendergast, *Venice*, ca. 1911–12, watercolor, 17⅛″ × 23⅛″, McNay Art Museum, San Antonio, Texas, bequest of Marion Koogler McNay; see also fig. 80.

metic images of the Grand Canal—an exercise that demanded extraordinary ingenuity. Sargent's *Grand Canal, Venice* (fig. 75) is, startlingly, as devoid of human life as it is of architectural monuments. From a low landing stage beside the Palazzo Pisani Moretta, his eye skirts along the range of facades on the right, so nearly perpendicular to the picture plane as to be unrecognizable. On the left the view is cropped to exclude any palaces close enough to be familiar and heroic. The broad waterway, uninterrupted by the Rialto, as the facades are uninterrupted by recognizable palace or church, is the central element of the work. But more important, it is a painting that—with its emphatic title—points more to those things *not* being recorded than to those that are. Sargent is not just being visually "democratic" here, he is being self-consciously nonheroic.

In the *Rialto Market, Venice* (fig. 76; see also fig. 80) by Childe Hassam (1859–1935) there are figures, but no touch of modernity intrudes; the scene

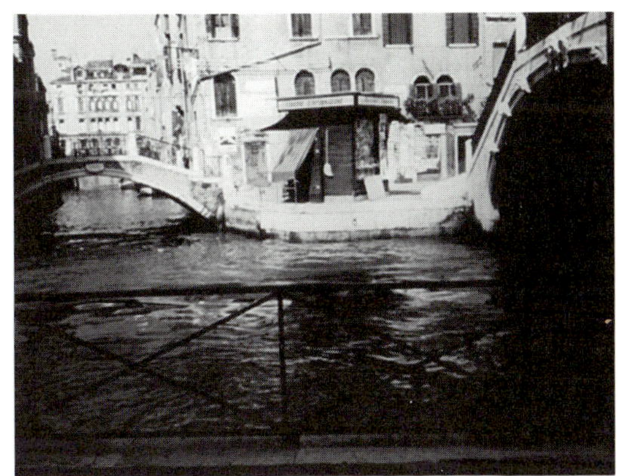

Fig. 74. Site of Maurice Prendergast, *Venice* (fig. 73).

is of a picturesque open-air market beside the (unseen) Rialto bridge. Most artists of Venetian scenes portray subjects in this mode with views of this type, preferring gondolas and fishing boats to vaporetti, fishwives and artisans to hotel managers and hawkers, the marketplace to the waterbus stop. In this sense the low mimetic mode tends toward

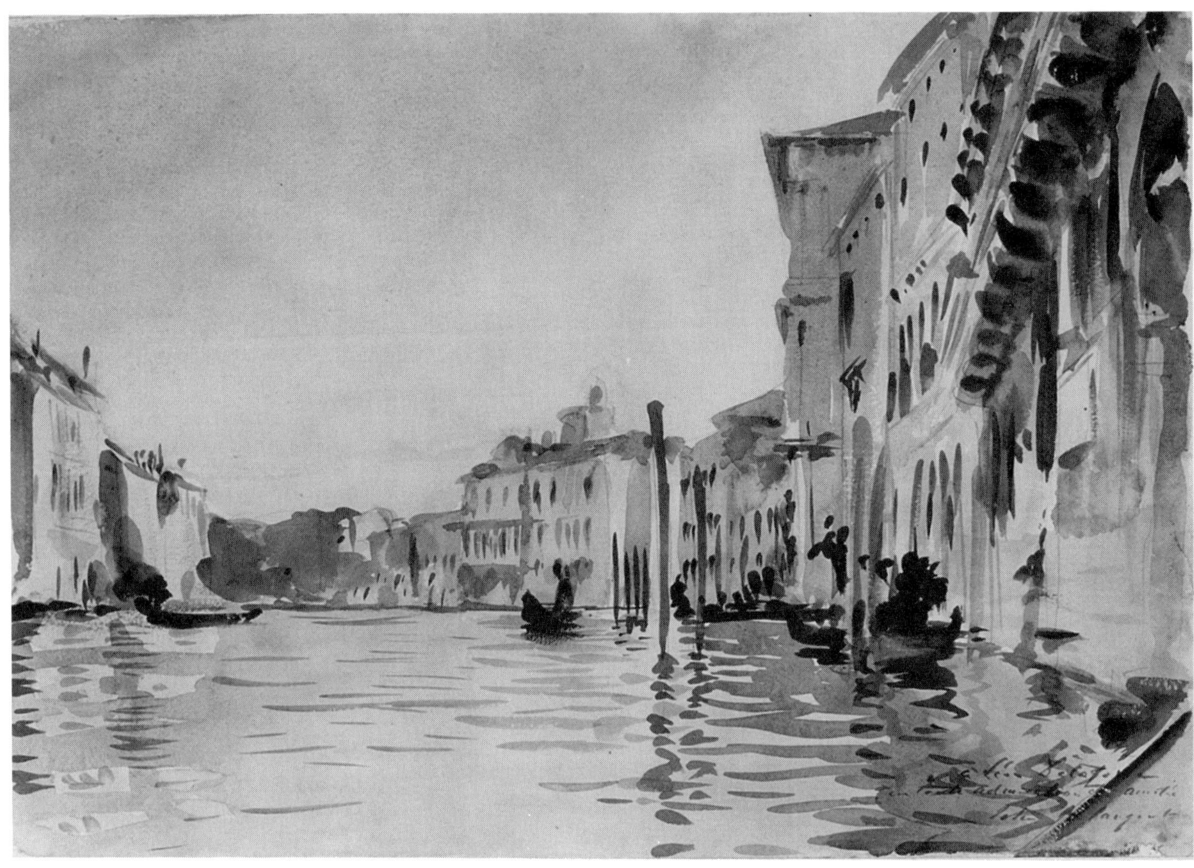

Fig. 75. John Singer Sargent, *The Grand Canal, Venice*, ca. 1903–13, watercolor, 9⅝″ × 13⅞″, Fogg Art Museum, Harvard University, Cambridge, Bequest of Grenville L. Winthrop; see also fig. 80.

a more conservative frame of reference, a more archaic interpretation of human activity. The view includes a range of fine but indistinct buildings, the soaring spire of Santi Apostili, and some local women poised on the bundle-strewn flagstones. Although the scene is set beside the Grand Canal, the water is not seen; it is sensed only as a wide gulf which separates the foreground campo from the buildings opposite. In this Hassam has devised yet a third strategy for deheroicizing the grand waterway.

Venice's small open paved spaces, or campi, were not frequently painted, even by those who shared the low mimetic vision of Howells, a self-confessed, not infrequent "prisoner" in their surrounding walls. The campi, which invariably include a well near the center and a church facade on one long side, are more the province of the people, less aristocratic, less touristed than the canals. Here Howells's "interesting squalor and picturesque wretchedness" are to be found. They tend to be hot and airless spaces. No watery reflections or

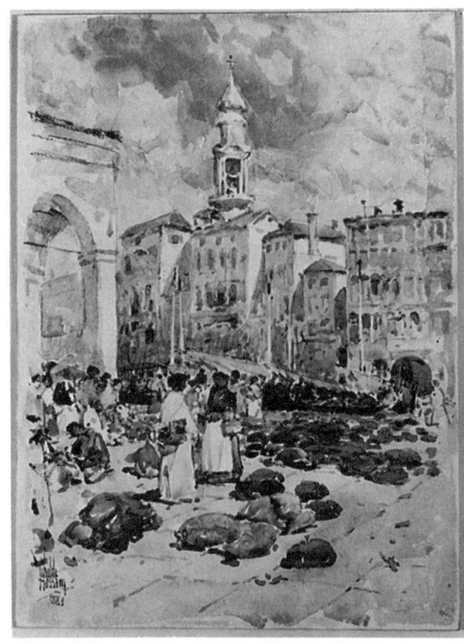

Fig. 76. Childe Hassam, *Rialto Market, Venice*, 1883, watercolor, 14″ × 9½″, Mead Art Museum, Amherst College, Amherst, Massachusetts; see also fig. 80.

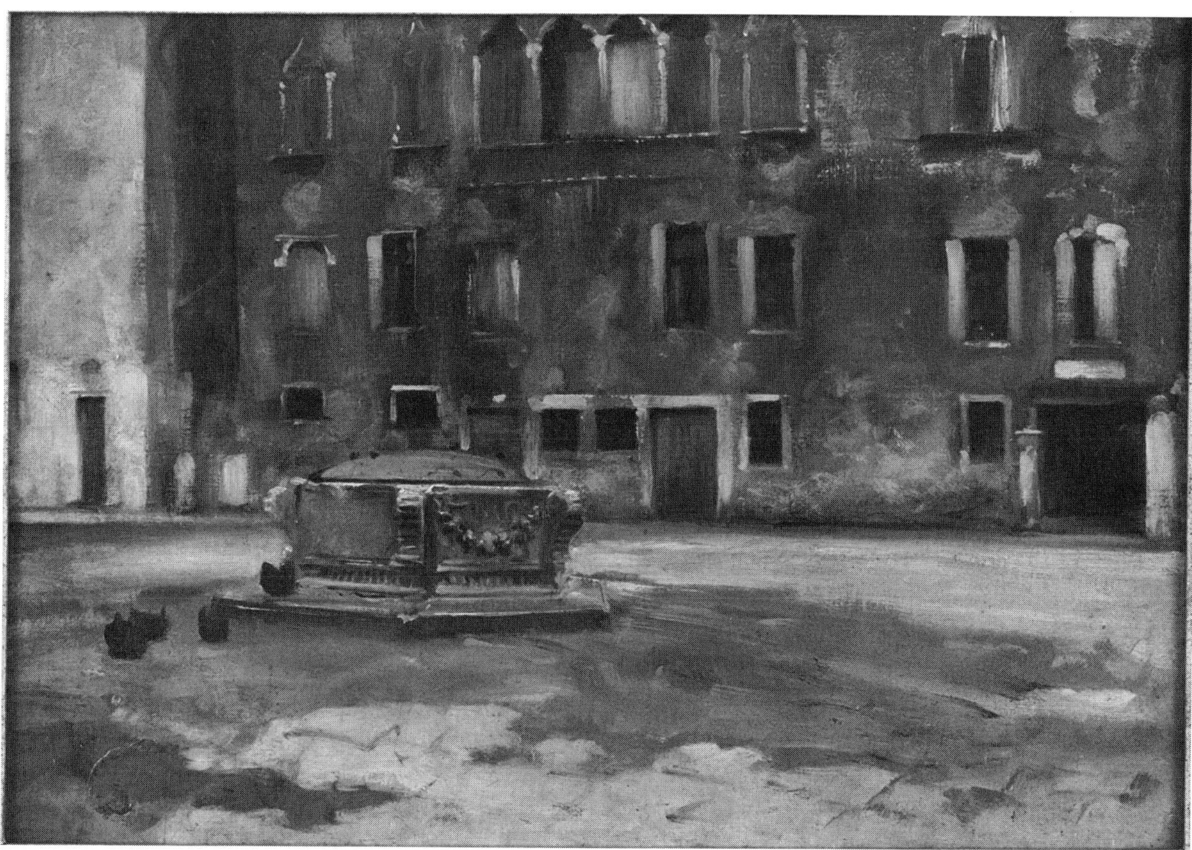

Fig. 77. John Singer Sargent, *Campo Sant' Agnese, Venice*, ca. 1890, oil on canvas, 17½" × 25", Wellesley College Museum, Wellesley, Massachusetts; see also fig. 80.

shimmering leaves break up the light and suggest respite from land-locked, man-made stone enclosure. Unlike the axial canal spaces, no pictorial conventions suggested themselves and became firmly established. Two of those who essayed the subject (with radically differing strategies) were Sargent in *Campo Sant' Agnese, Venice* (fig. 77) and Prendergast in *Festival, Venice* (fig. 78).[29] The first portrays the southeast corner of a small campo behind the Accademia (see fig. 80). The long façade of a Gothic palazzo, shabby for the loss of much of its stucco, and a stubby corner of a blank vernacular structure caught in the morning sunshine occupy the background. Unseen on our left is the small church of Sant' Agnese, and on our right the noble Gesuati (introduced in abbreviated form in Chase's *In Venice*, fig. 43). In the foreground an elaborate baroque wellhead, supported by marble scrolls and adorned by an opulent floral swag tied with delicate marble ribbons, is the focus of our attention and the roost for four fat Venetian hens. Our point of view is low, entirely human, even rather henlike in this context. The little drama (as all low mimetic scenes are *little* dramas) is acted out entirely with nonhuman protagonists. It is a phenomenon we have seen over and over again, one peculiarly suited to and well developed in Venice.

In a distinct minority in this respect is Prendergast, whose works are almost invariably well-peopled. *Festival, Venice* (fig. 78) portrays the small square-shaped Campo San Maurizio (fig. 79), its modest space dressed out in flags and lanterns and populated by numerous denizens of the neighborhood. Warmly shawled women, small clusters of men, and a whole flock of children converse or walk randomly through the space. It is twilight—the festive lamps are lit and the last rays of the sun just catch the upper wall and chimney pots of the corner building. The whole scene is cast in a chill shadow which belies the gaiety of the banners and lamps. The viewer's vantage point is high, evidently from a tall stage or ladder placed against the wall of the modest church that crowds the square

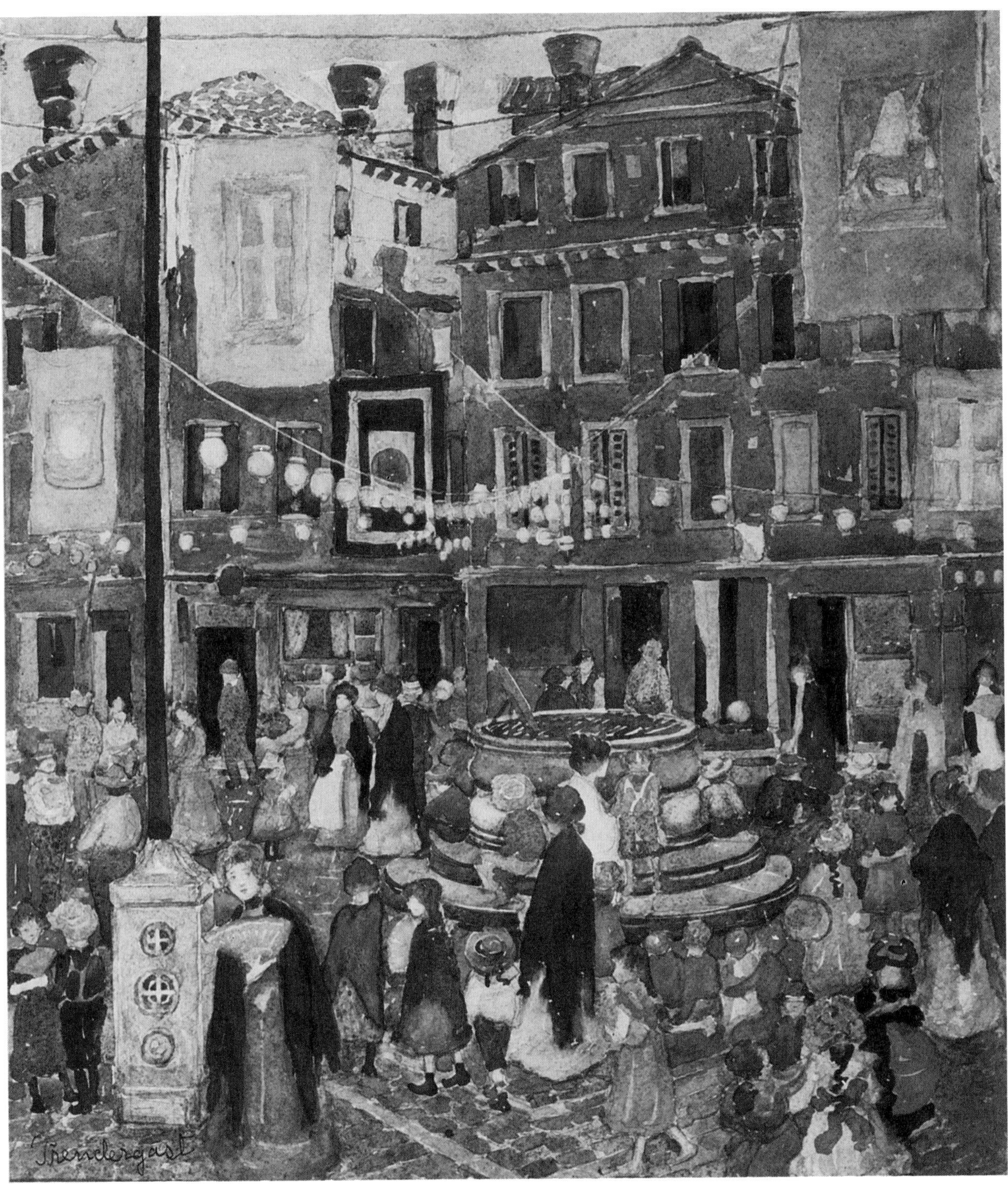

Fig. 78. Maurice Prendergast, *Festival, Venice*, ca. 1898–99, watercolor, 16⅝″ × 14″, Collection, Museum of Modern Art, New York, gift of Abby Aldrich Rockefeller; see also fig. 80.

on its northern boundary. Prendergast seems to prefer this high vantage point and seems to have repeatedly gone to great trouble to achieve it. What it does for him is give him a wide, complex stage for his figures. In complicated overlapping layers they mark a steep recession into space, dramatizing what is, in fact, a rather shallow space, one marked out for us more regularly by the wonderful swooping line of the lanterns. Howells tells us that by his time (thirty years before Prendergast's first visit to Venice) the festivals for which the city was internationally famous, indeed infamous, had shrunk to rather tawdry anticlimactic affairs.[30] No one is having a whooping good time here (the only adult

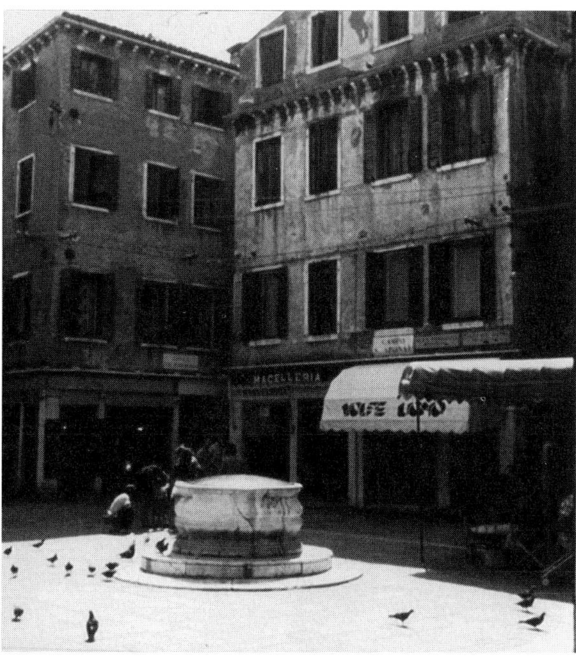

Fig. 79. Campo San Maurizio, site of Maurice Prendergast, *Festival, Venice* (fig. 78).

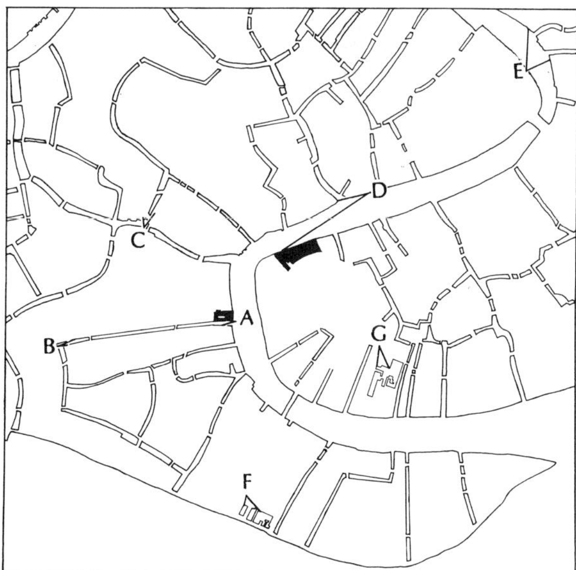

A. Moore, *San Barnaba, Venice,* fig. 65
B. Sargent, *Venetian Canal,* fig. 66
C. Prendergast, *Venice,* fig. 73
D. Sargernt, *The Grand Canal, Venice,* fig. 75
E. Hassam, *Rialto Market, Venice,* fig. 76
F. Sargent, *Campo Sant' Agnese, Venice,* fig. 77
G. Prendergast, *Festival, Venice,* fig. 78

Fig. 80. Map of sites of figs. 65, 66, 73, 75, 76, 77, 78.

clusters are monosexual; nothing at all resembling intrigue or courtship is going on); however, there is a certain sense of spirit and specialness about the affair, which one reads as much in the upper reaches of the picture as in the lower. The microcosm portrayed in both the Prendergast and the Sargent campi pictures is of a world living more in its memories than in its traditions.

It often surprises visitors to find that Venice is basically a pedestrian city. While it is easier to travel to some destinations by vaporetti, few people hire gondolas and most walk. What one sees in these canal and campi views is a pedestrian's-eye view of a newly discovered realm, one characterized by an extraordinary sense of urban quiet, sudden narrow vistas, unthreatening disorientation, and a sense that one is encouraging surprise and experience while deliberately avoiding both Objects of Interest and a culture "morally and materially . . . in good repair."

Apertures

One of the curious things about nineteenth-century Venice is the noticeably prominent role foreigners played in stirring up Venetian memories. Howells (and other travelers) give instance after instance in which even vaguely informed visitors know historic figures and places that are completely unknown to Venetians.[31] Tied to the facts of daily experience, they seemed (to these visitors with their eyes on specific historic facts and on the general sweep of historic events) startlingly ignorant—we might say innocent—of the large historic "case" that their city offered to the rest of the world. They dated their decline (insofar as they saw it at all) not from the fifteenth century (or more specifically, as Ruskin put it, "I date the commencement of the Fall of Venice from the death of Carlo Zeno, 8th May, 1418")[32] but from the inception of the Austrian occupation in 1797. Howells condenses these two differing interpretations of the Fall and the present dull sober bitterness of the city in his observation, "The causes of this change lie partly in the altered character of the whole world's civilization, partly in the increasing poverty of the city, doomed four hundred years ago to commercial decay, and chiefly (the Venetians would be apt to tell you wholly) in the implacable anger, the inconsolable discontent, with which the people regard their present political condition."[33]

So the city was then two distinctly different entities to these two populations, the visitors never unaware of the Venetian past, and the local people rarely aware of it. The material mediating for the visitors between the past and themselves was the

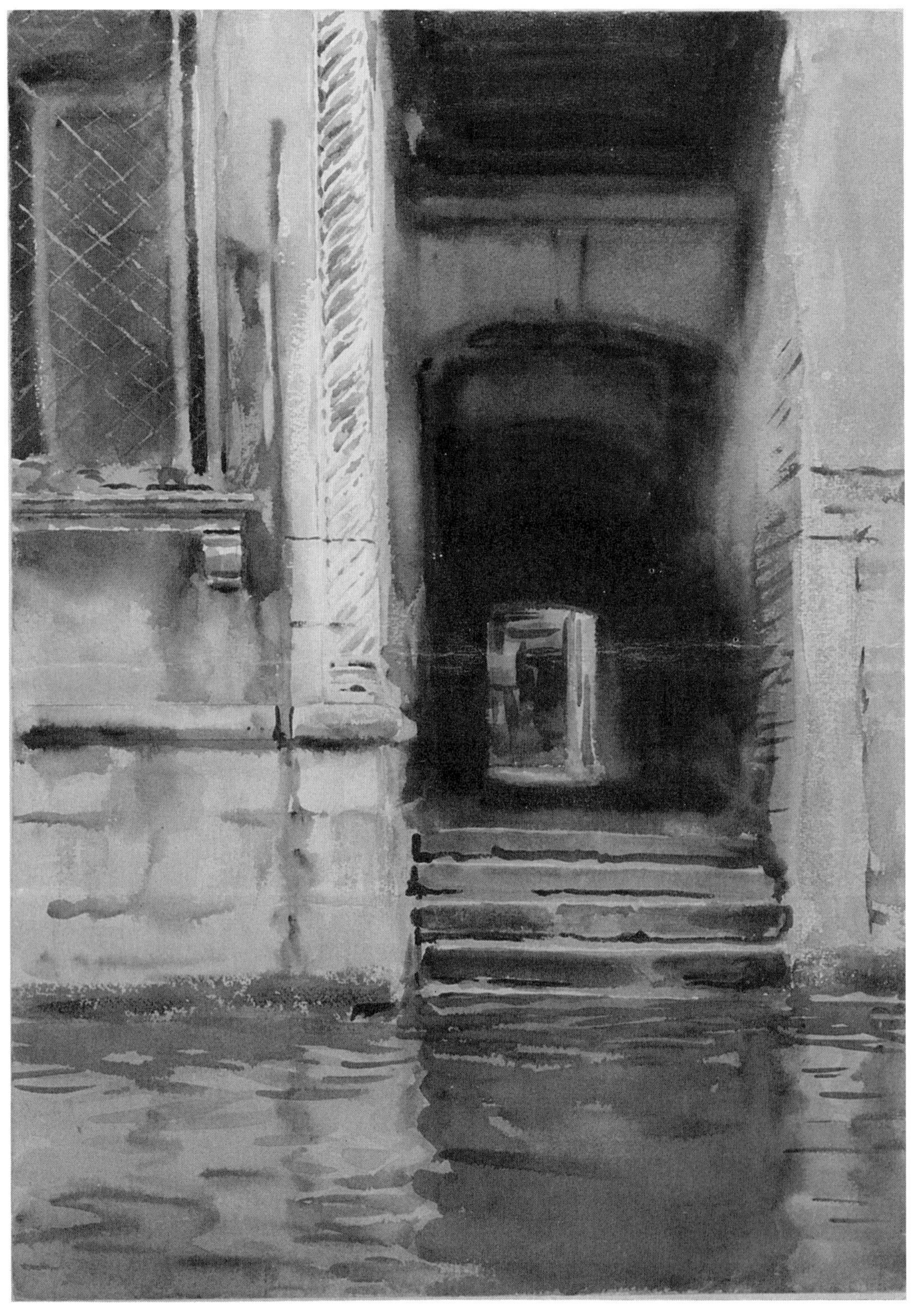

Fig. 81. John Singer Sargent, *Venetian Doorway*, ca. 1905, watercolor, 20 15/16″ × 14 1/4″, Metropolitan Museum of Art, Gift of Mrs. Francis Ormond, 1950.

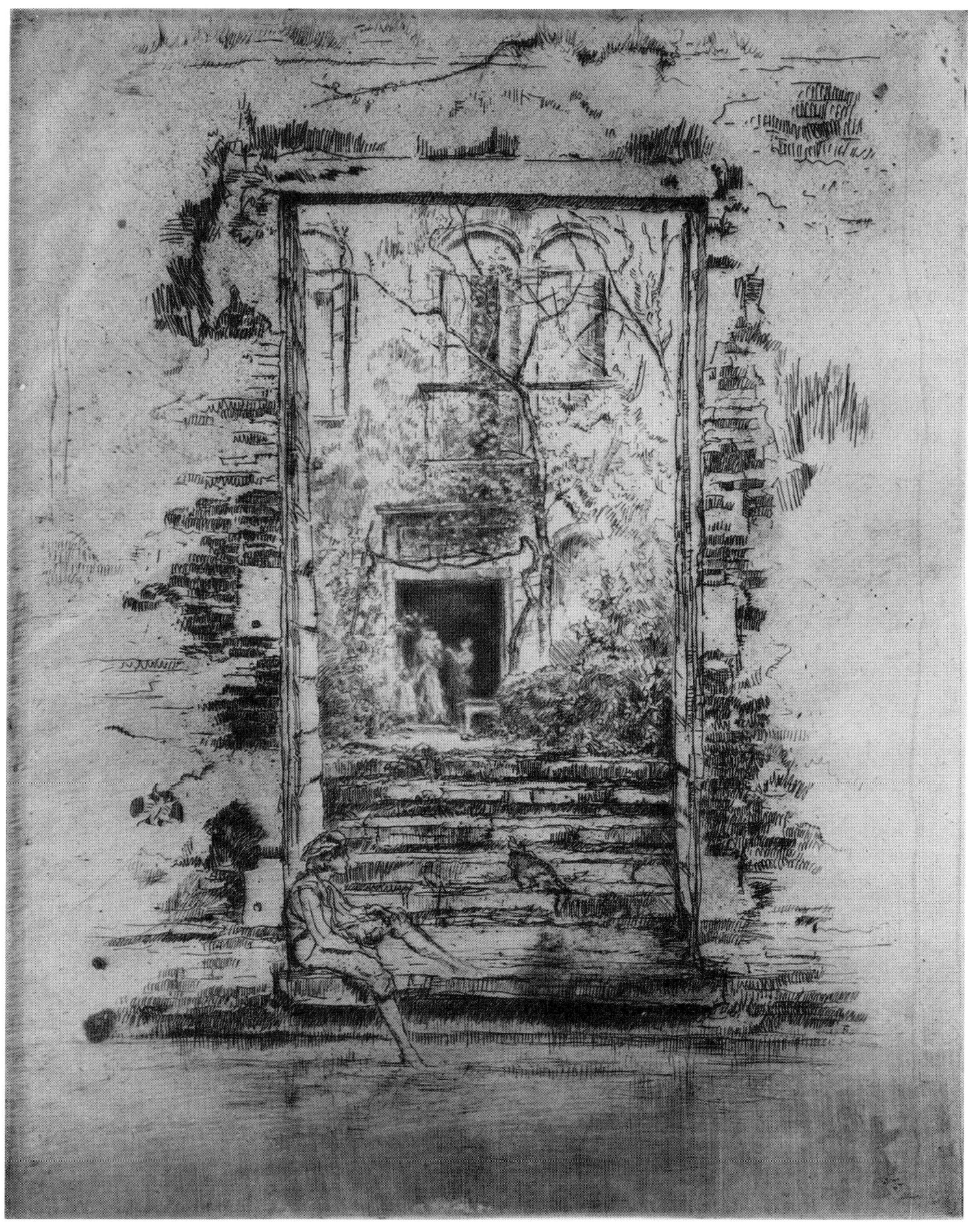

Fig. 82. James McNeill Whistler, *The Garden*, 1880, etching and drypoint, Fine Arts Museums of San Francisco, Achenbach Foundation for Graphic Arts, purchase.

fabric of the city—its stones—testifying silently but eloquently, to the informed or imaginative, about a reality beyond the visible present. Painters in the low mimetic mode who sought to find an objective correlative for the native sense of unhistoric space hit on an ingenious but simple visual structure. They not only avoided the monuments, they also avoided, in large part, portraying the vernacular physical fabric of the city as well. Instead these images are structured around apertures, openings, and cleavages. As the emphasis is on negative space and empty voids, the sense of time past, of historic time one reads in noble structure and decayed vernacular structure alike, is minimalized. Instead the emphasis is on the present moment, on human action within the human-scaled aperture. These narrow negative spaces have extraordinary visual power; as in Sargent's *Venetian Doorway* (fig. 81), they pull the viewer's eye down into their depths with an intensity and velocity that are surprising. Hesitating only momentarily on the wall surface parallel to the picture plane, our eye plunges straight as an arrow deep into mysterious space. Often the very partial glimpse we get through the yawning opening is extremely complex, with layers of light and dark, of rooms and spaces made more interesting by the meagerness of our view. Whistler's etching *The Garden* (fig. 82) and his pastel *The Doorway, Venice* (fig. 83) are, with the Sargent *Venetian Doorway* (fig. 81), good examples of this complex layering.[34] Because doorways and steps are usually in a very human scale (no matter how grand the building), our empathetic participation in these images is rapid and total. Unaware and uninterested in the two-dimensional facade of the building—its height, width, architectural details—we fix on the narrow three-dimensional volume opened up and offered to us. Empathetically we mount the stairs and enter, finding ourselves in successive areas of tunnellike darkness, open courtyard, or enclosed interior space with further apertures suggested beyond. The point of view is low; the format mimics our standing posture. This is a very personal mode, appealing more than anything else to our sense of discovery. Unlike the Dutch genre scenes which they superficially resemble, these aperture images are seen with the curious eye of a quickly passing stranger, not the affectionate descriptive, domestic eye of a habitué. The sense of mystery, of cursory, spontaneous impression is cultivated, not the familiar inventory of space, object, and kin that we admire in the Dutch masters. The fact of otherness, interesting cultural otherness, is dramatized; the figures and their environment are not described, only suggested, inferred, as though seen quickly and recorded rapidly. The emphasis is on the quality, aura, and size of spaces more than on architectural fabric or social fact.

Even when the opening is so dark as not to admit our curious eye, as in Whistler's *Bead Stringers, Venice* (fig. 84), the wall is almost not drawn, almost nonexistent.[35] The effort of the artist has been to fix the apertures, to see them as principal characters in his brief pantomime. One pictorial means by which Whistler consciously draws our eye away from surface fabric, away from the stones and stucco, is by avoiding cornice and corner edges of his structures. Secondly, and more distinctively Whistlerian, he vignettes the wall surface within the picture frame. The bricks and mortar are suggested near the openings, as in *Bead Stringers, Venice* and *The Garden* (fig. 82), but they are only implied toward the edges of the picture frame. This device of vignetting is one that is especially suitable to aperture-oriented views, and Whistler explored its possibilities again and again. There is a dark void at the center of these compositions, which we read as deep space, and a paper-colored void at their edges, which we read as solid wall. It is part of Whistler's magic that, with the few strokes describing the aperture surround, we readily grant him both.

In most of these aperture compositions Whistler includes figures. They are to be found at the most "real" part of the composition, at the opening, usually to one side as though stepping aside to let our eye pass beyond. Doorways suggest human posture and human action. They suggest entering and exiting and everyday life. Unlike the heroic and many low mimetic views in which the Ruskinian sense of history, read through architectural substance, is paramount, here the subject is not just "ordinary" (nonmonumental), not just seen from a merely human point of view with a merely human cone of vision, it is also an image of daily human life existing less in an aura of past history than in an envelope of present time. The architectural fragments he offers us are dilapidated, decayed, even postlapsarian in tone (as the Fall, whether dated from 1418 or from 1797, is inescapably part of the

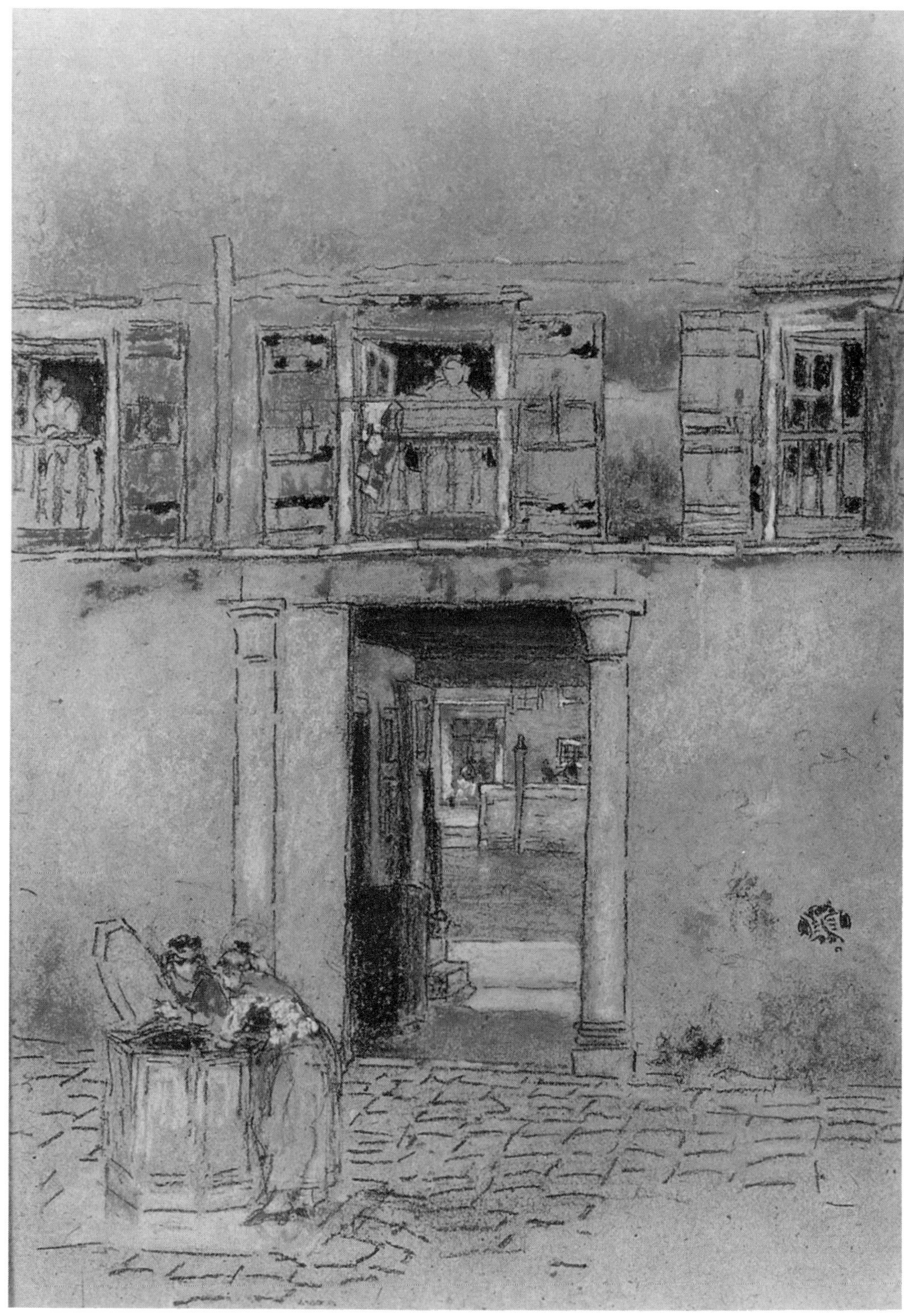

Fig. 83. James McNeill Whistler, *The Doorway, Venice,* ca. 1879–80, pastel and charcoal on gray-brown paper, 11¾″ × 7⅞″, St. Louis Art Museum, Gift of J. Lionberger Davis.

present), but they are containers for, rather than surrogates for, human activity. And that activity is primarily a present one, conscious of its chores and sometimes not unaware of the staring artist.

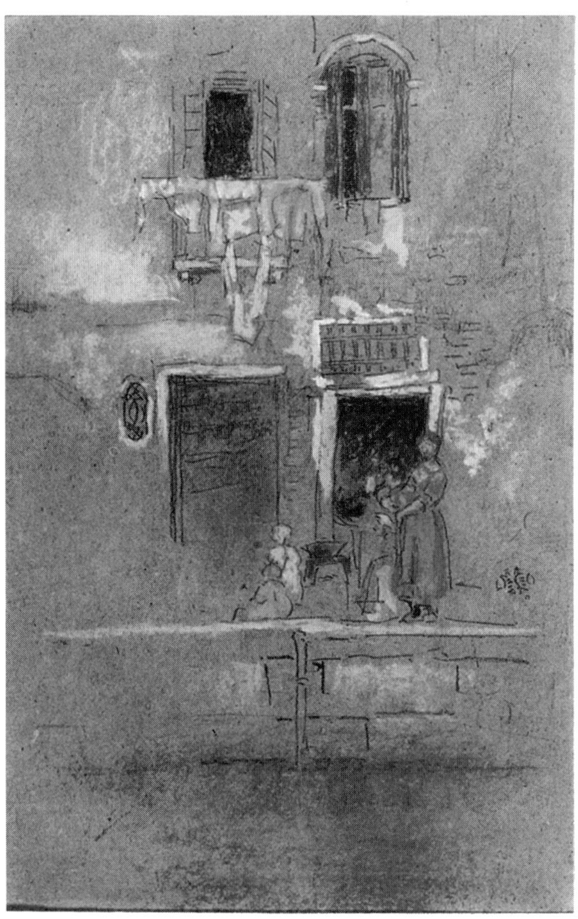

Fig. 84. James McNeill Whistler, *Bead Stringers, Venice*, ca. 1879–80, pastel and charcoal on brown paper, 11¾" × 7¼", Metropolitan Museum of Art, Harris Brisbane Dick Fund, 1917.

Among other opportunities, the aperture composition allows the artist to create a frame within a frame or a tale within a tale. These two spaces, interior and exterior, can offer differing and juxtaposed microcosms—the characters in one frame ignorant of but often contrasted with those outside, including ourselves. In such an image as *The Garden* (fig. 82), the image offers a sanctuary, an experience unlike that offered by the canal. By contrast *Nocturne: Furnace* (ca. 1880, etching and drypoint, Second Venice Set) and *The Two Doorways* (ca. 1880, etching and drypoint, First Venice Set) by Whistler and *Street in Venice* by Chase (fig. 85) show men hard at work in their shops, blowing glass, hammering copper, and sorting goods.[36] They are both antithetical to and paradigms for the artist hard at work outside the second frame. In these cases, where the male worker is the discovery and the focus of interest, the figure is centered within the frame of the door and offered to us as a small sample of life in modern Venice.

It is a curious fact of Venice's social geography that the paved ways, the many *calli* (alleys) are the zones of the poorer Venetians. It is here on dry land rather than on the waterways that many images of contemporary Venetian folk, especially Venetian womenfolk, necessarily concentrate. As is clear from Whistler's *Bead-stringers, Venice* (pl. 5), these narrow lanes are places of existence, not of transition. They are as much social space contained as a series of architectural facades contain-

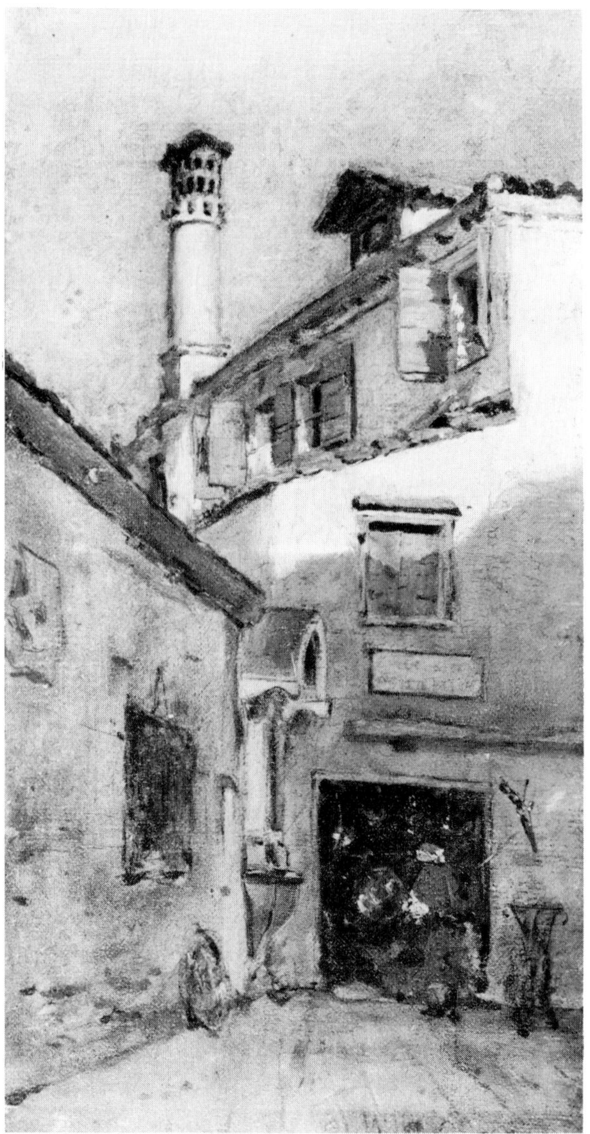

Fig. 85. William Merritt Chase, *Street in Venice*, ca. 1877, oil on board, 12½" × 6", Lyman Allyn Museum, New London, Connecticut.

ing. In these shady alleys one is very aware, as one artist put it, of "the children, bareheaded, barefooted, and most of them barebacked; . . . their mothers and sisters chok[ing] up doorways, stringing beads, making lace, sitting in bunches listening to a story by some old crone."[37] This choking up of doorways and narrow streets gives the artist a necessarily human subject in these areas. In Whistler's *Bead-stringers, Venice*, most figures sit or stand with an idleness of demeanor and an absence of purpose which no commentator on nineteenth-century Venice failed to observe. In the foreground, however, one woman lifts high her right hand. In her lap rests a bright pouch and we can infer that she is, as the title suggests, stringing colored glass beads. They form a very complete harmony, the visual structure (low narrow cone of vision), the architectural subject (narrow calle and modest courtyard), and the human subject—characteristic Venetians engaged in characteristically Venetian occupations.

Figures

There are relatively few compositions that focus on Venetians—single or clustered figures. It is perhaps surprising that even in the low mimetic mode, the spatial and architectural context of the city seemed to translate more easily into suitable and meaningful and saleable compositions than did genre scenes. And those genre scenes that were painted point to a truncated vision of Venetian society. The absence of "the better sort" of Venetians from these paintings points as much to the low profile that the surviving aristocracy maintained as to its apparent extinction. The Venetians the artists did see were working men and women, people distinguished from their observers by levels of wealth, idiosyncrasies of dress, and by the types of work they undertook. Shopkeepers, restaurateurs, hotel managers are among those invisible in the painters' Venice, a fact harmonious with the silent interdiction to keep other artists and most tourists out of the picture. The Venetians we see are gondoliers, glassblowers, bead stringers, lacemakers, laundresses, people who work with their hands rather than with the managerial and merchant skills for which their (generalized) ancestors were so justly famous. Of course these hand skills are more visible, and more available to the perambulating artist; however, they also represent the important concepts of art and craft and manual skill, quantities threatened in the late nineteenth century and ones which the artists themselves had a stake in championing.

In the background of Duveneck's *Canal Scene with Washerwomen, Venice* (fig. 86), on the left-hand side, a bead stringer holds up and checks her strands. Balancing this seated figure is a swarthy man on the opposite side, leaning on a fishnet-strewn parapet. He smokes a pipe and looks at the large, buxom, beautiful washerwoman who is silhouetted against a dark aperture at the center of the picture. The male figure is most probably a self-portrait, gaining the advantage of a double prospect on the object of his admiration. Her attendants on the steps compose with her the sort of triangle we are accustomed to see in Renaissance Madonna altarpieces. She is, in a sense, a sort of low mimetic Madonna of the canal, a personification of beauty and wholesomeness flanked by art on one side and craft on the other, with youth and industry at her feet. Duveneck did seem to strive repeatedly for heightened meaning and emotional effect in his paintings, interpreting the Venetians in such an image as *Venetian Shrine, Sketch* (fig. 87) as a gently beatific folk. Here the husband cradles a young child while the wife mounts a short ladder to pay her respects to an aquatic version of a roadside shrine. Duveneck's *Shrine* is an image, above all, of domestic tranquility and simple naive faith, qualities attributed to "simple," poetic people by many (including the artist's Cincinnati patrons) who might have felt their own lack of "simplicity" an inevitable fault of their prosaic modernity.

In contrast to these self-consciously posed vignettes of daily life among the Venetians, in which high mimetic structures are employed and a romantic sense of loss is felt, Sargent's two compositions entitled *A Street in Venice* (pl. 6, fig. 88) are far more natural, far more inscrutable compositions.[38] They have an air of daily experience about them, of half-finished sentences. We even catch a glance, not over-friendly, signaling our visual intrusion. The setting is in one case a narrow shaded calle, in the other a slightly wider undistinguished street, the dry land and obscure territories in which the Venetians (rather than their visitors) are in full possession. We see the figures from the vantage point of a fellow pedestrian. Sargent's monochromatic treatment of the subject—varieties of grey with

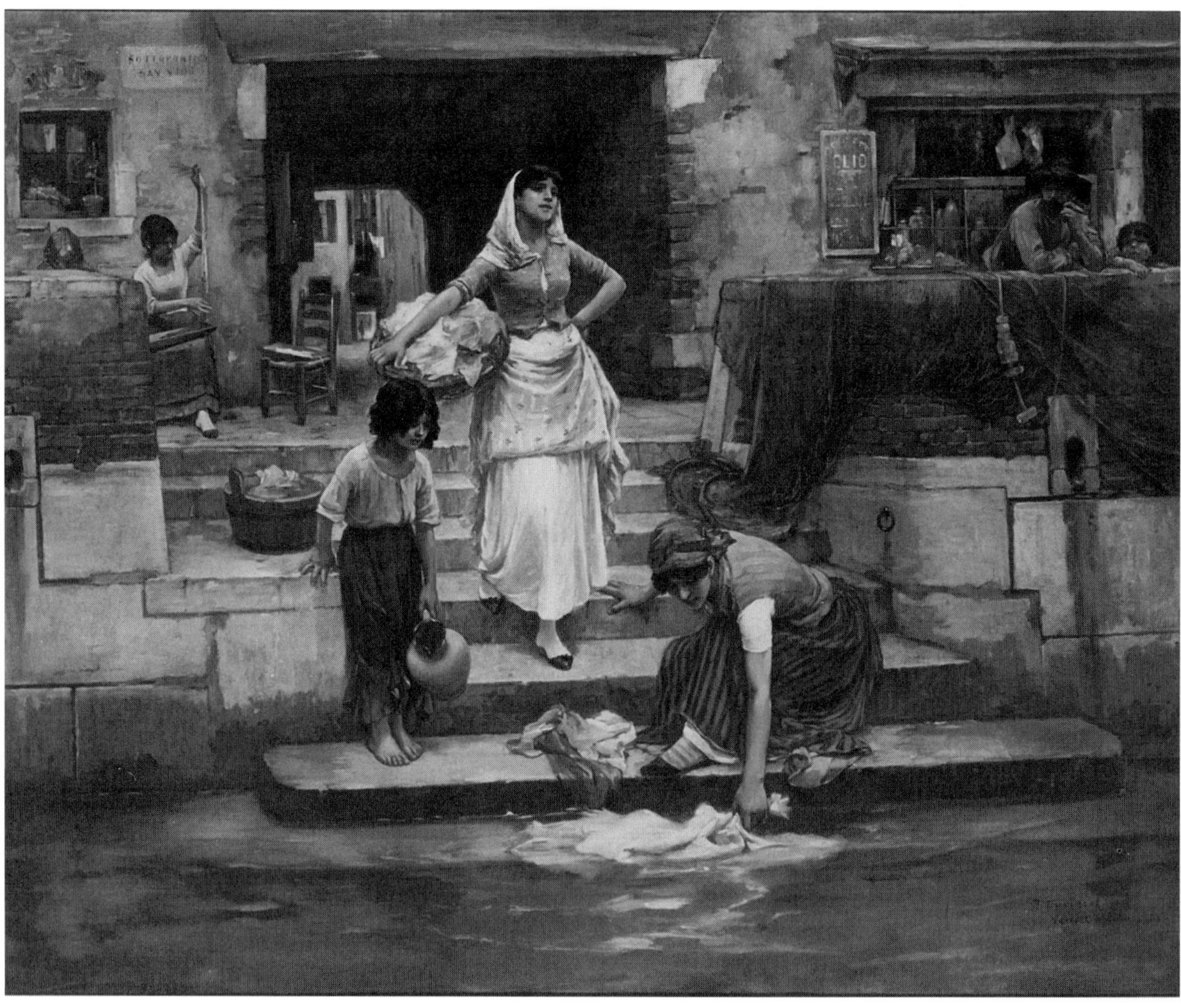

Fig. 86. Frank Duveneck, *Canal Scene with Washerwomen, Venice,* 1885, oil on canvas, 37½″ × 45″, Canton Art Institute, Canton, Ohio, gift by an anonymous donor.

black figures and a few touches of white and dull brick red—and the narrowness of the physical setting seem to suggest the general narrowness of these people's lives. But Sargent leaves little doubt that they are as psychologically complex as we, as full of investigative intensity, of clandestine and uncertain relationships, as we. The central figure in plate 6 is, like the central figure in Duveneck's *Washerwomen*, a wistful beauty. But here the wistfulness is underdramatized as she moves quietly along, deeply enwrapped in a long shawl. A fellow artist, Francis Hopkinson Smith, recorded his impression of a similar woman in one of his gilt-edged travel books: "Such a vision of beauty! Such a wealth of purple—grape purple—black hair; such luminous black eyes, real gazelle's, soft and velvety; so exquisitely graceful; so charming and naive; so unkempt,—so ragged,—so entirely unlaundered, unscrubbed, and slovenly!"[39] An equivocal description, it points up the double message that the Queen of the Adriatic and these allegorical personifications of the city delivered to the late nineteenth-century Anglo-American visitor: beautiful but ragged and unlike the observer in both respects. Almost more than any other quality, these women and Venice were very other. The collision was double: between Venice's past and its fallen present, and between the culture interpreted and the observer's. We have a slight sense here of painterly anthropologists moving among aborigines—half admiring of, half revolted by the culture they have bound themselves to observe and interpret. The painters do not want to *be* Venetians, they do not even want to be very close to them, if the number of surviving figure images is any indication. Some, like Duveneck, seem to dictate too actively the terms on which Venetians are seen. Others, like Sargent, appear to seek out the characteristic pose, gesture, or situation, to catch them at rear entrances, against dark walls, in narrow sunlit winter alleys, encountering one another. In this he appears to interpret less than to record. Like Henry James in such late works as *The Awkward Age,* he gives us almost pure "dialogue" and little narrative description or obvious interpretation. And hence the sense of irresolution and ambiguity which thrusts much of the interpretive task on the viewer.

Of the two sexes, women seem to be, by far, the preferred figurative subject. Their industries, so important to Venice's economy, continued to flourish during this period. Baedeker reports that in 1906 more than four hundred women were employed by the principal lace-making concern alone.[40] And among these populations of workers, several artists seem to have set up their easels. Robert F. Blum's *Venetian Lacemakers* (fig. 89) and two paintings by John Singer Sargent, *The Bead Stringers of Venice* (fig. 90) and *Venetian Glass Workers* (fig. 91) give some sense of the artists' interpretations of these social and economic groups.[41] Blum's women are young and handsome, their ruffled, gossamer, brightly colored clothes fit well, and they chat over their bobbins with obvious delight. The vantage point is that of a seated onlooker with whom one girl gaily flirts. The figures are ranged in a shallow diagonal recessing along the exterior wall back into space. By contrast Sargent's damaged *Bead Stringers* (fig. 90) is a much more subdued work with a superficially very similar subject and composition. The space is an odd-shaped room with heavy sheets of fabric hanging in an alcove and along the wall which plunges diagonally across the picture. Two young women in the foreground turn their backs to us and face a dark aperture, edged by a heavy, tassel-tied curtain. A group of women cluster in the far corner. There is no visible communication between any of the figures, or between any of the figures and ourselves. The women thread their beads in long bags which sit in rectangular trays on their laps. Something in their silence and slumped pos-

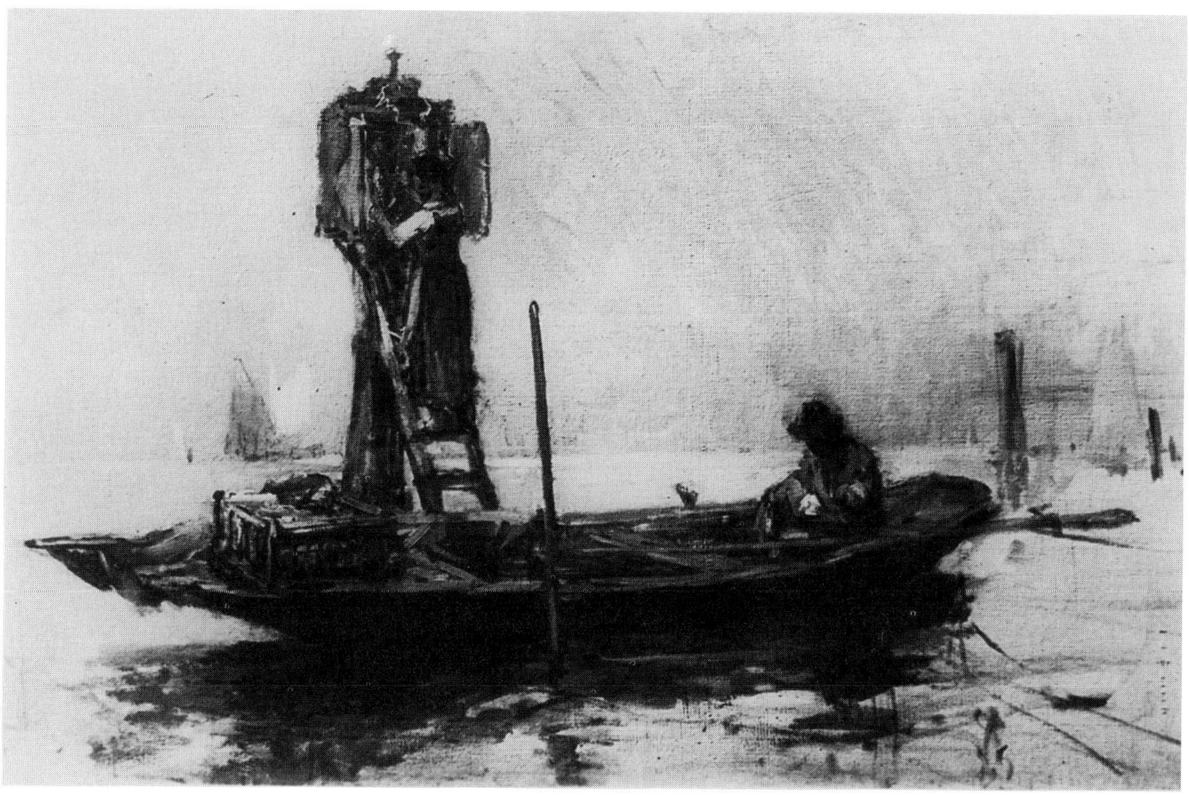

Fig. 87. Frank Duveneck, *Venetian Shrine, Sketch,* ca. 1885, oil on canvas, 25″ × 37″, Cincinnati Art Museum, Gift of Frank Duveneck.

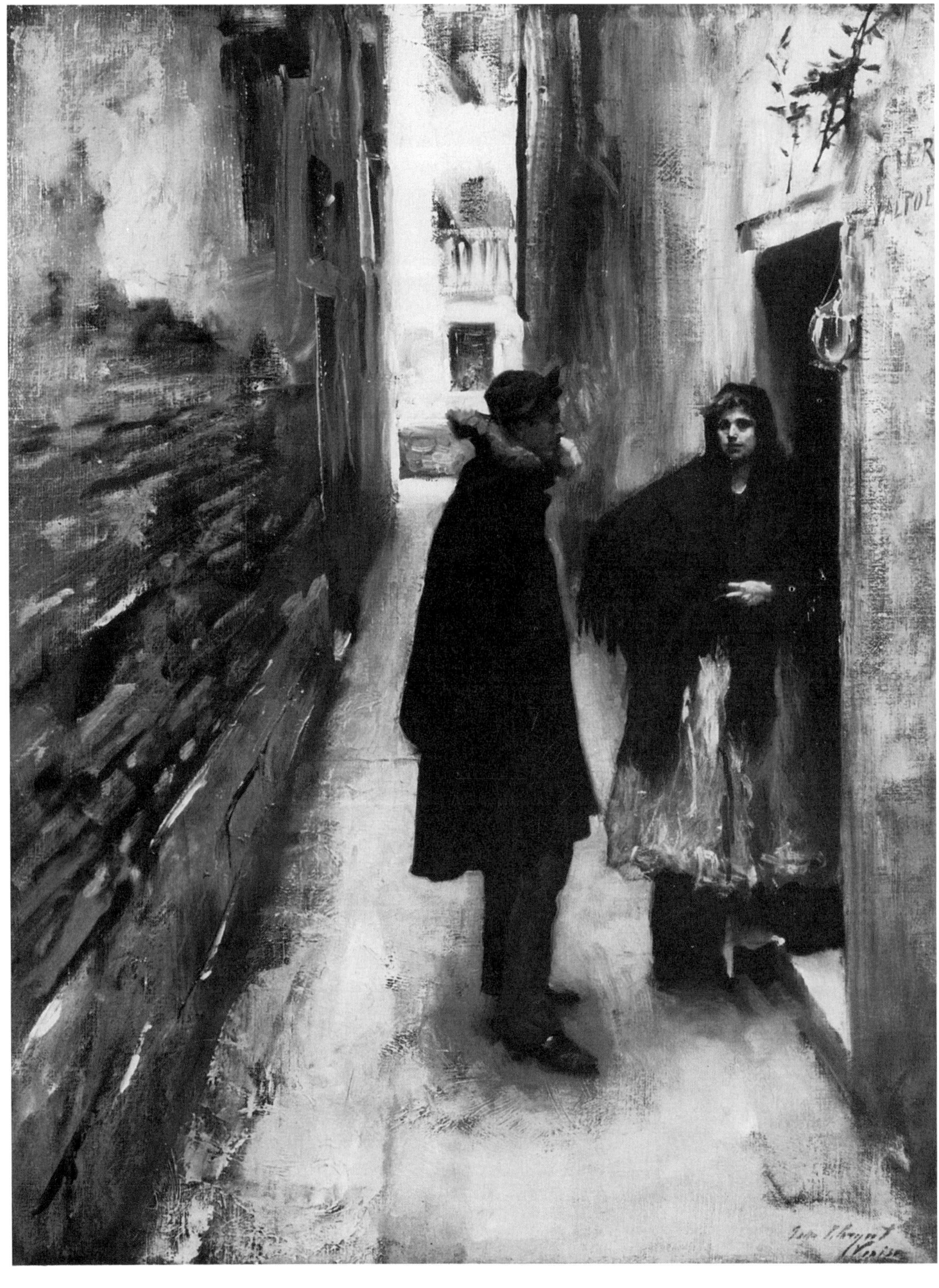

Fig. 88. John Singer Sargent, *A Street in Venice,* ca. 1882, oil on canvas, $27\frac{9}{16}'' \times 20\frac{5}{8}''$, Sterling and Francine Clark Art Institute, Williamstown, Massachusetts.

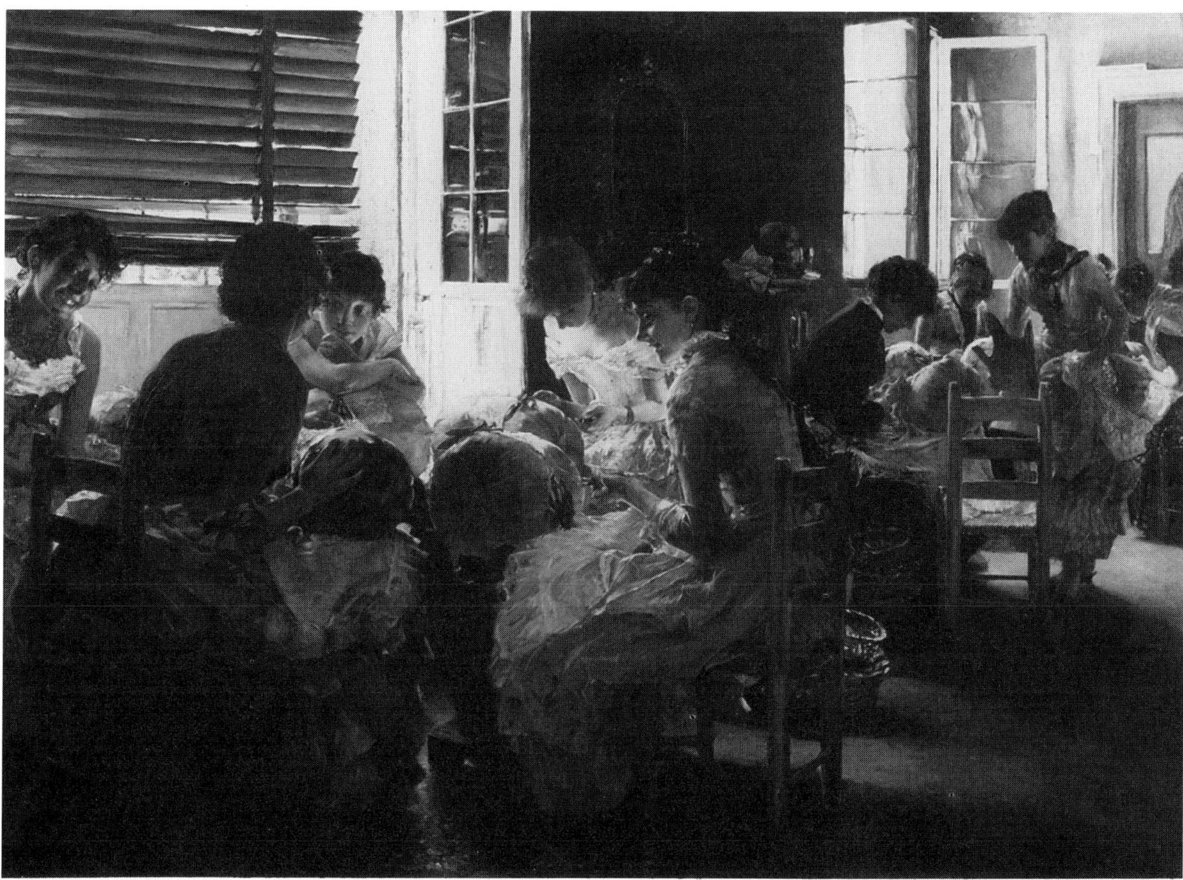

Fig. 89. Robert F. Blum, *Venetian Lacemakers,* 1887, oil on canvas, 30⅛" × 40¼", Cincinnati Art Museum, Gift of Mrs. Elizabeth S. Potter.

ture and in the disconcertingly wide and empty foreground suggests the tediousness of this labor. Not a simple local affair, these inexpensive glass beads, once strung, reached all the corners of the earth and constituted a primary trade medium with indigenous populations in the remotest of newly explored continents. The sheaves of thin glass rods the male and female workers are handling in *Venetian Glass Workers* (fig. 91) were composed into bundles that were cut to make beads or delicate stylized flowers, most familiar to us inside paperweights. In Sargent's image the darkness of the interior, the remoteness of the barred window, and the unhandsome solemn face of the only distinct worker combine with our high point of view to suggest difficult and onerous work under unpleasant circumstances. Visually, the painting comes alive through the shimmering bundles of glass—bright, hard, and one of Venice's remaining precious means of livelihood.

Sargent's interpretations of these spaces and these women and these chores are considerably more ambiguous than Blum's. Certainly many of his figures are young and handsome, but they are also slatternly. The compositions seem dark and haphazard, like bad snapshots taken under difficult conditions. Sargent appears not to manipulate his subjects or their spaces, yet the images hold us with their rather haunting inscrutability. It is a perfectly ordinary sort of place with perfectly ordinary sorts of tasks (for Venice), yet Sargent has managed to jar us into a more serious reconsideration of the social realities involved than Blum, whose elegant women seem more like boarding school girls on holiday than craftspeople at work. While Blum appeals to a host of given positive qualities—youth, beauty, happiness, even sensuality—Sargent constructs his art, his object of value, out of a much more meager visual and emotional vocabulary. Sunlight does not caress his beauties, it slices in-

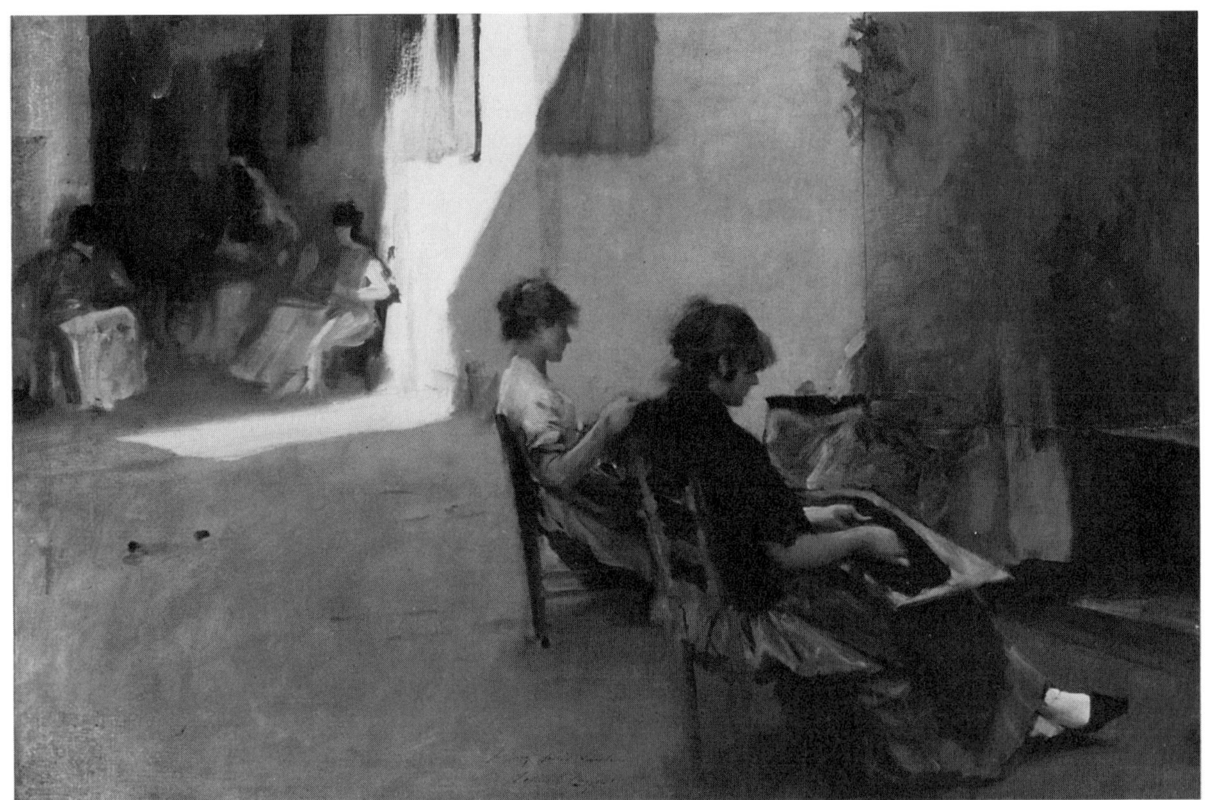

Fig. 90. John Singer Sargent, *The Bead Stringers of Venice,* 1880 or 1882, oil on canvas laid on board, 22⅛″ × 32¼″, National Gallery of Ireland, Dublin.

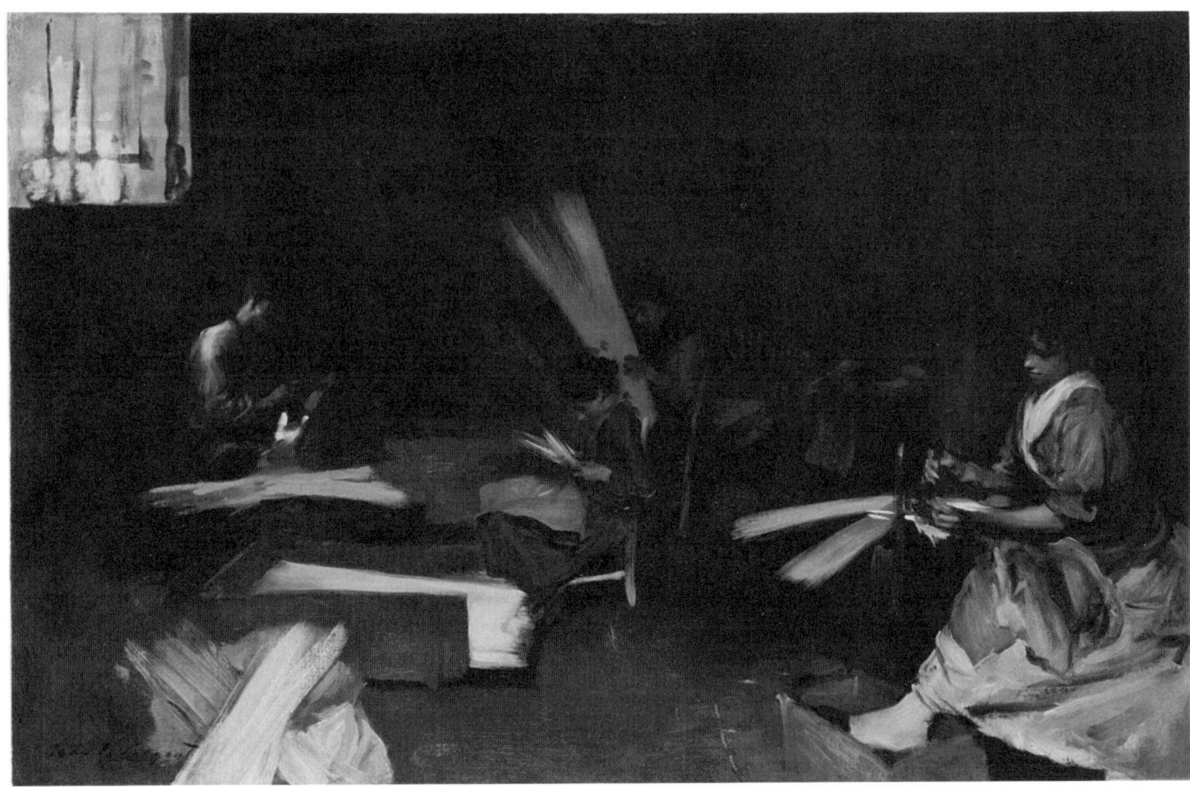

Fig. 91. John Singer Sargent, *Venetian Glass Workers,* 1880 or 1882, oil on canvas, 22¼″ × 33¾″, Art Institute of Chicago, Mr. and Mrs. Martin A. Ryerson Collection.

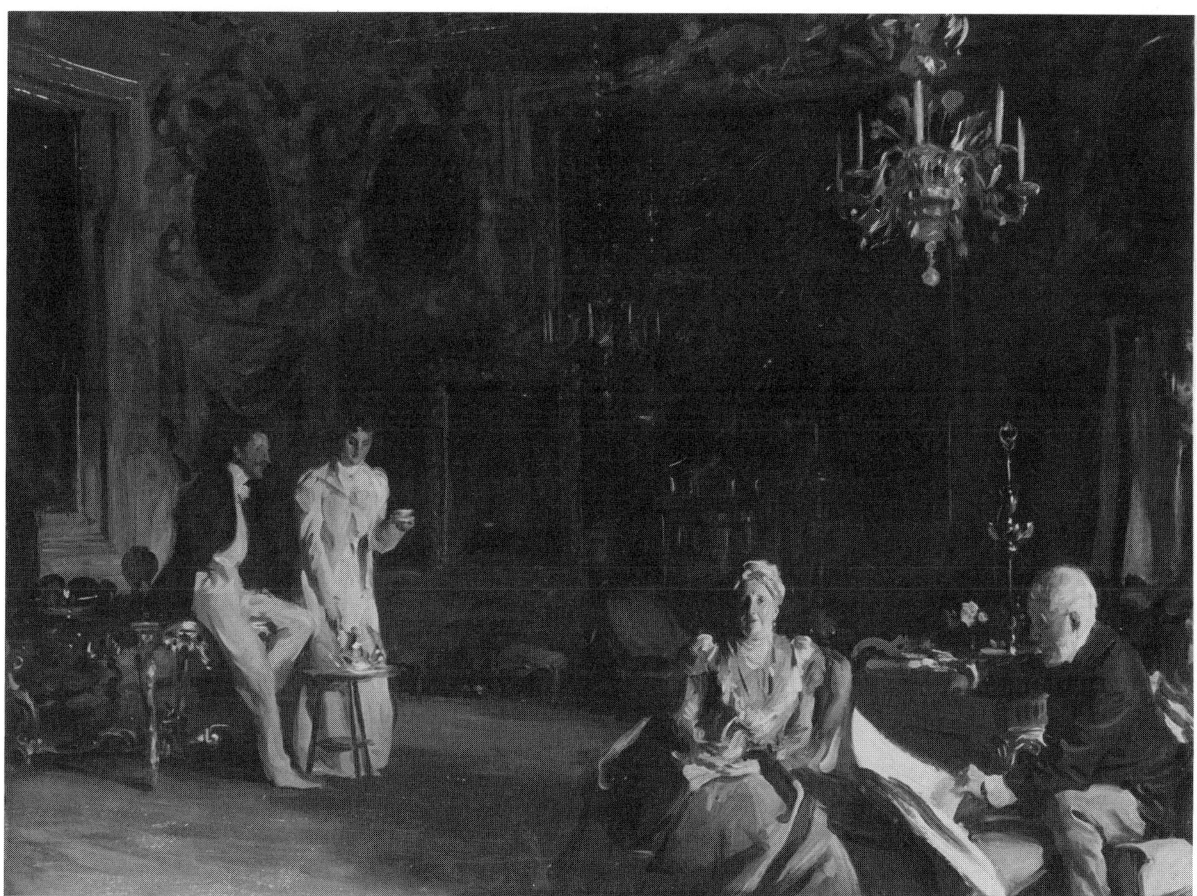

Fig. 92. John Singer Sargent, *An Interior in Venice,* 1899, oil on canvas, 25½″ × 31¾″, Royal Academy of Arts, London.

trusively and irrationally through his pictures, glaring in an intense but meaningless pattern on wall and floor and shoulder. The colors are subdued, the scene almost static, the characters make no direct appeal to our senses. Yet by this seeming inversion of pictorial strategy, our curiosity is aroused, our participation insured.

Insofar as Sargent's compositions are less "artful" than Blum's or Duveneck's, seemingly a more literal translation of the objective scene than we have come to expect, less replete with conventions and expectations confirmed, they embody a greater verisimilitude. We sense, when we look at these Venetian figure compositions of Sargent's, a world not unlike our own puzzling, partial, disorienting daily experience in a foreign country, or even in an unfamiliar part of our own city. They evoke a sense of daily experience not unlike that which Edgar Degas (1834–1917) explored a decade earlier in Paris. These are images of women working and relaxing, in characteristic poses, from the particular strains caused by their particular type of work. We are strangers to the figures and know about them and their environment only through their gestures, postures, and the relationships they form with each other and with their interior space. And like Degas's these genre scenes are enigmas, full of obscure observations partially made, of questions raised and not answered. Even his group portrait of the elegant American Daniel Curtis family (fig. 92) is not without ambiguity and visual dissonance.[42] It contains symptoms of this willed irresolution, this lack of a clearly ordered, flattering artistic arrangement, in the framing which slices the principal figures' feet with the bottom edge of the canvas, and in the harsh light which rakes their elderly features.

Far more ambiguous is a series of three oil paintings of women in a palace hall: *Venetian Interior* (fig. 93), *A Venetian Interior* (fig. 94), and *Venetian Bead Stringers* (pl. 7).[43] In the *Venetian Bead Stringers* we recognize the familiar tray in the lap of one

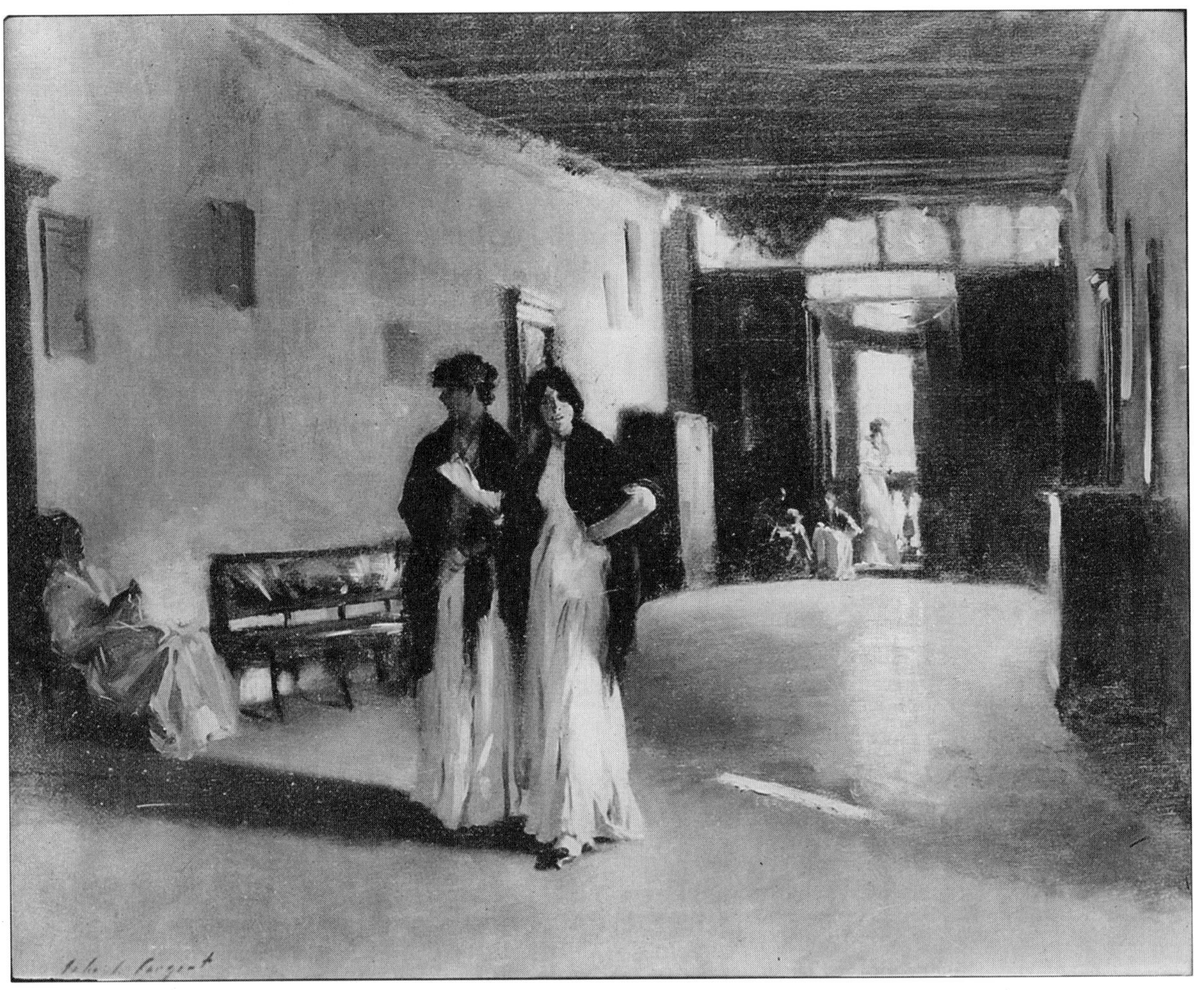

Fig. 93. John Singer Sargent, *Venetian Interior,* ca. 1882, oil on canvas, 27″ × 34″, Museum of Art, Carnegie Institute, Pittsburgh, Pennsylvania, Museum Purchase, 1920.

of the figures, and in the Clark Institute picture (fig. 94) a bead bag lies on a precarious table (we see only one of its legs) while two girls raise their arms with ropes of strung beads. In the Pittsburgh painting (fig. 93), one woman is engaged in some sort of handwork, perhaps crochet, but by and large these women are idle. Pictorially this is an all-female society and an indolent society. In fact there is something of the suggestion of a seraglio here.

The setting is the central hallway of the principal floor of a large-scale palace. Architecturally it is consistent with Ruskin's brief description: "the interior apartments always consist of one noble hall on the first story, often on the second also, extending across the entire depth of the house, and lighted in front by the principal groups of its windows, while smaller apartments open from it on either side. The ceilings, where they remain untouched, are of bold horizontal beams, richly carved and gilded."[44] By the "first story," he means the first floor above ground level or, in this case, above canal level. The entrance floor often contains a similar but barer space with a low ceiling and a long axis from water entrance to a back court which contains the stair. The principal central room upstairs is entered from a well-lit stair in the center of one short side, visible in the Albright-Knox picture (pl. 7) and the Clark Institute picture (fig. 94). To the right we see a dark room, and to the left is a second staircase rising to the floors above. The Pittsburgh picture (fig. 93) appears to be of the same hall from the opposite vantage point at the foot of these stairs, looking toward the heavily curtained window wall with its balcony overlooking a canal. (Whistler appears to have portrayed the same scene from midway on the rising stairs in

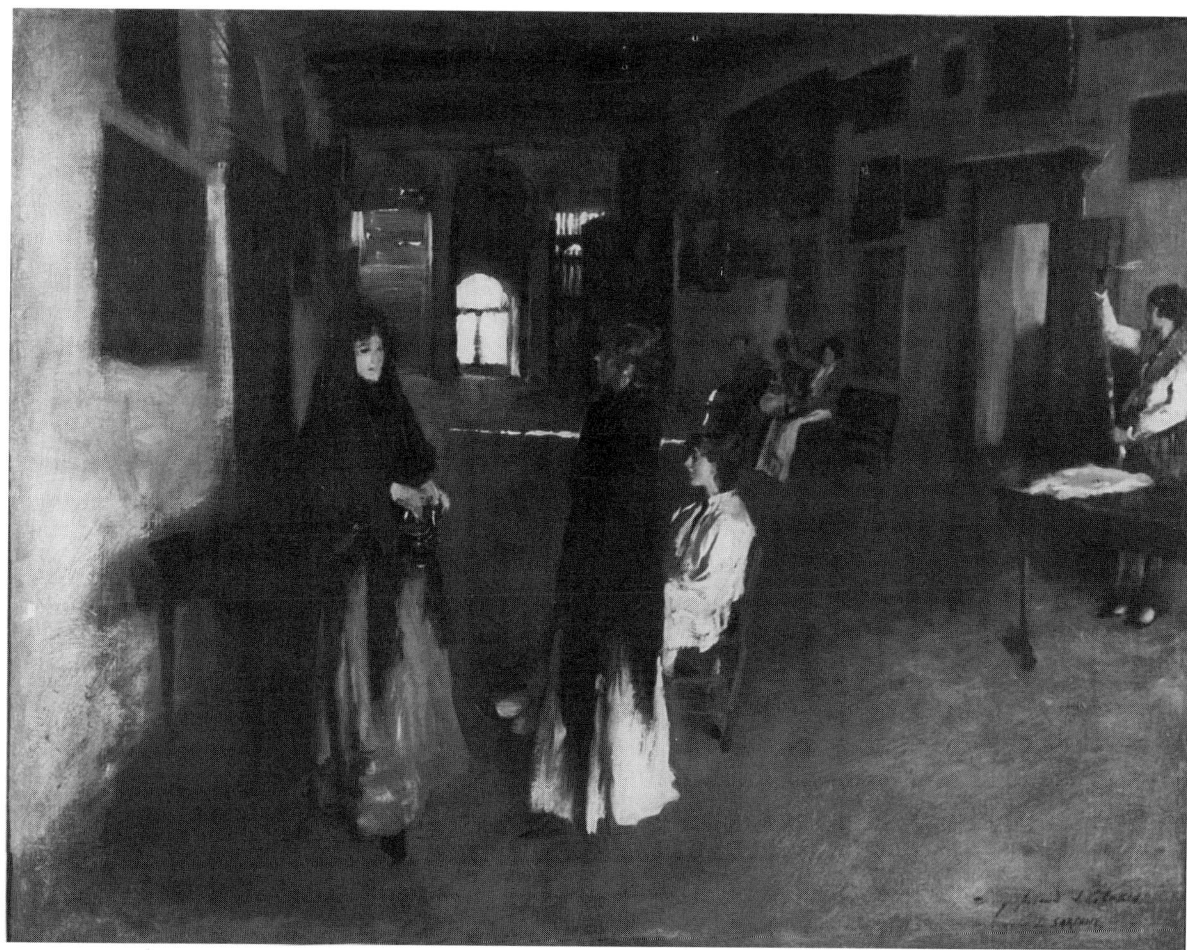

Fig. 94. John Singer Sargent, *A Venetian Interior,* 1882, oil on canvas, 19¹⁄₁₆" × 23¹⁵⁄₁₆", Sterling and Francine Clark Art Institute, Williamstown, Massachusetts.

Palace in Rags.)[45] The space is sparsely furnished with a long saber-legged leather-upholstered sofa bench along one wall; a wardrobe, a chest, and some flimsy chairs and table make up the rest of the furnishings. Paintings appear (but not consistently) on the walls. The denizens of this space are slim and young, uniformly costumed in dark shawls, and sometimes carry fans, familiar from other paintings and from period photographs as part of the female Venetian costume. One carries a teapot and several, as we have noted, appear to be working. The compositions are much more straightforward than in *The Bead Stringers of Venice* (fig. 90); here the principal figures are centered and address us. Their space is a clear prismatic rectangular volume seen from easily comprehended points of view. The viewer is standing and, for the most part, ignored. The ambiguity here is one of tone, not of pictorial structure. Who we are and why we have come to this "palace in rags" is an open question. It is possible that this is a bead-stringing headquarters and the indolence we see and find so perplexing is the same that maddened Mark Twain throughout his European tour in *Innocents Abroad* (1869). Simultaneous indolence and starvation seemed inconceivable to him as they are strange to us, but familiar to Europeans who had struggled with an insufficiency of work and a surfeit of workers for centuries.[46] However, the lassitude may also be a suggestion of a profession on the part of these women for which Venice is even more famous than for its bead stringing.

The two elements that are most striking about Sargent's Venetians are their readiness to return our gaze with an inquisitive and not altogether sociable stare (as in *A Street in Venice,* pl. 6, *Venetian Interior,* fig. 93, and *Gondolier's Siesta,* pl. 8) and their willingness to assume ungenteel "natural" poses, as in *The Sulphur Match* (fig. 95) and *Venetian Women in the Palazzo Rezzonico* (pl. 9). Sargent's Venetians lounge, sprawl, lean against walls, place their hands on their hips, tip back their chairs, and generally treat us, their observers, with as little dignity in their body language as in their challenging stares. The fact that they perceive us and tolerate our intrusion, casting us in the role of an observed urban stranger, is unusual in nineteenth-century genre work. Edouard Manet also uses this direct device, permitting us to see ourselves—or rather to see ourselves in the distinct fictive persona of a solitary male observer—in the returned look of the figures within the scene. But Manet's starers are women, and the drama, then, has the air more of an adventure than the silent challenge Sargent permits his Venetians of both genders to issue. Sargent bestows upon his Venetians the air of resourceful urbanites, incompletely aware, perhaps, of the past through which they daily make their way but hyperaware of contemporary Venice with its daily facts of work, boredom, and intrigue within an eccentric physical shell, and a haunting sense of being constantly observed.

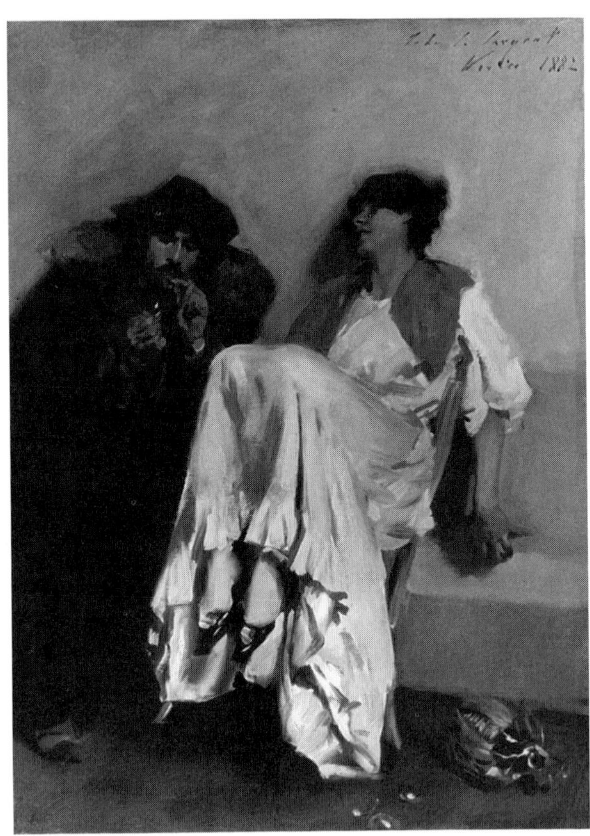

Fig. 95. John Singer Sargent, *The Sulphur Match,* ca. 1882, oil on canvas, 23″ × 16½″, private collection.

In all these low mimetic images, whether of figures or of their architectural context, both the subject and the vantage point of the viewer are deliberately nameless and nonheroic. The focus is on unimportant and unrecognizable subjects, although in many instances the artist's strategy has been to depict the heroic subject as though it were unimportant and unrecognizable. This deliberate avoidance of "proper" point of view, this low mimetic appropriation of the high mimetic subject (whether Daniel Curtis or the Salute or Venice itself) is the distinctive hallmark of a huge body of work at this period. From a merely human point of view, with a narrow cone of vision or an expanse too wide and thin to render the monuments heroic, artists of low mimetic views insisted on reseeing, on rediscovering and reinterpreting Venice. Part of the artists' strategy was modesty (of posture, tone, subject, even medium), but in a very real sense, their intent was to capture the ordinary and catapult it to resonance and extraordinary value by purely artistic means. Working with the materials and points of view and visual limitations of daily, momentary experience, the artists in this mode effectively avoided the pressure of the predecessors whose paintings in the Accademia and Doge's Palace could not have escaped their notice. They also, and perhaps more important, offered an appropriate interpretation of a "fallen and forlorn" Venice. Corollary, of course, is the assumption that if the Venetian moral fiber had held out, the Fall would not have occurred and the reins of power would not have passed into Anglo-American hands. So in a sense the interpretation involves a dual sense of pathos in the loss that has occurred and a possessiveness in the gain that has been won. This is a gain that seemed to entail the leisure, in fact the responsibility, for careful observation and interpretation of the "case" of Venice as a historic lesson with a displaced contemporary resonance.

FOUR

No Object but the Subject: The Ironic Mode

In Greek drama the *eiron,* while small and weak, consistently outwits the *alazon,* the bullying braggart. By indirection and feigned powerlessness the *eiron* defeats his more powerful, more brashly straightforward opponent. Irony, then, whether of dramatic situation, rhetoric, or image, involves a strategy of dissimulation, of self-denigration, of apparent retreat. The *eiron,* as protagonist, takes on a posture of limitation, of inferiority. The "inferiority" of the character springs from the loss of those conventions with which even the low mimetic artist clothes and dignifies his characters: "in low mimetic modes characters are usually presented as they appear to others, fully dressed and with a large section of both their physical lives and their inner monologue carefully exercised." However, an "intensification of low mimetic, an attempt to describe life exactly as it is . . . ends, by the very logic of that attempt, in pure irony."[1] Inclusion of the inconsistencies, the trivia, the fuzzy-headedness, the fragmentation that freight every individual existence produce the effect, in literature, of irony and the absurd. We seem—even while we feel that this is "life exactly as it is" and that we "might be in the same situation"—to be experiencing a fiction characterized by frustration and absurdity. The applicability of this mode to the visual arts becomes clearer in light of Frye's amplification of the situation emphasizing not the protagonist (to whom we will return shortly), but rather the artist:

> The conception of irony meets us in Aristotle's *Ethics,* where the *eiron* is the man who deprecates himself, as opposed to the *alazon.* Such a man makes himself invulnerable, and, though Aristotle disapproves of him, there is no question that he is a predestined artist, just as the *alazon* is one of his predestined victims. The term irony, then, indicates a technique of appearing to be less than one is, which in literature becomes most commonly a technique of saying as little and meaning as much as possible, or, in a more general way, a pattern of words that turns away from direct statement or its own obvious meaning. (I am not using the word ironic itself in any unfamiliar sense, though I am exploring some of its implications.)
>
> The ironic fiction-writer, then, deprecates himself and, like Socrates, pretends to know nothing, even that he is ironic. Complete objectivity and suppression of all explicit moral judgements are essential to his method. Thus pity and fear are not raised in ironic art: they are reflected to the reader from the art. When we try to isolate the ironic as such, we find that it seems to be simply the attitude of the poet as such, a dispassionate construction of a literary form, with all assertive elements, implied or expressed, eliminated. Irony, as a mode, is born from the low mimetic; it takes life exactly as it finds it. But the ironist fables without moralizing, and has no object but his subject. Irony is naturally a sophisticated mode, and the chief difference between sophisticated and naive irony is that the naive ironist calls attention to the fact that he is being ironic, whereas sophisticated irony merely states, and lets the reader add the ironic tone himself. (Pp. 40–41)

This expanded definition brings up the important elements that one might call the psychology or posture of irony and the artistic technique and structure of ironic fictions. The ironic artist "deprecates himself," "pretends to know nothing, even that he is ironic." The irony of the work of art is generated out of his attitude toward art, toward his specific subject, and toward the general social and physical world around him, and of these he pretends to have no opinion. This posture is that of "a detached recorder of the human scene" (p. 49). He is a transparent sheet on which mere facts are recorded: "complete objectivity and suppression of all explicit moral judgements are essential to his method." The artist becomes, then, a window through which one may look in and see a small sec-

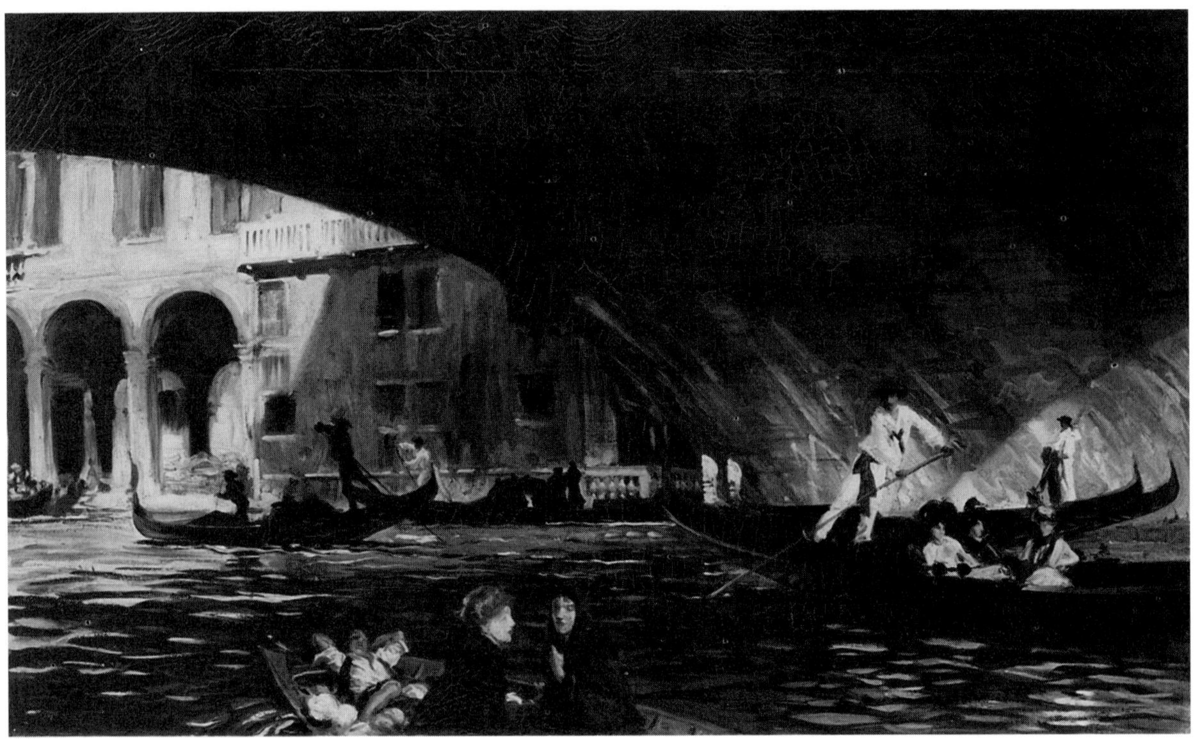

Fig. 96. John Singer Sargent, *The Rialto, Venice,* ca. 1911, oil on canvas, 22″ × 36″, Philadelphia Museum of Art, George W. Elkins Collection.

tion of social reality or look out and see a small section of physical reality. The artist deprecates himself and his role as intermediary, emphasizing his identity as a recorder, a craftsman, over that as a creator or inventor.

Frye dates the shift to the ironic mode in English literature "around 1900 (several decades earlier in French literature)" (p. 63). He also characterizes it as extremely sophisticated, with—originally—a small circle of appeal. It is not, then, surprising that few American artists painting Venice should have worked in this mode. Venice was, after all, an intrinsically high mimetic subject with a wealth of low mimetic appeal. Irony was present in the city's situation, as all falls—whether Adam's, or Lear's, or Venice's—have a strong element of irony. However, in Frye's sense of the term, which emphasizes irony of structure over irony of tone, Venice was not a natural subject. Several artists ventured in the direction of the ironic (Bunner, for instance, in his *Rio Santa Croce e Santa Maria della Salute,* fig. 42, is a naive ironist), but only two worked extensively in this mode, John Singer Sargent and Maurice Prendergast.

It has been often said that the Venetian subjects that Prendergast and Sargent selected were random and unimportant, that the "real" subjects of their works were light and color and pure paint (grand displays of craftsmanship).[2] There are several reasons critics have taken this line. First, it seemed important to associate these artists directly with French impressionism (the most significant development in painting during their period), and the impressionists are generally thought to paint pure light (scientifically, objectively) rather than subjects. Second, by stressing the insignificant nature of Sargent's and Prendergast's subjects, they were placing these artists in the vanguard of twentieth-century art, which is, in fact, subjectless. However, if one were to postulate that these literally meaningless, beautifully crafted works were fundamentally, profoundly, perhaps even unknowingly, ironic, one would be placing them more accurately in the context of their time while retrieving the intellectual dignity of the artists. In a sense the critics are right; the subjects in Sargent's *Rialto, Venice* (fig. 96) and Prendergast's *Piazza di San Marco* (pl. 10) are in themselves unimportant, even absurd, but the assumption that this meaninglessness springs from nonchalance or ignorance on the part of the artist is to accept the *eiron's* self-deprecating posture at face value. The architectural protagonists they portray are partial, fragmentary, inexplicable; and consistent with the ironist's strategy, all overt, interpretive, assertive, emotional elements are eliminated. The work appears as "pure" art, untrammeled by social message or personal judgment. In fact, this meaninglessness is not without pattern or meaning. The interpretation of what are essentially high mimetic objects with sub–low mimetic narrowness of vision and fragmentariness of subject points to a broader interpretation of physical (and by extension, of social) reality as fragmentary and essentially incomprehensible.

Monuments Re-viewed: Maurice Prendergast

Prendergast is one of the few artists who worked extensively in all three modes that we have been considering. While each painting is distinctly in one mode which constitutes its underlying structure, traces of other modes coexist in almost every work. One of the extraordinary features of Prendergast's achievement is his versatility, his inventive ingenuity with pictorial syntax. In *Piazza di San Marco* (pl. 10), *Market Place, Venice* (pl. 11), *The Grand Canal, Venice* (pl. 12), and *Rainy Day, Venice* (pl. 13), the artist's vantage point is high, much higher than ordinary human height, and this we have taken as a characteristic of high mimetic design.[3] However, it is clear that Prendergast's repeated preference for this high point of view constitutes not an acceptance but rather a manipulation of the familiar convention. He uses it not to look expansively across a superhuman panorama as in Canaletto's *Bacino* (fig. 3) but rather to look down at a scene spreading itself beneath his feet, almost we might say, beneath his toes. Unlike the high mimetic usage of the high vantage point, Prendergast repeatedly uses it in conjunction with a very high horizon line. Any expanse of open space or sky is almost eliminated as the distant buildings bump their roofs along the top of the frame. We are forced to drop our eyes to a scene not generously spreading itself before us but confusedly layered below us. In this instance a high mimetic convention has been appropriated, radically reinterpreted, and readjusted so that its original tone is seriously undercut.

One also notices in these works a return to high mimetic subjects—the first portrays a fraction of the Campanile, the second the Rialto, and the fourth the Salute. In part this is a reaction "against the mode immediately preceding" and a return to some aspects of what Frye calls "the modal grandfather."[4] In literature this takes the form of a "nostalgia for the aristocratic" in such writers as Yeats, Eliot, Pound, and Proust. In painting (in the universe of Venice views) it takes the form of a return to monumental subjects. In fact, however, in the case of these American Venetian views, this is a "return" not so much in the temporal sense as in a spatial sense. From frontal monuments in the heroic mode, the artist moves to back alleys and small canals in the low mimetic mode, and in the ironic mode there is a return (with a difference) to the subject of monuments, the subjects of the "modal grandfather." In these American views of Venice we see a simultaneous concurrence of the three modes; temporally one could describe them as old-fashioned, contemporary, and avant garde. And yet, taking our period as a whole, they coexist, each responding to different aspects of the same transitional aesthetic era.

The artist working in the ironic mode self-consciously resees and reinterprets the high and low mimetic modes in his revision of the monument's character. He simultaneously denies the frontal, *alazon*, view and the "backwards" low mimetic view. Instead his strategy is to find and portray a "wrong" point of view, one so seemingly random, absurd, and disconcerting that most critics discount its importance. Prendergast's *Piazza di San Marco* (pl. 10) gives us a view not of that extraordinary expanse of processional space familiar to us from Bellini's *Procession in the Piazza* (fig. 12), Canaletto's *Piazza San Marco* (fig. 19), and Turner's *Juliet and Her Nurse* (fig. 23), but a small wedge of that pavement. From our vantage point on the clock tower, our eye is aimed not westward down the grand expanse of the Piazza, not due south where our view would include the full Piazzetta, framed by the Ducal Palace, with the noble San Giorgio on the horizon. Rather, the view is southwest (see fig. 97), a view oblique to the architectural framework; it takes in a fraction of the Piazza, a slice of the Piazzetta, three bays of the Procuratie Nuove, and a disconcertingly two-dimensional chunk of the massive Campanile. It is late afternoon and all the architectural facades are

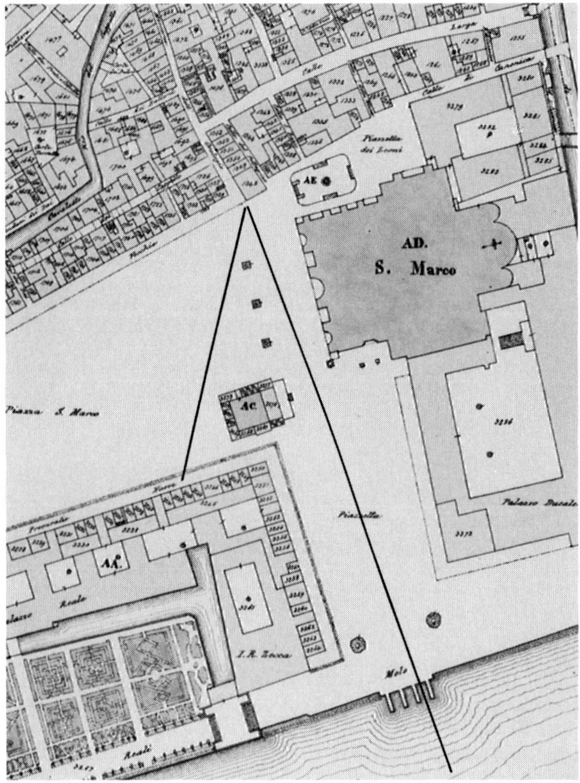

Fig. 97. Map of site of Maurice Prendergast, *Piazza di San Marco* (pl. 10).

cast in deep shadow. The image seems to be "about" three Italian flags, ranged rather redundantly across the middle of the picture. This is the same general prospect that Tintoretto used to dramatize and localize his *Doge Alvise Mocenigo Presented to the Redeemer* (fig. 15). In that painting the architectural orientation of the image imitates that of the space before the viewer, framing and lending stature to the central human action. Tintoretto's elimination of the Campanile from its appropriate position on the right-hand side of his composition was probably the result of his realization that its inclusion would necessarily be vertically partial. Vertical slicing of buildings seems to be absent from almost all pre-nineteenth-century views, which suggests a deliberate avoidance, in fact, a "rule" or proscription against its use. Prendergast's deliberate use of the truncated Campanile in *Piazza di San Marco* suggests not only acceptance of a truncated building as a pictorial element but also a manipulation of our modal expectations. Although topographically accurate, the view is disorienting. We have no proper footing; the spaces and structures are fragments and, within the fiction of the picture space, incomprehensible. Moreover, the various pictorial elements seem disproportionately treated. Mere flags dramatically upstage the intrinsically more important architectural structures and spaces. *Piazza di San Marco* is, in fact, a marvelously crafted image of an objectively portrayed set of monuments. Beyond that, it is an image in which ironic tone and structure give us a sense of bafflement and, simultaneously, a sense of the artist's wit.

Only slightly less dramatic and disorienting are *Market Place, Venice* (pl. 11) and *Rainy Day, Venice* (pl. 13). In *Market Place, Venice,* a broad flight of stairs becomes—only if we are knowledgeable of the topography and willing to allow the artist this synecdochic substitution—the Rialto. The lateral covered sections of the bridge by which it is usually recognized (see figs. 28 and 38) are invisible, cut off from our field of vision on each side. Only the precipitous stairs and the flank of San Giacomo enable us to identify the locale (see fig. 98). Moving a few feet to the west and turning his gaze perpendicular to the bridge, Prendergast in *The Grand Canal, Venice* (pl. 12) looks down from the

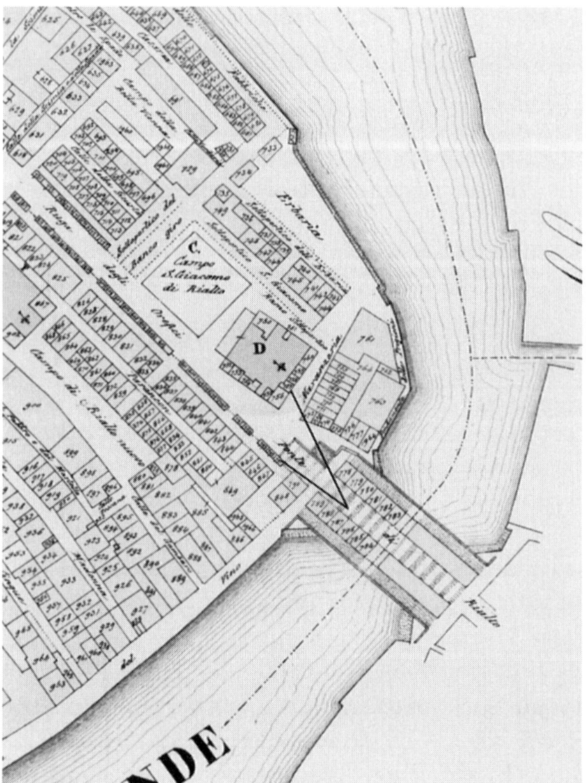

Fig. 98. Map of site of Maurice Prendergast, *Market Place, Venice* (pl. 11).

Rialto's parapet onto the Fondamenta del Vino and a narrow stretch of the great waterway. Unlike G. L. Brown's high mimetic *On the Grand Canal, Venice* (fig. 24) with its moody grandeur, its broad expanse of water and majestic structures, and equally unlike Sargent's expansive but vacant and curiously unmonumental *The Grand Canal, Venice* (fig. 75), Prendergast's is a vertical slice, equally blue-yellow water and mauve pavement, in which the disorganized moving variables (gondolas, pedestrians, shimmering water) upstage the sober dignity of the architectural setting. The most insistent fact about the view in Prendergast's interpretation is not the identity of the spaces or structures, or the resonance of their assembled dignity, but the curious juxtaposition of real verticals (lampposts, mooring posts, buildings, figures, the format of his image) with the assertive apparent vertical of the fondamenta edge that severs the image abruptly and irreparably. He presents us here with a symmetry of cleavage rather than the symmetry of identity that we expect in high (and many low) mimetic images. Symmetry here produces not an effect of hierarchy and order but rather an interrogation of the fact of symmetry in his startling and repeated equation of unequals. Similarly, *Rainy Day, Venice* (pl. 13) is an image that, despite its extraordinary craftsmanship and apparent complete objectivity of tone, raises more questions than it answers. Here the slice of vision is taken from an uncomfortable height, and again this height is not an aid to the descriptive scope of the scene. As there is no structure from which one can obtain this prospect we are figuratively perched on one of the extraordinarily tall ladder-platforms used by photographers above the edge of the narrow pavement (see fig. 99). The Grand Canal spreads before us, busy with gondolas. Just outside our cone of vision on the right is the front portal of the Salute in the foreground; and in the background, the Doge's Palace, the Campanile, and domes of San Marco are just excluded by the right-hand margin. Invisible though it is, the implied presence of the Salute is as powerful an aspect of this image as the arch of the Rialto is of *Market Place, Venice.* We see only one small aspect of the monument here, the inlaid colored marble of a piece of the Salute's fondamenta, as in *Market Place, Venice* we saw only a small area of the Rialto's steps. The artist helps us with neither a name nor a mnemonic profile (arch or dome)

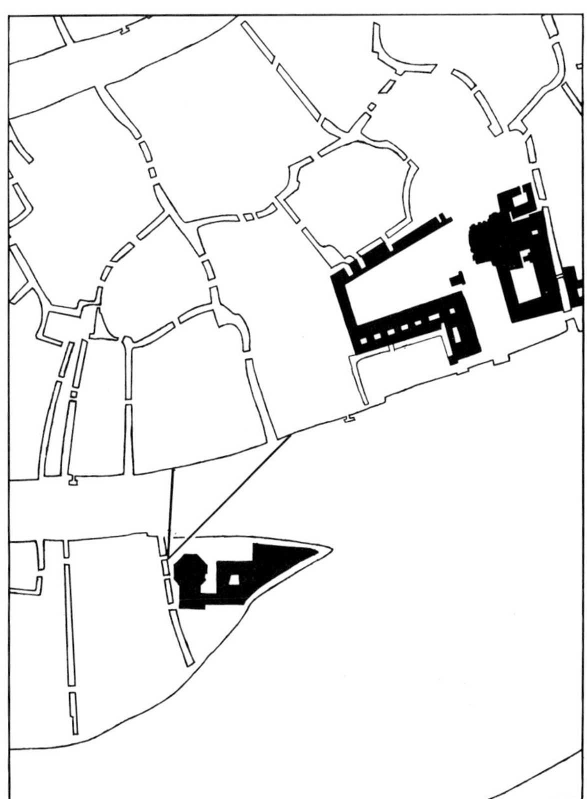

Fig. 99. Map of site of Maurice Prendergast, *Rainy Day, Venice* (pl. 13).

that would enable us to recognize the site. Yet he insists on "doing" monuments, or rather pieces of them, in this quizzical, unsettling way.

The difficulty, the source of bafflement that we felt in some low mimetic views, is intensified in the ironic mode. In Lévi-Strauss's discussion of miniaturization, he suggests that the effect of image making is to make "the object as a whole seem less formidable. . . . The quantitative transposition extends and diversifies our power over a homologue of the thing" (see chap. 2, p. 27). By making a model or a miniature image, the object becomes simplified and the object viewer goes through the reverse of the natural process of understanding. He or she moves immediately to comprehension of the whole without passing through what Lévi-Strauss considers the necessary steps of a careful investigation of the parts, which only gradually produces comprehension of the whole. The reason these two Prendergast images are ironic and leave us in a state of bafflement despite their crystalline objectivity is because he simulates not Lévi-Strauss's process of miniaturization but Lévi-Strauss's process of understanding (investigating, comprehending isolated fractions that together compose into a whole) and then truncates the process. There is no homologue of the object, just a fraction; hence there is miniaturization without explication or comprehension. The fact that the viewer tolerates this incompletion, this precipitous point of view, and even enjoys it, speaks for his or her general toleration for bafflement, irresolution, and tension. One might say that the fundamental difference between the Colman view of *San Giorgio Maggiore* (pl. 2) and such an image as *Rainy Day, Venice* is to be found not so much in the image itself but in the model that the image reflects back of the viewers' ideas of physical and social order. The Colman image points to a reality full of discoverable order, hierarchy, and resolution, the Prendergast to a reality no less crystalline in its details but bristling with ambiguity, tension, bafflement, and irresolution, a world in which knowing is always a partial solution, knowledge an open question.

It might be said that Prendergast's images are "photographic," and there is no question about the frequent use of photographs by these artists.[5] However, the ironic mode in the visual arts is not simply a function of the discovery of photography. Even the most cursory survey of early professional architectural photographs indicates consistently low mimetic or the conservative, high mimetic nature of their visual syntax. At this time, and long after, photographers still carefully respected the vertical integrity of structures and, where possible, their horizontal edges as well (see figs. 10, 49, and 59). Nor are Prendergast's eccentric cones of vision caused by "snapshot" errors which the photographer discovers and the artist mimics. The significant point is not the mere availability of a visual organization or motif but the need and appropriation of that organization by an artist and, beyond that, the recognition (on some level) of its elements by a comprehending public. An artist's visual syntax (his manner of composing pictures) and his visual vocabulary (his subjects) are not mere tools in the picture-making process. If they are vital they will echo, will contain metaphors for, larger models of the nature and principles of the physical and natural world. Without this broad common base they could build responsiveness in others only on the most superficial level.

Images in the ironic mode can be read, then, as symptoms of a world in which the dark complexities of post-Lyellian geology, post-Darwinian biology, post-Newtonian physics, and post-Nietzschian social history were making themselves felt. For the layman as for the professional, the models by which one understood the physical and social world were being replaced, not so much by new whole models as by a deep sense of complexity, even profound incomprehensibility. If we read these images as symptoms or paradigms for a new order in which only glimpses of the knowable are possible and tension certain, then we cannot help also seeing a certain enjoyment, a certain level of actual comfort, with irresolution and fractional insight. Just as the Fall of Venice offered artists of the low mimetic a historic trauma that translated well into a "relaxed charm," so modernism (if we may so call the late nineteenth-century epistemological trauma) translated well into fragmentary brilliance.

Monuments Re-viewed: John Singer Sargent

Far more extensively than Prendergast, Sargent pursued the subject one might call the Venetian fragment. Working primarily in watercolor in the ironic mode he produced a substantial portfolio of oblique images of some of the city's best-known structures. *The Rialto, Venice* (fig. 96), for instance, with its horizontal format and monument-oriented title, suggests the epic mode, but the image itself confounds these expectations with its fish's-eye view of the great Renaissance marble bridge.[6] We look obliquely across a small section of the great, cavernous space from an eccentric, low aquatic viewpoint. The arch of structure on the left and the arch of shadow on the right meet and balance delicately on a short stretch of water where three gondolas cross. Neither the structure above nor the volume below is explained; just this one point of balance is described. The soaring Rialto has here been portrayed as a dark cavernous void, in fact a fragment of a void and nothing more. We are offered a piece of a shadow instead of the substance. The viewer (at gondola-seat level) and his fellow excursionists have only this great negative space in common as an organizing principle. The margins of the cone of vision appear to be arbitrary, as does the location of objects in space within the picture frame, outside the picture frame, and crossing the fragile boundary between the two.

A decade before Sargent began these images and three decades before this one was painted, Degas recorded in his notebook a series of possible artistic subjects, suggesting "no one has ever done monuments or houses from below, from beneath, up close, as one sees them going by in the streets."[7] Degas, who preferred interior scenes with figures, did not take up this subject, but it is significant that this extraordinary innovator in the area of pictorial composition should have articulated the problem. "No one has ever done monuments . . . from below" he notes and includes a sketch of a domed structure from a pedestrian viewpoint. It seems extraordinary to us that this view—as an artistic subject—is novel to him; it is, after all, life and structure exactly as we find and experience them daily. However, when miniaturized and transposed into art, it becomes clear exactly how hostile and disproportionate and nonhuman a building, especially a monument, is when seen partially, obliquely from close by. Sargent's interpretation of architectural void and aperture is as bizarre as that of architectural facade, as we have seen in *Doorway of a Venetian Palace* (fig. 11). As a human surrogate the Palazzo Balbi is a cold anonymous incomprehensible other. Known only from the fraction of knowledge we have here, those attributes that humanize a facade or a bridge—symmetry, proportion, relationship, and gesture—are forever absent. The homologue is incomplete; we are left in permanent knowledge of the fraction and permanent ignorance of the whole.

More the province of the local inhabitants are the narrow paved calli and courtyards that were the sites of numerous low mimetic images. Sargent's views of these areas include hauntingly empty spaces as in *Venice* (pl. 14). Our first instinct is to see this watercolor as unfinished or as a preparatory drawing for a projected (peopled) work, but if we permit ourselves to see it as a finished architectural drawing, not random but deliberate and well calculated, we see the vernacular equivalent of *Doorway of a Venetian Palace* (fig. 11). There the facade and here the aperture are objectively drawn, beautifully executed and at the same time profoundly inhuman. Full of the robustness and brilliance of sunshine and the interest of shadows, they nevertheless remind us more than anything else of what is absent—figures from the one, completeness of empathetic form from the other. The vacancy and shoebox closeness of *Venice* and the overscaled architectural presence of *Doorway* both thwart our expectations and comment on those expectations without departing from a tone of ingenuous candor. While seeming to have "no object but his subject," Sargent has succeeded in commenting on the conventions of high and low mimetic image making, of grand and vernacular subject portrayal. If we read these architectural objects and space empathetically (and it is only with difficulty that we do not), we are struck by the baffling and oppressive nature of these sun-filled pictures. The image we see of ourselves, the view reflected back, from these pictures, is that of a solitary alien wandering through an interesting but baffling series of experiences, an individual of acute sensitivity, but one who can know only one thing at a single moment.

Although Sargent made other studies of empty alleys and foreshortened palace facades, repeating the pictorial structure and syntax of a narrow cone of vision, with a partial and baffling effect, these images do not repeat the same subject. However, in at least two instances he seems to have embarked on a series, making numerous images (over a considerable period of time) of a single structure, a few high mimetic, some low mimetic, and many in the ironic mode. One senses that a multiplicity of fractions, a plurality of parts, seems to substitute for a comprehensive whole. *Café on the Riva degli Schiavoni* (fig. 100) is a view from the Danieli Hotel tables on the Riva looking toward Santa Maria della Salute on the left (here brought forward and greatly enlarged), and the Libreria on the right. These are the two structures to which he returned again and again for subjects. Both are richly sculptured white marble, monumental in size, position, and statement. In these and most other paintings of Venetian monuments Sargent avoided Gothic structures and dwelt on the Renaissance-baroque buildings so abhorrent to Ruskin.[8] The Libreria is a thin building; its long flank closes one side of the Piazzetta (see fig. 1). It is closely abutted on the western boundary, however, by the Treasury building, and only three bays are visible from the Grand Canal. It is this end-on view with a long vista down the Piazzetta that Sargent paints at least half-a-dozen times. In selecting this subject Sargent seems to be going in the very teeth of Ruskin's teachings. In a discussion of architectural paintings of Venice Ruskin mentions "the case of the palaces of the

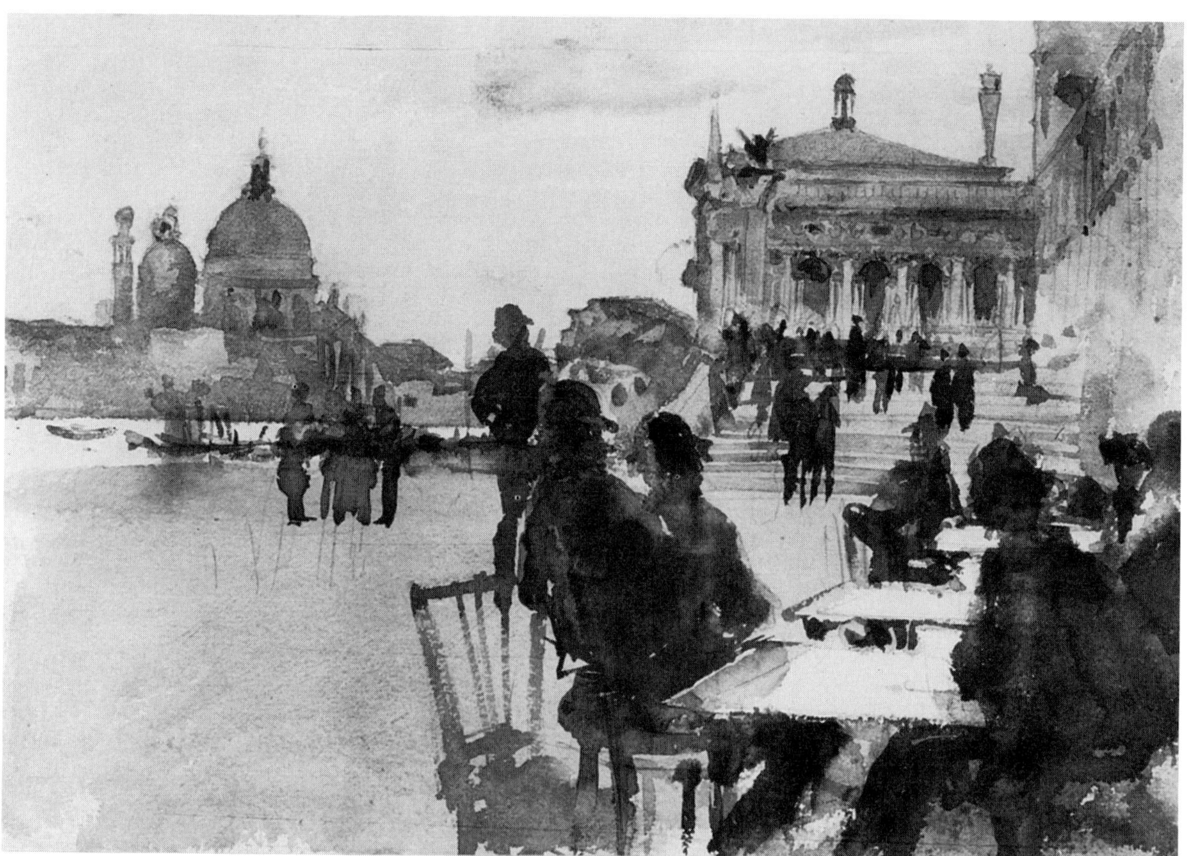

Fig. 100. John Singer Sargent, *Café on the Riva degli Schiavoni, Venice,* ca. 1900, watercolor, the Ormond Family.

Renaissance": "They are never drawn singly, or as the principal subject, nor can they be. The building which faces the Ducal Palace on the opposite side of the Piazzetta [the Libreria] is celebrated among architects, but it is not familiar to our eyes; it is painted only incidentally, for the completion, not the subject, of a Venetian scene."[9] Sargent (a half century later) seems to be challenging the idea that this building can never be "drawn singly, or as the principal subject." In maintaining that it can be so drawn, that it does make a fine subject, Sargent celebrates not just the building itself (and the architectural classicism of his own day) but also the decadence of Venice for which it is an objective correlative in Ruskin's cosmology and, it can be argued, in the popular imagination.

The rich tactile surface of the Libreria with its bold relief sculptural swags, balustrades, and finial figures is emphasized in each of these several images. Our point of view is low, just above the water, in *The Piazzetta, Venice* (pl. 15), the prow of our gondola prominent in the foreground, and considerably higher in *A Note* (fig. 101).[10] In both we look up at the white mass of the building against a blue sky (in each of the many Libreria images, even that dated 1913, the Campanile is absent).[11] The monument is always partial, the vantage point usually low, and the cone of vision narrow. *A Note* (unlike the others) is seen from a high viewpoint and may be an excerpt taken from one of the early photographer's ladder-borne views of the building. We see only the top half of the facade and a fragment of Saint Theodore on his pillar nearby. The whole composition floats uncomfortably in the billowy sky, uprooted from the earth. *The Piazzetta, Venice* (pl. 15), on the other hand, slices the building horizontally, eliminating the upper story. Except for this architectural fragment, which is stable, calm, repetitive, and parallel to the picture plane, the image is alive with diagonals. A jumble of gondolas (this area of the Molo is a gondola "cab stand") occupies the lower half of the image, intrudes into the upper half, and sends our eyes into the distance along the length of the Piazzetta. It has been said that "Sargent almost never altered a scene or a building, or its proportions, to suit his compositions, scrupulously adhering to observed fact."[12] However, here, as in *Café on the Riva degli Schiavoni, Venice* (fig. 100), he has made significant alterations. He has moved the pillar of Saint Mark from its place directly to our right (due east) of the Saint Theodore pillar to the further end of the Piazzetta, where it stands in for the clock tower and its flanking horizontal structures. This substitution has two effects. First it simplifies the composition, repeating the columnar form in the right foreground, and second it offers one simple graphic high mimetic whole in a universe of fragments.

This general return to high mimetic subjects (monuments) and even to slyly introduced high mimetic statements (as in this pedestaled winged lion) is characteristic of the ironic mode. Here the modal grandfather is more graphically intrusive than one might expect. Gondolas alone would have been sufficient to signal "Venice" but not to suggest the weight of tradition, of extraordinary former preeminence symbolized by the lion of Saint Mark. And Sargent seems to want that allusion, avoiding here as always any direct comment on the Fall.

The cluster of gondolas, and specifically the prow of "our" gondola, in *The Piazzetta* dictates our point of view, our seated posture. Not just an instrument of our passivity, our nonactor observer status, this prow suggests a narrator, like that in Henry James's *The Aspern Papers,* who is also a character within the fiction. Sargent repeatedly uses this motif to establish in a concrete manner a very specific, unique point of view, to suggest (what the fragmentary, sliced composition of these ironic works further confirms) that the image represents the limited, isolated experience of a single glimpse, of a single consciousness. And like the single narrative perspective available to us in *The Aspern Papers,* it brings up the question of the trustworthy narrator. Unlike the omniscient narrator of high mimetic panoramas and epic fictions, the ironic narrator sees and relates only those truths available from a severely limited, merely human perspective. The return to the subject of monuments is altered, not only by their partial treatment, but also by the tone

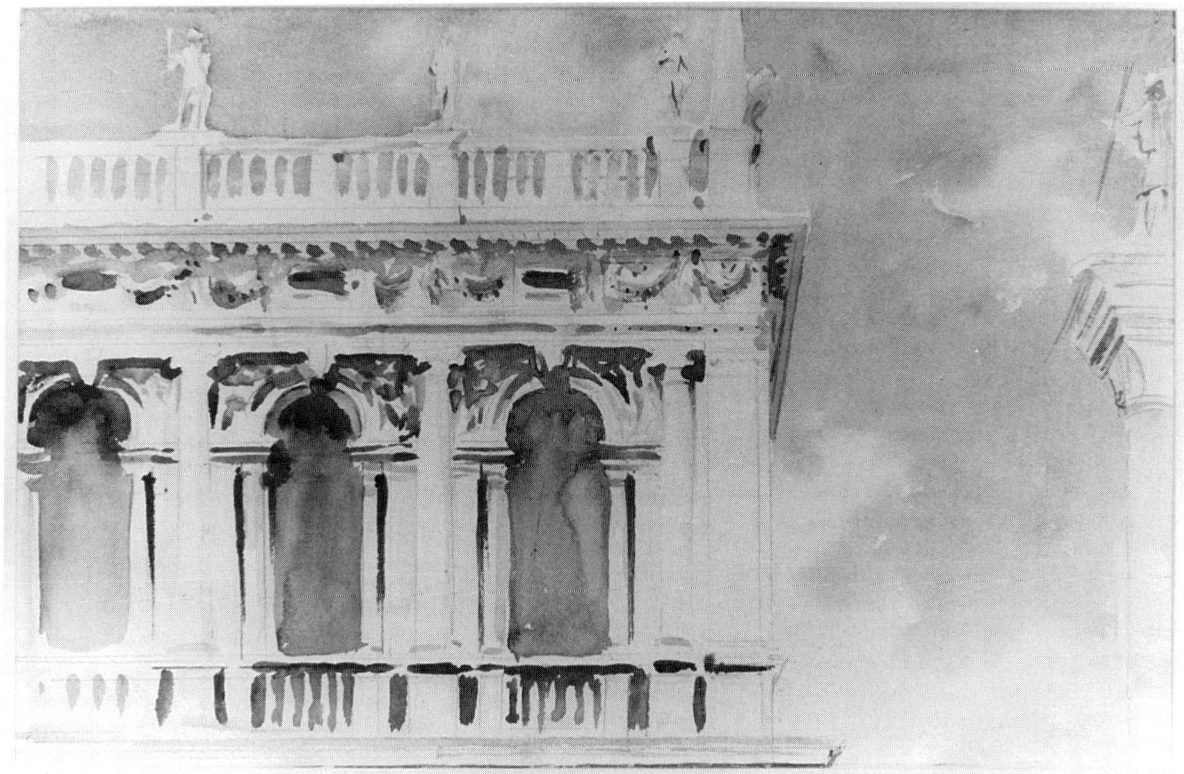

Fig. 101. John Singer Sargent, *A Note (Libreria, Venice),* ca. 1902–8, watercolor, 13⅜″ × 19¾″, Fine Arts Museums of San Francisco, Achenbach Foundation for Graphic Arts, Gift of George Hopper Fitch.

and perspective suggested by this gondola prow.

Even more than the Libreria, the Salute provided Sargent with multiple opportunities for pictures—at least a dozen survive. Like most of the Libreria views, they have a low vantage point and they emphasize the gleaming architectural elements in bright sun. But unlike the Libreria views, they are full of variety, because the artist circled the building noting different slices of the structure. Most are of the portal area, focusing on the sculptural and spatial elements near the facade pavilion. A second large group portrays the rear of the building, concentrating on the relationship of the domes and the towers. Rather than a single explanatory detailed overall view as in Francis Hopkinson Smith's *Venice: The Grand Canal with Santa Maria della Salute* (fig. 30), where a high mimetic inventory of elements from fondamenta to lantern are carefully rehearsed, here seemingly random, even incomplete, elements are isolated. They are abstracted from any meaningful relationship with the building as a whole, from its surroundings and from its meaning as a symbol of Venice.

In this method of multiple but disconnected views there is an analogy with what Frye sees as one of the primary aspects of the poetry of this period, "poetry which is encyclopaedic and yet discontinuous."[13] The crystalline but fragmented objectivity of the ironic artist has an analogy in the literary "practice of cutting out predication, of simply juxtaposing images without making any assertions about their relationship."[14] This technique of silent juxtaposition is used within single works (see fig. 105) and within a series. In both cases the artist's posture is that of a recorder-craftsman, not an interpreter or synthesizer of material.

The rear view of the Salute that Bunner made from the Rio Santa Croce (figs. 42 and 44) is startling in some respects, but it retains a sense of the integrity of the structure and of its tremendous size. In Sargent's rear views of the Salute (as in *Santa Maria della Salute, Venice,* fig. 102) the four parts of the building that are visible (large dome, small dome, pair of stair towers) are confused with one another and with the rigging of moored ships.[15] The viewer is slightly above water level in the Giudecca Canal, looking through spars and bowsprits which confuse not only the outlines of the architectural features but also our sense of proportion. The image is disorienting, but even more so is *Rigging* (fig. 103; see also fig. 104).[16] Although undoubtedly faithful to optical reality, Sargent here has shifted position so that the two separate domes—behind a tower and a mast—appear to converge into a single form. Part of the ironic stance is to see discontinuity where "ordinary" vision (or knowledge) sees wholeness, and a second, minor aspect sees, as in this case, false continuities, false syntheses as wholes.

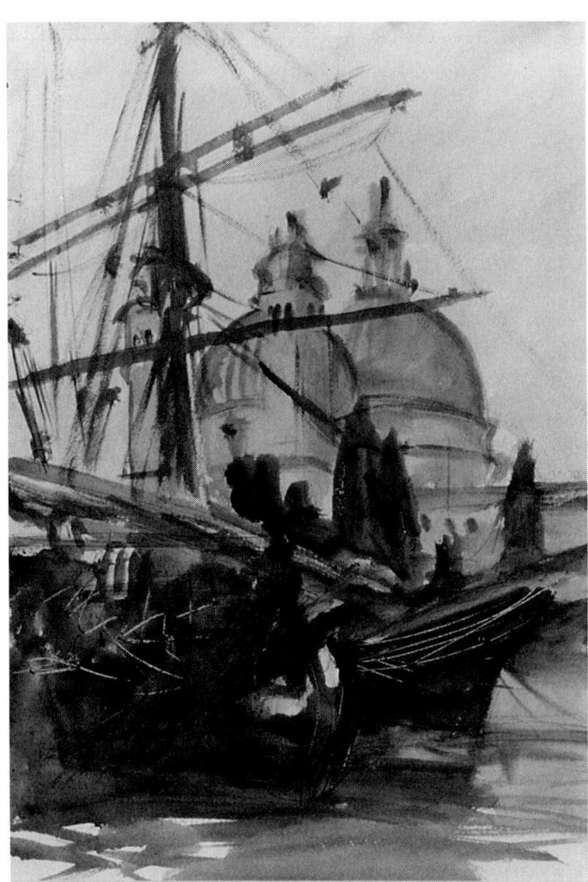

Fig. 102. John Singer Sargent, *Santa Maria della Salute, Venice,* before 1909, watercolor, 18″ × 12″, Victoria and Albert Museum, London; see also fig. 104.

Far more typical of the ironic mode is *The Dogana* (fig. 105), which contains three disparate elements: the small temple structure on the Punta della Dogana surmounted by kneeling bronze figures supporting a gold ball on top of which Fortuna (here invisible beyond the frame) greets shipping entering the Grand Canal; a large yacht, which drifts by with slack jib sails; and a man who siestas in the prow of a (our) gondola, attentive to neither boat nor building (nor us). We struggle to find or create an organizing principle, yet it seems beyond

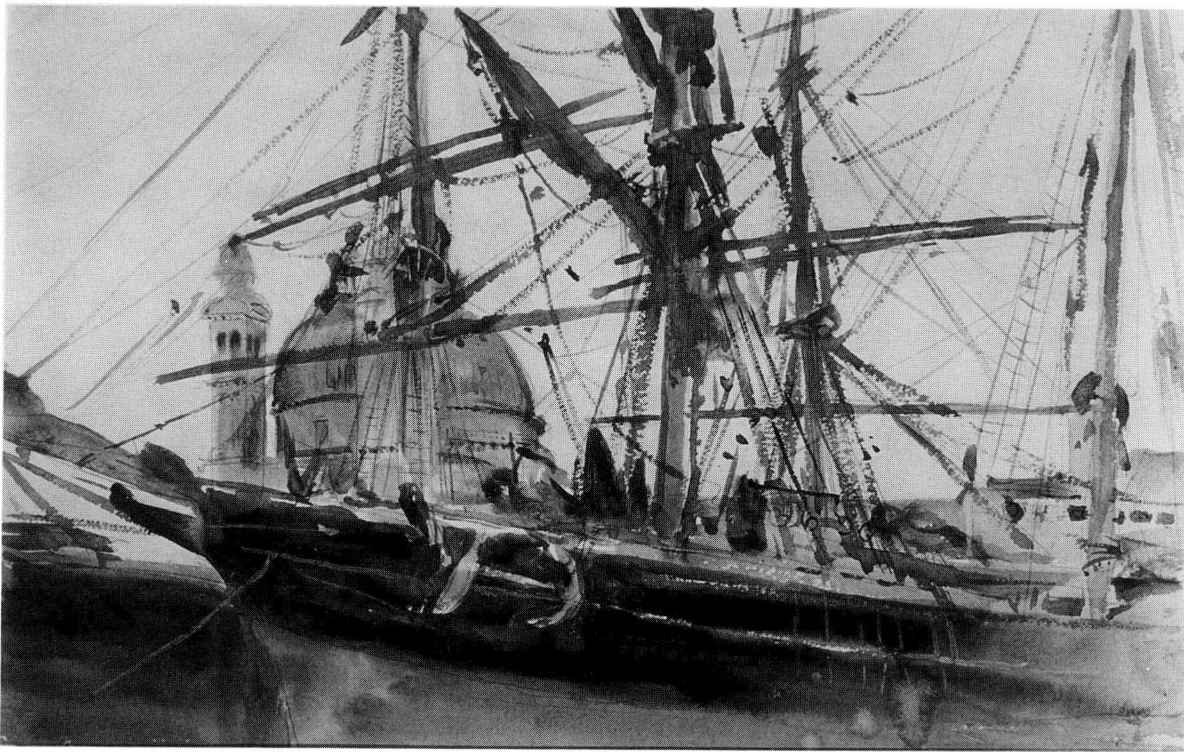

Fig. 103. John Singer Sargent, *Rigging,* ca. 1905–8, watercolor, 11⅛″ × 18″, Brooklyn Museum, purchased by special subscription; see also fig. 104.

our mental effort to see any but a superficial spatial and temporal relationship between these elements. Oddly yoked, disproportionate fractions, these elements coexist, comment on each other only because the artist insists they do so.

A second picture of this same area is equally startling for different reasons. In *Venice: La Dogana* (fig. 106) Sargent seems to have heeded Degas's injunction to "do monuments . . . from below, from beneath, up close."[17] In a narrow, oblique cone of vision that shoots up at a remarkable angle, we catch Fortuna on her golden ball against a Tiepolo sky. Simultaneously grand and odd, we have a double impression of the brilliant note she makes in the sky and the meager note we must make to her. The ironic celebration of the monument—unlike the high mimetic—involves a corresponding diminution of the viewer.

We have not lost our meager persona, what we might call our damaged self-esteem, in *Venice* (fig. 107), where we stand on the water steps below the Fondamenta della Salute and look east to the golden ball, now distantly resting (within the fiction of the image) on the roof of the long low customs building (see fig. 104).[18] Our horizon is crowded

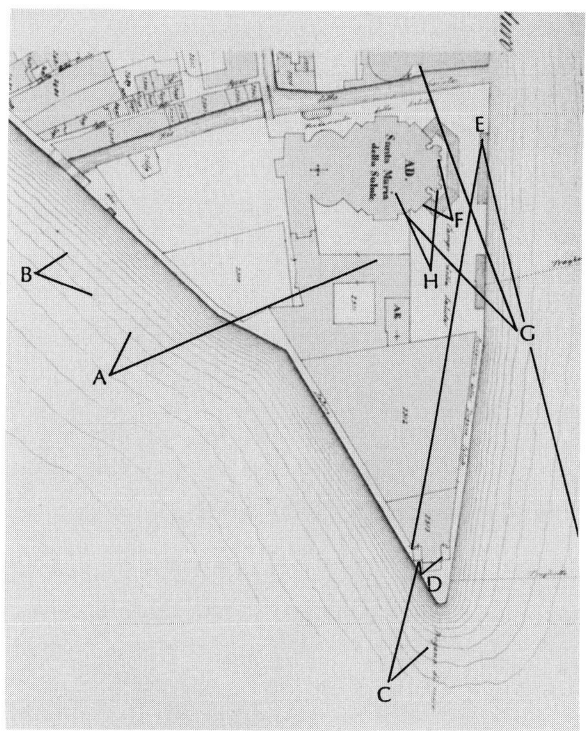

A. *Santa Maria della Salute, Venice,* fig. 102
B. *Rigging,* fig. 103
C. *Dogana,* fig. 105
D. *Venice: La Dogana,* fig. 106
E. *Venice,* fig. 107
F. *Santa Maria della Salute, Venice,* fig. 108
G. *The Salute, Venice,* pl. 16

Fig. 104. Map of sites of Sargent images, figs. 102, 103, 105, 106, 107, 108, and pl. 16.

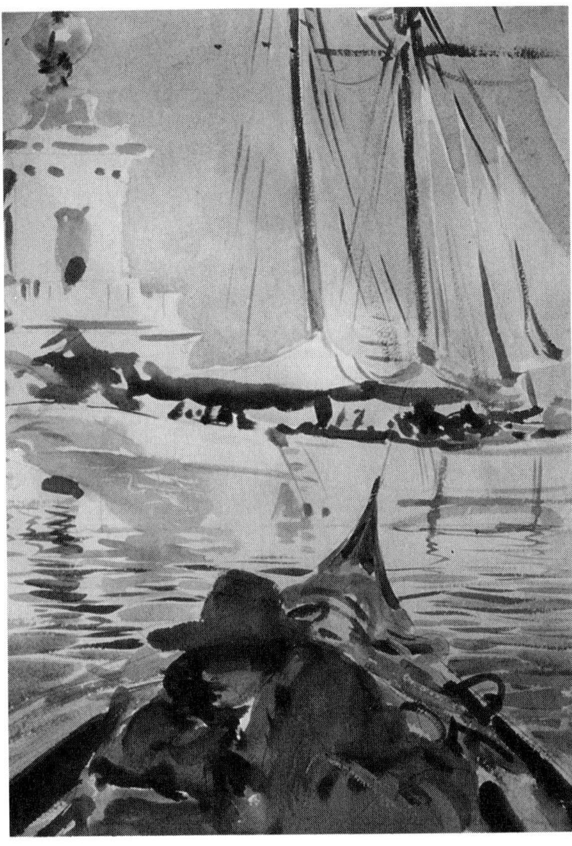

Fig. 105. John Singer Sargent, *The Dogana*, ca. 1904–8, watercolor, 13½″ × 9″, the Ormond Family; see also fig. 104.

with steps—they fill almost half the image—and although the field of vision is wide, it is not expansive. It does not even take in the statue that crowns the ball and that would lead our eye skyward, up from the low horizontal bars of repetitious steps. Nor do things improve when we mount up onto the Campo della Salute and turn to the facade of the church itself in *Santa Maria della Salute, Venice* (fig. 108). From a seated position on the campo our eye level reaches only the tenth of sixteen approach steps. Nor are there pedestrians to comfort us in this difficulty of incommensurate scale. Lifting our eyes we can see three complete plinths, several columnal fragments, and indistinct statuary. The architectural world that completely fills the visual field is a jumble of disconnected prismatic shapes—all angular, incomplete, and unsymmetrical. Nothing is so complete a loss in the ironic mode as the loss of symmetry, that architectural attribute that mimics our human form and instantly engages our sympathy and empathy. Nothing so comforting, so orienting is permitted here. Even when we move back in space as in *Santa Maria della Salute* in the Brooklyn Museum collection, the architectural composition does not recompose. Here figures enter, but they are as out of scale with the monument as we and, moving in the dark, watery foreground, have as little relation to the huge bright marble forms.

In an effort to gain the scope of a structure that towers so high above our meager human height that even its plinths, even its column bases, are above our eye level, one alternative—the one used in *Venice: La Dogana* (fig. 106)—is to tilt back our head and look up. An image almost half sky with a tumbling cascade of volutes, carved saints, and crisp, angular but unrelated architectural details, *The Salute, Venice* (pl. 16) slices off and offers up a corner of that grand church.[19] It is splendidly portrayed—warm shadows and bold sculptural forms stand out against a crisp blue sky. It seems an accident, a happy accident, that Sargent should have

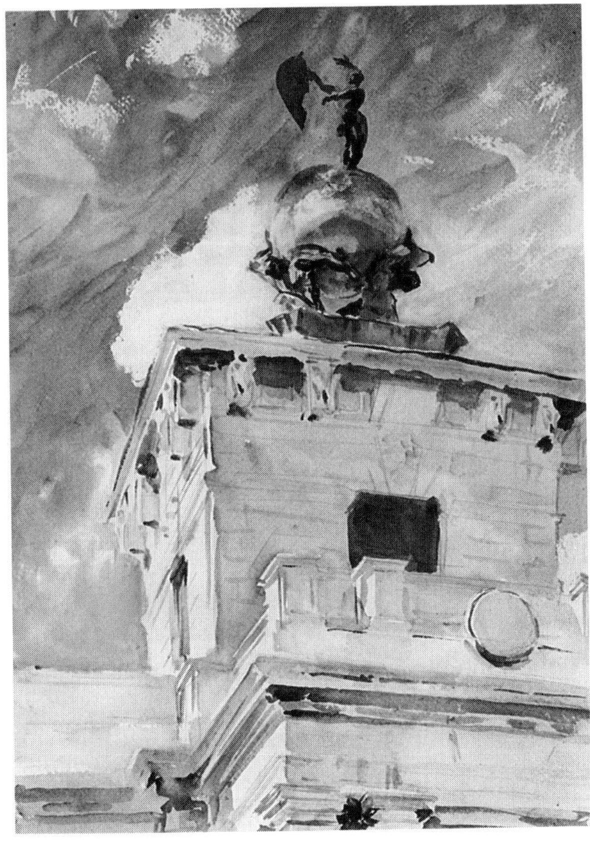

Fig. 106. John Singer Sargent, *Venice: La Dogana*, ca. 1911, watercolor, 19¾″ × 14″, Museum of Fine Arts, Boston, Charles Henry Hayden Fund; see also fig. 104.

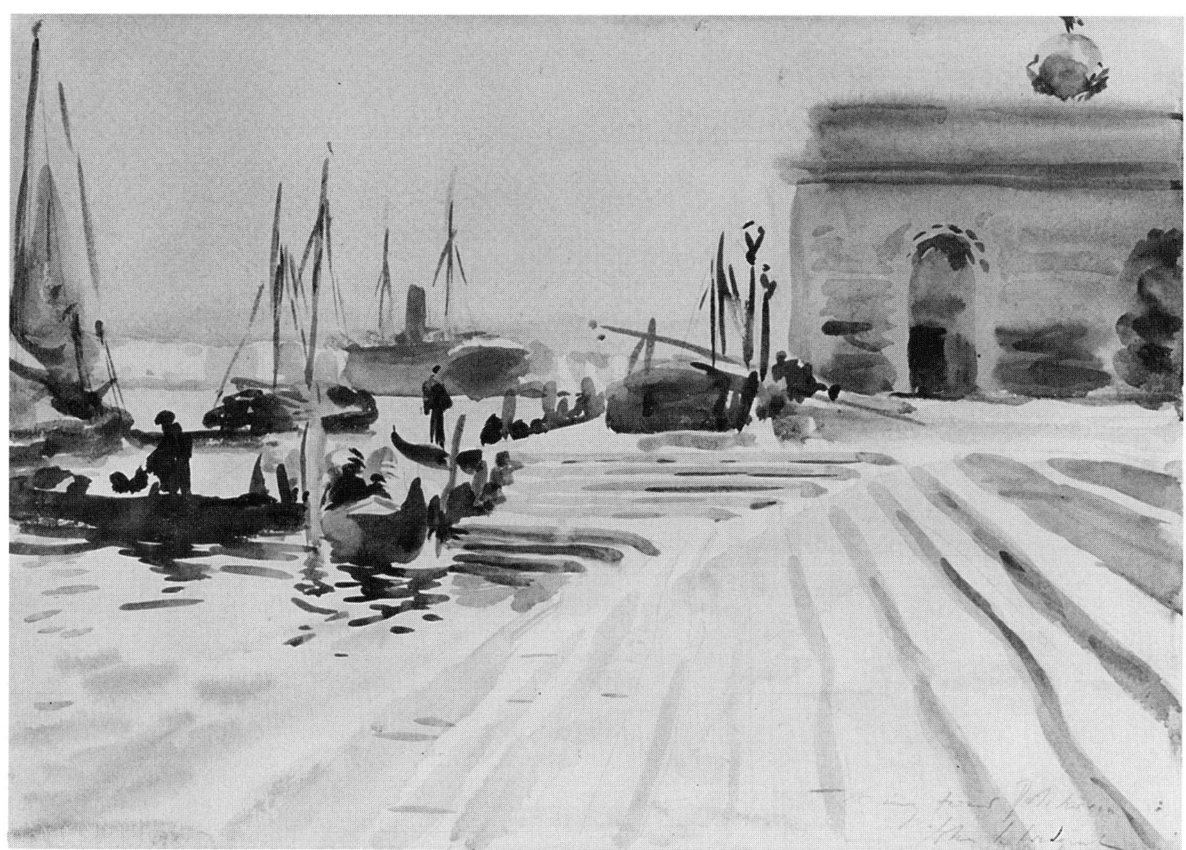

Fig. 107. John Singer Sargent, *Venice,* ca. 1903–12, watercolor, 9⅞" × 14", Worcester Art Museum, Worcester, Massachusetts, Gift of Mr. and Mrs. Stuart Riley, Jr.; see also fig. 104.

chosen "at random" this treasury of baroque architectural detail, yet it clearly was not an accident but a sought-for, struggled-over achievement. It is not a view from the ground; that would be entirely too foreshortened, too mechanically difficult to execute (see fig. 109). The view was taken from some height, possibly from a photographer's ladder-platform.[20] In this we can see the deliberate and painstaking selectiveness behind the cool pose of Frye's ironist simply recording "life as it is," maintaining a posture of noninvolvement, even nonchalance about subject, questing only after noninterpretive objective craftsmanship. Executed with infinite care and enthusiasm, *The Salute, Venice* is nevertheless as unsettling and disorienting as Sargent's other images of this church. Together they do not compose into that whole that knowledge of many parts of an object ought to produce in Lévi-Strauss's paradigm: "To understand a real object in its totality we always tend to work from its parts. The resistance it offers us is overcome by dividing it" (see p. 27). Despite multiple clear, objective views, Sargent's Salute is still an inscrutable and overwhelming object. In the ironic mode the dividing of the object, the multiplication of episodes, does not produce comprehension and wholeness but rather an effect analogous to Frye's "poetry which is encyclopaedic and yet discontinuous." Each image is a lonely isolated episode, and the bafflement it insists we feel is not dispelled by multiplied instances.

Images of monuments in the ironic mode such as this series by Sargent seem to follow a uniform strategy in their approach to the heroic structure. The primary ascribed value of the monument is denied by fragmentation, by a low or "inappropriate" vantage point, or by a suppression of setting, leaving the structure transformed, even unrecognizable. But simultaneously, within the view chosen, the artist appropriates the structure anew and, by the sheer power of his art, creates value in the image. The artwork then is absolute and in-

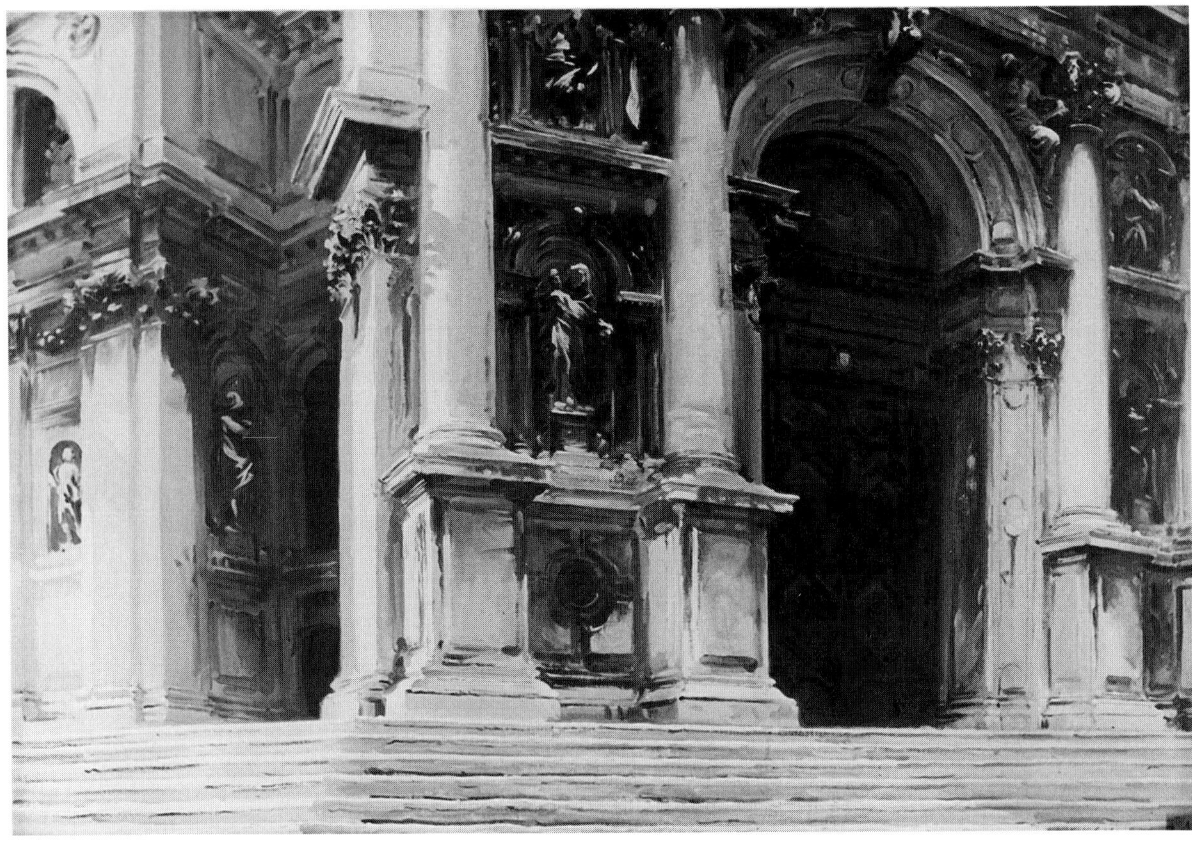

Fig. 108. John Singer Sargent, *Santa Maria della Salute, Venice,* ca. 1905, oil on canvas, 28⅛″ × 39⅜″, Johannesburg Art Gallery; see also fig. 104.

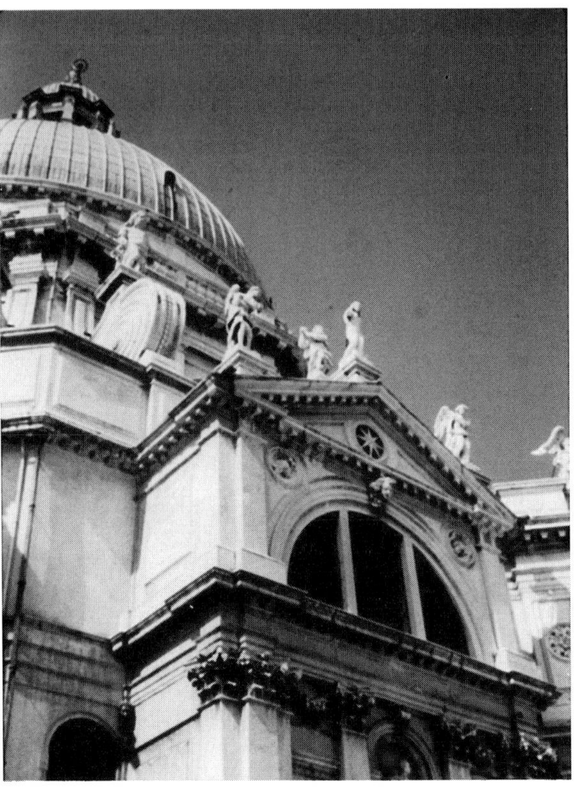

dependent; it is replete with its own and not with borrowed resonance. This insistence that the artist create value and significance by purely artistic means is what Henry James refers to as "the literal squeezing out of value."[21] And rarely in the painterly mode is this squeeze, this strategy of denial, appropriation, and revaluation, so successful as in Sargent's *The Salute, Venice.*

Fig. 109. Site of John Singer Sargent, *The Salute, Venice* (pl. 16).

FIVE
The Ozymandias Problem

Seen in isolation or in relationship to the hundreds of other images that share its wider subject, Venice, Sargent's *The Salute, Venice* (pl. 16) is an extraordinary work, full of visual brilliance and conceptual opacity. It is both self-explanatory, self-referential, and extremely dependent on a huge corpus of work—painterly, historic, and literary. It not only exists, it also answers and rebuts. It avoids alternatives; it is the end product of deliberate selection, a selection guided by cultural as well as visual forces.

When the "discovery" of the subject of the city of Venice occurred—and we can regard Thomas Rossiter's 1843 letter from Venice to John F. Kensett ("It is not . . . the place to paint original pictures in, unless it be architectural compositions")[1] as the somewhat reluctant opening gun—no one could have predicted that Sargent's Salute series seventy years later would sound the final salute. Taken together, these several thousand images represent an unusual and telling concentration of energy, curiosity, and talent, and a broad spectrum of visual experience and intellectual assessment.

That a single subject, Venice, had appeal over a considerable length of time, that artists made an effort to be there—not to gain instruction as in Paris, or to seek out patronage and each other's fellowship as in Rome, but to see and reinterpret the city itself—speaks for the painters' engagement with the subject. That these visions and revisions exhibit multiple but clustered and related characteristics, points to questions larger than mere personal artistic idiosyncrasies and individual visual problems.

Complicating and complementing the issue of shifting visual interpretations of the city is the question of Venice's reputation: Venice's history is not a fixed chronicle of dates and meanings. Like all histories, that of Venice is rewritten and reinterpreted generation by generation, each generation dwelling on those elements, occurrences, and cultural institutions that are exemplary for or antithetical (and therefore possibly threatening) to its own patterns of life and habits of thought. These interpretations, whether historic, literary, or pictorial, point back to the interpreters, illuminating their own concerns as clearly as the purported subject.

As it was Ruskin's enterprise to read in the stones of Venice a tale written by long-gone and otherwise inarticulate artisans, it has been our enterprise here to read in images of Venice certain patterns of expression and habits of mind that might otherwise have gone unrecorded. But where Ruskin's quarry was a moral one (seeing evidences of stalwart virtue and harmony with nature), ours is a more broadly cultural one. The investigation has focused on modes suggesting mental attitudes, preoccupations, and meanings beyond the artists' obvious subject. For a high mimetic image involves the viewer in a different set of assumptions about the nature of the world, of the observer's place in that world, and the place of image making within that culture, than does an image in the low mimetic or ironic mode.

In making these pictures these American artists were involved in two kinds of discovery, the physical discovery of a foreign territory and the meaning of that adventure to them, which might be called their self-discovery. Each painting is a condensation of felt experience and a fictionalization of that experience. It represents both a record of observed fact and a projection of qualities that touched a responsive chord within the artist's self-definition. That these were not idiosyncratic, merely personal visions and projections is suggested by the repetition of patterns of vision, subjects, and artistic structures within this universe of Venetian views. These works fall into larger groups that appear analogous to the categories that Frye perceived in his analysis of literary fictions. That all three modes—high mimetic, low mimetic, and ironic, representing three discrete types of response to a single physical reality—were present during this relatively short period points to the richness of American response to large and complex problems of history, culture, and personal memory.

Paintings in the high mimetic mode portray a world that is basically aristocratic. It is beautiful and superhuman and adopts the historic Venetians' view of themselves. Buildings are recognizable, significant, and portrayed in a serious manner. The artist accepts the architect's intentions about the viewing of his structure—frontal, heroic, symmetrical, and comfortably framed by sea and sky. Forms are complete, especially in the vertical dimension, and the image is informed by a clarity, a rationality, a sense of consequence, and a sense of shared social experience. The vantage point is usually high, the format often a stable horizontal rectangle, and the cone of vision wide, suggesting a superhuman breadth of visual experience. The viewer picks up and appropriates many of these aspects of the images. His discovery is of a foreign city full of large-scale monuments which suggest a past in which the space was inhabited by giants—not just magnificently large but also artistically gifted and materially successful. The adoption of this stance by Americans in their abundant self-mythologizing can also be seen in the plans for the Chicago World's Fair of 1893—a Great White City full of heroic Old World posturing, rational axial spaces, and poetic lagoons. The adoption of this visual vocabulary suggests a will, even a cultural need, to inherit the artistic heritage, physical architectural grandeur, and material success that these predecessors so ably represented.

As the high mimetic represents a giant's-eye view of Venice and suggests a corporate social experience, a consensus and hierarchy of value, the low mimetic repudiates this stance and this view of social and artistic relationships. Here the artist is not so much a discoverer of grand monuments, a confirmer of values ascribed and understood; he is a discoverer of the nonmonumental aspects of life. His "blundering steps" take him on journeys into *terre inconnue,* into small alleys and campi where monuments are seen from behind or where natives in their "interesting squalor and picturesque wretchedness" go about their daily chores, oblivious of artists, of history, even of the fall of their city. This is a pedestrian's-eye view, a private view, democratic in its subject matter. Aware of a sense of belatedness, the artists' strategy is not to strike the resonant chord of the familiar mnemonic monumental facade but to defamiliarize the city and reappropriate it on different terms. The city is seen from normal human height, usually through a restricted cone of vision; the scale, media, and subject are modest. In this common-humanity point of view the artist discovers both the postlapsarian nature of the city—peopled now by poor and ragged folk with narrow personal horizons—and also the commonness of his own humanity with theirs. To maintain that Venice is a city in which one can be lost, in which the unextraordinary events of daily life continue, is to say that it is not unlike America although, perhaps, morally and materially "in ill repair." In his self-discovery here the artist finds an analogue in the ahistoric spaces and lives of the calli and campi for his own painterly activity. This is a self-discovery by the artist of the artisan and, on a larger scale, the discovery by a culture fast eradicating the last vestiges of artisan values and artisan economy, of the stability and personal satisfactions inherent in a handwork culture. In this the low mimetic mode captures a nostalgic view, but it is very different in quality, even antithetical, to that inherent in the high mimetic nostalgic view.

An intensification of all the characteristics seen in the low mimetic mode results in a shift into the ironic. Where in the low mimetic mode one had a sense of private vision, in the ironic mode the note is, above all else, of isolation. The artist's arena of physical discovery returns to the monument, but he sees it from a sub-pedestrian's-eye view, often from a barnacle's-eye view. The narrow cone of vision has been still further constricted until one sees only fractional and ambiguous sections of architectural substance and space. The sense of possession and comprehensibility seen in the high mimetic mode, and still present but on a smaller scale in the low mimetic mode, is here absent. Symmetry and completeness are lost. Topographically accurate, these views are harmonious with neither our expectations nor the architect's intentions. Our expectations are thwarted, and in that loss we see a comment on those expectations, on our assumptions about physical order and pictorial order, about fictions, and about the nature of our own lives. Here the object of value is devalued and its value reconstituted only within the terms of the specific artwork, the specific interpretation. This devaluation and revaluation is a commentary not just on the physical objects portrayed but also on the predecessor modes—their messages and assumptions. The self-discovery we see a symptom of here is that of an individual or a culture that senses a fundamentally undecodable reality. This is a reality that can be seen clearly in parts but that resists clarity in the whole. Implied here is also the notion that bafflement, ambiguity, and irresolution, while uncomfortable on one level, are also clearly in some way pleasurable. It is a transfer not unlike that of fear into pleasure, which was so characteristic of romantic fictions. For those with an ironic point of view, tension can, in an equally bizarre twist, confer pleasure.

It is important to note that while high mimetic and low mimetic points of view have passed into popular culture, the ironic has only made slight incursions. One can, that is, purchase high and low mimetic postcards of Venice, but ironic popular images—in photographic or painterly form—are rare. It remains a somewhat privileged mode, one which enjoyed a short life span in painting, supplanted after World War I by truly subjectless works which represent an interiority beyond the ironic that we are investigating here.

Modes have been invoked in this analysis because a reading from a modal perspective appears to account for more in more interesting ways than other possible readings of these images. The concept helps us see beyond the presumptions and difficulties inherent in more traditional interpretations and clarifies the means by which artists create meaning in pictures. It also presses us toward a more useful synchronic understanding of the images and assists us in disengaging ourselves from our own cultural relativism. Because it is physical, a painting is, unlike a stage play which must be reenacted, contemporary with both its initial primary audience and with all subsequent audiences. It is continuously contemporary. And in it each audience necessarily sees not only its physical self but also a mirror of certain preoccupations, hopes, and appetites that they sense and respond to even without complete examination or articulation. As the cultural equipment that these eyes bring to this seeing of the object shifts, the relevance and importance of the object and its various components alter. Most recent commenters—because of their greater sensitivity to issues of technique and abstract composition and their lack of a modal framework—have undervalued the subject of these works, especially those in the ironic mode, and therefore have not reached into issues of stance and point of view. In doing so, they have denied such artists as Sargent and Prendergast not only their literal architectural subjects, but also their dialogue with their predecessors and their engagement with large questions of history and the past, insisting that their paintings are "about" light and color and paint. The achievement of these artists is usually measured only within the protomodernism which they come to represent in a view of art history that sees that history as an unfolding self-referential, solely diachronic drama. In other words, their critics have denied the artists their ironic stance, their careful, artful thoughtfulness, and their temporal embeddedness.

A modal reading can usefully enlarge our understanding of other artworks as well. The versatility or vacillation between modes that we see not only in the work of these artists but also in that of their European contemporaries points to a deliberate testing and manipulation of the modes, a questioning of assumptions, especially those implicit in the high and low mimetic modes. In this larger model, late nineteenth-century artistic ventures into the ironic mode represent a final remark on and critique of the other two, a solution or resolution, one could say, with a question mark.

The object of this study has not been to imply or establish any degree of discovery, originality, or "firstness" on the part of these American artists—taken singly or as a group. In painting as in literature the French have precedence in the use of the ironic mode. As early as the late 1860s the low mimetic term "genre scene" begins to seem inappropriate when applied to the views of daily life portrayed by the impressionists, as these artists were already moving into the ironic mode. The difference, however, between the development and application of this novel toolbox by French artists and that by their American contemporaries is that the impressionists turned its extraordinary syntax and vocabulary on the railroads, leisure sports, and urban encounters of modern Paris while the Americans applied it, more incongruously, more startlingly, to the archaic subject of Venice. The urban novelties of New York and Paris did not pique the Americans with nearly the curiosity and intensity of that completely other world: the past.

These paintings, taken as a whole, are evidence of the exploration of a problem, a problem analogous to that of Shelley's traveler who comes upon a single sculptural fragment and reads on its pedestal,

> "My name is Ozymandias, king of kings;
> Look on my works, ye Mighty, and
> despair!"
> Nothing beside remains. Round the decay
> Of that colossal wreck, boundless and bare
> The lone and level sands stretch far away.

The traveler perceives, of course, impotent hubris—the assertion of pride and power within a vacuum of evidence—but he also (and more important for our purposes) is confronted with the fact of a discontinuous past. Neither verbal legend nor physical evidence bridges the void of mutual ignorance between himself and Ozymandias. The two routes to the past—history (tale, myth, or record) on the one hand and objects (pots, artworks, buildings, and cities) on the other—are unavailable. The first has evaporated with the death of those knowledgeable; the second has been reduced to sand. What Shelley's fictive traveler has come upon is a failure of public memory. If the evidence of monument erection is to be trusted, there is no period in history in which the desire to prevent the failure of public, cultural memory was as strong as during the nineteenth century. The civic monument is consciously both a mnemonic object and text, an active agent of public remembrance and instruction. It asserts that every generation must be reeducated and private memory inoculated with public memory so that the event and the place reverberate for those who have no personal experience of the glory, achievement, devastation, bravery, or betrayal of individuals and groups. The public tale and the public monument, taken together, insure that when a traveler arrives at the scene of public action, as Byron put it, on observing for the first time the fields of Marathon "the sense aches with gazing to behold / The scenes our earliest dreams have dwelt upon."[2] The sense cannot ache if it has not been educated; the beholding of the site has no resonance if it is unrecognizable. For Americans in the nineteenth century the sense of the possibility of a discontinuous past, a past unmarked and untold, seems to have pressed especially hard. And the rival natural "monuments," the newly appointed icons of the American wilderness such as Niagara and Yosemite, seem to have insufficiently quieted this terror of pastlessness. While they offered tangible evidence of a mighty geologic past and even a promise of divine favor, they could not answer the felt need for a continuous public past.

Feeling himself or herself to be genetically European but culturally other, the American traveler to lands beyond "the lone and level sands" surveyed both the historic record and the surviving structures for elements of continuity or analogy. But the appropriation of this newfound historical memory was problematic. Not only was it a forbidden memory because it was someone else's memory, but also, it simply didn't fit. None of the three kinds of memory analogous to the three fictive modes—costumed grandeur, nostalgic reverie, or ahistorical document—could easily chart a relationship, could bridge the temporal and spatial gap between the European past and the American present. What these images record is the search, its urgency, its restless parameters, and its astonishing aesthetic achievement.

NOTES

Preface

1. Margaretta M. Lovell, *Venice: The American View, 1860–1920* (San Francisco: Fine Arts Museums of San Francisco, 1984).

2. Jan Mukařovský, "The Essence of the Visual Arts," in *The Semiotics of Art: Prague School Contributions*, ed. Ladislav Matejka and Irwin R. Titunik (Cambridge, Mass.: MIT Press, 1976), p. 237.

Chapter 1

1. Examples of "Venetian" buildings include the National Academy of Design in New York City (Peter B. Wight, 1865) based on the Doge's Palace (the academy building was demolished in the 1890s; parts were salvaged and incorporated into Our Lady of Lourdes Church, 467 W. 142d St., 1904 [Norval White and Elliot Willensky, *AIA Guide to New York City* (New York: Collier Macmillan, 1978), p. 263]); the Montauk Club in Brooklyn (Francis H. Kimball, 1891), based on the Cà d'Oro; and Stoeckel Hall in New Haven (Grosvenor Atterbury, 1897), based on the Palazzo Contarini Fasan (Desdemona's house). An art academy, a club, and a fraternal organization commissioned these buildings, institutions in which theatrical design was especially permissible. Fenway Court in Boston (Edward H. Sears, 1902), built to house Isabella Stewart Gardner's art collection (including fragments of Venetian structures), employs Venetian architectural vocabulary but imitates no specific facade or interior. It might be noted, however, that many architects, including Henry Austin and Louis Sullivan, used characteristically Venetian fenestration systems and wall surface treatment in altered form.

2. George Inness, Jr., *Life, Art, and Letters of George Inness* (New York: Century Co., 1917), p. 75; and Nicolai Cikovsky, Jr., *George Inness* (New York: Praeger Publishers, 1971), p. 39.

3. Albert Bierstadt, *The Domes of the Yosemite* (1867; oil on canvas; St. Johnsbury Atheneum, St. Johnsbury, Vermont).

4. Albert Bierstadt, letter to *The Crayon*, July 1859, quoted in Nancy Heller and Julia Williams, "Albert Bierstadt: The American Wilderness," *American Artist* 40 (January 1976): 52–57, 96–97, 102. See also Gordon Hendricks, "Bierstadt's *The Domes of the Yosemite*," *American Art Journal* 3 (Fall 1971): 23–31.

5. Henry James, *The Wings of the Dove* (New York: Charles Scribner's Sons, 1902), 2:208; Henry James, *The Aspern Papers* (London and New York: Macmillan & Co., 1888), p. 134.

6. *Mappa del Comune Censuario di dorsoduro porzione della città di Venezia . . . 1847*, 1:1,000, forty sheets, Yale University Map Collection, New Haven, Connecticut. All the detail diagrams in this study are derived from this set of maps.

7. Exceptions include John Singer Sargent, *Sketching on the Giudecca*, ca. 1904, watercolor and gouache (William Rathbone, Oxfordshire, England, pictured in Lovell, *Venice*, p. 119), and Thomas Moran, *Splendor of Venice*, pl. 1.

8. George Kubler, *The Shape of Time: Remarks on the History of Things* (New Haven, Conn.: Yale University Press, 1962).

9. Harold Bloom, "*Clinamen* or Poetic Misprision," in *The Anxiety of Influence: A Theory of Poetry* (New York: Oxford University Press, 1973), pp. 19–45.

10. Heinrich Wölfflin, *Principles of Art History: The Problem of the Development of Style in Later Art*, translated by M. D. Hottinger ([New York:] Dover Publications, n.d.), p. 9.

11. Northrop Frye, *Anatomy of Criticism: Four Essays* (Princeton, N.J.: Princeton University Press, 1957).

12. Ibid., pp. 33–34.

13. Claude Lévi-Strauss, *Structural Anthropology*, translated by Claire Jacobson and Brooke Grundfest Schoepf (New York: Basic Books, 1963), pp. 21, 23.

14. See also Lovell, *Venice*, pp. 66–67, 69.

15. See ibid., pp. 134–38, 152–53.

16. See Dianne Hauserman Pilgrim, "The Revival of Pastels in Nineteenth-Century America: The Society of Painters in Pastel," *American Art Journal* 10 (November 1978): 43–62.

17. One scholar, Robert Getscher, says of this image, "Whistler worked directly on the plate from a gondola moored some fifteen or twenty feet across the canal" (Robert Getscher, *The Stamp of Whistler*, exhibition catalog [Oberlin, Ohio: Allen Memorial Art Gallery, 1977], p. 80). If this were the case he was standing in the gondola rather than sitting, as the eye level is about five feet above the water line. Characteristically Whistler and other artists found steps, doorways, and landings from which to work that gave the finished low mimetic work the appearance of a waterborne vantage point.

18. See Lovell, *Venice*, pp. 129–30.

19. See ibid., pp. 95–97, 121–22.

Chapter 2

1. Frye, *Anatomy of Criticism*, p. 15.

2. Ibid., pp. 34, 38, 41.

3. John Ruskin is particularly harsh on Tintoretto's architectural painting: "But whatever advances were made by Tintoret in modes of artistical treatment, he cannot be considered as having enlarged the sphere of landscape conception. He took no cognizance even of the materials and motives, so singularly rich in colour, which were for ever around him in his own Venice. All portions of Venetian scenery introduced by him are treated conventionally and carelessly, the architectural characters lost altogether" (*Modern Painters*, in *The Works of John Ruskin*, edited by E. T. Cook and Alexander Wedderburn, [London: George

Allen; New York: Longmans, Green & Co., 1903], 3:182–83).

4. See J. G. Links, *Canaletto and His Patrons* (New York: New York University Press, 1977).

5. Harold Bloom, "The Internalization of Quest-Romance," in *Romanticism and Consciousness: Essays in Criticism* (New York: W. W. Norton & Co., 1970), p. 7.

6. *Juliet and Her Nurse* is currently on loan to the Metropolitan Museum of Art in New York City.

7. John Ruskin, *Praeterita: Outlines of Scenes and Thoughts Perhaps Worthy of Memory in My Past Life*, in *Works* 35:217. Ruskin's letter in defense of Turner (October 1, 1836) reads in part:

> His imagination is Shakespearian in its mightiness. Had the scene of "Juliet and Her Nurse" risen up before the mind of a poet, and been described in "words that burn," it had been the admiration of the world: but placed before us on the canvas, it becomes—what critics of the brush and pallet may show their wit upon at the expense of their judgment; and what real artists and men of feeling and taste *must* admire, but dare not attempt to imitate. Many-coloured mists are floating above the distant city, but such mists as you might imagine to be aetherial spirits, souls of the mighty dead breathed out of the tombs of Italy into the blue of her bright heaven, and wandering in vague and infinite glory around the earth that they have loved. . . .
>
> This, oh Maga, is the picture which your critic has pronounced to be like "models of different parts of Venice, streaked blue and white, and thrown into a flour tub"! That this picture is not seen by either starlight, sunlight, moonlight, or firelight, is perfectly true: it is a light of his own, which no other artist can produce—a light which seems owing to some phosphorescent property in the air. This picture can be, and ought only to be viewed as embodied enchantment, delineated magic. (*Modern Painters*, in *Works* 3:638–39)

8. Ruskin, *Modern Painters*, in *Works* 3:639.

9. Thurman Wilkins, *Thomas Moran, Artist of the Mountains* (Norman: University of Oklahoma Press, 1966), pp. 6, 70.

10. Ibid., p. 184. While I have located almost a hundred, some of these, including *Venice* (n.d.) in the collection of the Fine Arts Museums of San Francisco and *Venice at Dawn* (1884; sold at Sotheby's London, January 18, 1978, and pictured in *Burlington Magazine* 112 [November 1977]: 889), do not include recognizably Venetian buildings or scenes. That Moran paintings were sometimes renamed to encourage sale is evident from such bizarre alterations as from *Childe Roland to the Dark Tower Came* to *The Lava Beds of Idaho* (ibid., p. 29). For a discussion of Moran in Venice see Lovell, *Venice*, pp. 66–70.

11. It might be expected that these images move from topographical fidelity to more visionary and imaginative interpretations as Moran's memory of direct experience of the city faded with time. However, this seems not to be the case: compare, for instance, the relatively accurate late *San Giorgio Maggiore* of 1905 (formerly at the Honolulu Academy of Arts, current location unknown) with the far more fictive version of the same church in *Venice* of 1887 (at the Pennsylvania Academy). It is not improbable that Moran used photographs of Venetian buildings to help construct his paintings. This would explain certain repetitious and at times illogical (within the framework of the individual picture) views. In "Stereoscopic Photography and the Western Paintings of Albert Bierstadt," *Art Quarterly*, 33, no. 4 (Winter 1970): 360–78, Elizabeth Lindquist-Cock suggests the importance of stereoscopic views to Bierstadt and to other artists of western scenes, including Moran (p. 378).

12. Wilkins, *Thomas Moran*, p. 195.

13. Ralph Waldo Emerson, "Nature," in *The Collected Essays of Ralph Waldo Emerson*, edited by Joseph Slater, Alfred R. Ferguson, and Jean Ferguson Carr (Cambridge, Mass.: Belknap Press of Harvard University Press, 1983), 3:104. The prototype for Moran's inclusion of the figure of an artist is J. M. W. Turner's first Venetian picture, *Bridge of Sighs, Ducal Palace, and Custom-House, Venice: Canaletti Painting* (1833, Tate Gallery).

14. See Lovell, *Venice*, pp. 70–71.

15. For a discussion of Maxfield Parrish's illustration for Edith Wharton's tale in *Scribners*, see Lovell, *Venice*, pp. 73–74.

16. Frye, *Anatomy of Criticism*, p. 37.

17. Henry James, "Preface to *The Aspern Papers*" (originally published in 1909), in *The Art of the Novel: Critical Prefaces by Henry James*, edited by Richard P. Blackmur, (New York: Charles Scribner's Sons, 1962), p. 161.

18. Ibid., pp. 166, 164.

19. Ibid., p. 164.

20. While we may associate large scale in an absolute sense and full scale (1:1) in a relative sense with the high mimetic mode, miniaturization or enlargement—unless exaggerated beyond norms—does not dictate mode. In painting the two genres we associate consistently with full scale are still life and portraiture, both low mimetic, while much twentieth-century painting, although enormous in absolute scale and enlarged in relative scale (as Roy Lichtenstein's work) is ironic. In sculptural form, a diner that presents itself as a giant duck is still low mimetic (Robert Venturi, Denise Scott Brown, Steven Izenour, *Learning from Las Vegas: The Forgotten Symbolism of Architectural Form* [Cambridge: MIT Press, 1977], pp. 87–127).

21. Claude Lévi-Strauss, *The Savage Mind* (Chicago: University of Chicago Press, 1968), pp. 23–24.

22. George Gaylord Simpson, *Principles of Animal Taxonomy* (New York: Columbia University Press, 1961), quoted in Lévi-Strauss, *Savage Mind*, p. 9.

23. Rudolf Arnheim, *The Dynamics of Architectural Form* (Berkeley: University of California Press, 1977), p. 140.

24. Samuel Colman, *Nature's Harmonic Unity: A Treatise on Its Relation to Proportional Form*, edited by C. Arthur Coan (New York: Benjamin Blom, 1971), p. 6.

25. See Henry Glassie, "Folk Art," in *Folklore and Folklife: An Introduction*, edited by Richard Dorson (Chicago: University of Chicago Press, 1972), p. 264.

26. David Park Curry and Patricia Dawes Pierce, *Monument: The Connecticut State Capitol* (Hartford, Conn.: Old State House Association, 1979), pp. 52–73.

27. See Lovell, *Venice*, pp. 51, 77–80, 88.

28. See ibid., pp. 151–52.

29. John Ruskin, *The Stones of Venice*, in *Works* 10:145.

30. James, *Wings of the Dove*, 2:167, 195.

31. Ruskin, *Modern Painters*, in *Works* 7:299.

Chapter 3

1. Frye, *Anatomy of Criticism*, pp. 33–34.

2. Warren Adelson, *John Singer Sargent: His Own Work*, exhibition catalog (New York: Coe Kerr Gallery, 1980), unpaginated; Evan Charteris, *John Sargent* (London: William Heineman, 1927), p. 172; Richard Ormond, *John Singer Sargent: Paintings, Drawings, Watercolors* (New York: Harper & Row, 1970), p. 69.

3. Henry James, "Preface to *The Spoils of Poynton*," in Blackmur, *Art of the Novel*, p. 119.

4. Ibid., p. 129.

5. Ruskin, *Stones of Venice*, in *Works* 9:410–12. Ruskin entitles the three volumes *The Foundations, The Sea-Stories,* and *The Fall.*

6. Ruskin, *Stones of Venice*, in *Works* 9:23.

7. William Dean Howells, *Venetian Life* (London: N. Trübner & Co., 1866), p. 126.

8. See Lovell, *Venice*, pp. 88–89.

9. Other examples include *Over a Balcony, View of the Grand Canal, Venice*, ca. 1890, watercolor on paper, Walters Art Gallery, Baltimore, Maryland, by Francis Hopkinson Smith, and *Venetian Scene*, ca. 1910, oil on canvas, in the Reading Public Museum and Art Gallery, Reading, Pennsylvania, by an unknown artist (see Lovell, *Venice*, pp. 127–28).

10. Ruskin, *Stones of Venice*, in *Works* 9:184.

11. Pilgrim, "Revival of Pastels," pp. 43–62.

12. Ruskin, *Stones of Venice*, in *Works* 9:38; see Lovell, *Venice*, pp. 80–83.

13. The major differences between the unfinished painting and the finished version are (1) the exclusion of the large arches of the Ducal Palace's ground-floor arcade from the finished version, (2) the inclusion of a corner of the prisons in the final version, (3) the movement of the lamppost from its actual position in the unfinished work to a fictional position where it functions as a fulcrum at the peak of the bridge's arch, and (4) a rearrangement of figures including the removal of all adults from the foreground. In general these changes simplify the three-dimensional space portrayed and clarify the two-dimensional picture surface, helping to concentrate our attention on the moving wave of bright umbrellas over the bridge. It has been quite reasonably suggested that Prendergast made use of architectural photographs to construct his images (it is easier to imagine a photographer than a watercolorist perched on the eight-to-ten-foot ladder-platform necessary for many of his views); see Eleanor Green, *Maurice Prendergast: Art of Impulse and Color* (College Park: University of Maryland Art Gallery, 1976), pp. 15, 16.

14. See Lovell, *Venice*, pp. 84–86. A second version, of *Ponte della Paglia* is in the Phillips Gallery, Washington, D.C.

15. Ruskin, *Stones of Venice*, in *Works* 9:17.

16. See Lovell, *Venice*, pp. 42–45.

17. See ibid., pp. 39–41.

18. Andrew Jackson Downing, *The Architecture of Country Houses* (New York: D. Appleton & Co., 1850; reprint, New York: Dover Publications, 1969), p. 263.

19. "Nobody," Ruskin reminds us, "is to be expected to live in the spire" or turret, but it should be fenestrated as though it were habitable (*Stones of Venice* in *Works* 9:402–3.

20. Downing, *Architecture of Country Houses*, pp. 344–45.

21. See Lovell, *Venice*, pp. 136–38, 149.

22. James McNeill Whistler, "Ten O'Clock," lecture 1885, reprinted in *The Gentle Art of Making Enemies* (New York: Dover Publications, 1967), p. 144.

23. Howells, *Venetian Life*, pp. 24–25.

24. Ibid., p. 29.

25. See Lovell, *Venice*, pp. 125–26.

26. The Metropolitan Museum of Art records note that "No. 5, Venetian Canal, John S. Sargent" was written on the backing, "probably in Sargent's own writing." However, this document is not now with the drawing.

27. See Lovell, *Venice*, pp. 130–31, 23–25, 48, 162–63.

28. Howells, *Venetian Life*, p. 27.

29. See Lovell, *Venice*, pp. 60, 124–25, 90–91.

30. Howells, *Venetian Life*, pp. 8, 13–14.

31. One particularly extended example is the incident recorded in Howells, "Some Memorable Places," in *Venetian Life*, pp. 208–21.

32. Ruskin, *Stones of Venice*, in *Works* 9:21.

33. Howells, *Venetian Life*, p. 8.

34. See Lovell, *Venice*, pp. 122–23, 165–66, 147.

35. See ibid., pp. 146.

36. See ibid., pp. 156–57, 166–67, 32–33.

37. Francis Hopkinson Smith, *Gondola Days* (Boston: Houghton Mifflin & Co., 1897), p. 90.

38. See Lovell, *Venice*, pp. 95–99.

39. Smith, *Gondola Days*, p. 184.

40. Karl Baedeker, *Italy: Handbook for Travelers* (Leipzig: Karl Baedeker; New York: Charles Scribner's Sons, 1906), p. 344.

41. See Lovell, *Venice*, pp. 26–28, 49, 102–5.

42. The Curtises hosted both Sargent and Henry James in their expatriate home in the Barbaro Palace pictured here. It is probable that Milly Theale's Palazzo Leporelli in *Wings of the Dove* is based on this grand palace. Ralph W. Curtis, pictured here with his wife, Lisa, in the middle ground, also was a painter and has left us one of the few instances (outside of Prendergast's work) of images of tourists in his *The Gondola* (1884, Isabella Stewart Gardner Museum, Boston). His decision to abandon an artistic career is fictionalized in Edith Wharton's "The Verdict"; see ibid., pp. 107–9.

43. See Lovell, *Venice*, pp. 99–102.

44. Ruskin, *Stones of Venice*, in *Works* 10:326–27.

45. James MacNeill Whistler, *Palace in Rags*, ca. 1880, pictured in *Whistler: The Graphic Work—Amsterdam, Liverpool, London, Venice*, Margaret F. MacDonald (London: Arts Council of Great Britain, 1976), figure 99.

46. Mark Twain [Samuel Clemens], *The Innocents Abroad, or the New Pilgrims' Progress* (Hartford, Conn.: American Publishing Co., 1869), pp. 209, 262, and *passim*.

Chapter 4

1. Frye, *Anatomy of Criticism*, pp. 49–50.

2. See chapter 3, p. 38, n.2; also Green, *Maurice Prendergast*, pp. 16, 18; and *American Impressionist and Realist Paintings and Drawings from the Collection of Mr. and Mrs. Raymond J. Horowitz* (New York: Metropolitan Museum of Art, 1973), p. 44.

3. See Lovell, *Venice*, pp. 80–81, 89–90, 86–87.

4. Frye, *Anatomy of Criticism*, p. 8.

5. See Green, *Maurice Prendergast*, pp. 16, 40, and Ormond, *John Singer Sargent*, p. 71.

6. See Lovell, *Venice*, pp. 119–21.

7. Theodore Reff, ed., *The Notebooks of Edgar Degas:*

A Catalogue of the Thirty-eight Notebooks in the Bibliothèque Nationale and Other Collections, 2 vols. (Oxford: Clarendon Press, 1976), 1:134–35 (Notebook 30, p. 196), vol. 2, n.p. ("on n'a jamais fait encore les monuments / ou les maisons, d'en bas, en dessous, de près / comme on les voit en passant dans les rues"). See also Linda Nochlin, *Realism* (New York: Penguin Books, 1971), p. 19.

8. Ruskin asserts early in *The Stones of Venice* that his purpose in writing the work is as much a wish to destroy the reputation of the Renaissance as to celebrate the achievement of Venetian Gothic builders: "Now Venice, as she was once the most religious, was in her fall the most corrupt, of European states; and as she was in her strength the centre of the pure currents of Christian architecture, so she is in her decline the source of the Renaissance. . . . It is in Venice, therefore, and in Venice only, that effectual blows can be struck at this pestilent art of the Renaissance. Destroy its claims to admiration there, and it can assert them nowhere else. This, therefore, will be the final purpose of the following essay"; *Works* 9:46–47.

9. Ruskin, *Stones of Venice*, in *Works* 10:271.

10. See Lovell, *Venice*, pp. 108–11.

11. The fourteenth-century structure collapsed in 1902; rebuilding commenced in 1905, and the facsimile Campanile we see today was completed in 1912. The absence from these views confirms their dating to the first decade of the twentieth century. The 1913 painting is pictured in *John Singer Sargent,* Adelson, unpaginated, entry no. 57.

12. Ormond, *John Singer Sargent*, p. 75.

13. Frye, *Anatomy of Criticism*, p. 61. The examples that he cites are T. S. Eliot's *The Waste Land* (1922) and Ezra Pound's *Cantos* (1917–25).

14. Frye, *Anatomy of Criticism*, p. 61.

15. See Lovell, *Venice*, p. 117.

16. See ibid., p. 117–18.

17. See ibid., p. 116.

18. See ibid., pp. 115–16.

19. See ibid., pp. 112–14, 58.

20. The only permanent high point from which this view is possible is the roof of the customs building, but that is 175 feet away, and details that Sargent includes are not visible from that distance. More logically the view is excerpted from a photograph (Sargent is known to have worked from photographs; see Ormond, *John Singer Sargent*, p. 71) or drawn from a movable platform.

21. James, "Preface to *The Ambassadors*," in Blackmur, *Art of the Novel*, p. 312.

Chapter 5

1. Thomas Brendle Brumbaugh, "A Venice Letter from Thomas P. Rossiter to John F. Kensett—1843," *American Art Journal* 5 (May 1973): 74–78.

2. Lord Byron, *Childe Harold's Pilgrimage*, canto 2, stanza 88.

SELECTED BIBLIOGRAPHY

Adelson, Warren. *John Singer Sargent: His Own Work.* New York: Coe Kerr Gallery, 1980.

American Impressionist and Realist Paintings and Drawings from the Collection of Mr. and Mrs. Raymond J. Horowitz. New York: Metropolitan Museum of Art, 1973.

Americans at Home and Abroad, 1870–1920. Houston: Meredith Long & Co., 1971.

Americans in Venice: 1879–1913. New York: Coe Kerr Gallery, 1983.

Arnheim, Rudolf. *The Dynamics of Architectural Form.* Berkeley: University of California Press, 1977.

Ashbery, John. "The Indian Summer of Frank Duveneck." *Artnews* 71, no. 2 (April 1972): 27–29, 69–71.

Bacher, Otto Henry. *With Whistler in Venice.* New York: Century Co., 1908.

Baedeker, Karl. *Italy: Handbook for Travelers, First Part: Northern Italy.* Leipzig: Karl Baedeker; New York: Charles Scribner's Sons, 1906.

Blackmur, Richard P., ed. *The Art of the Novel: Critical Prefaces by Henry James.* New York: Charles Scribner's Sons, 1962. First published in 1934.

Bloom, Harold. *The Anxiety of Influence: A Theory of Poetry.* New York: Oxford University Press, 1973.

Bloom, Harold, ed. *Romanticism and Consciousness: Essays in Criticism.* New York: W.W. Norton & Co., 1970.

Boorstin, Daniel Joseph. *America and the Image of Europe: Reflections on American Thought.* New York: Meridian Books, 1966.

Bowers, David F. *Foreign Influences in American Life: Essays and Critical Bibliographies.* Edited for the Princeton Program of Study in American Civilization. Princeton, N.J.: Princeton University Press, 1944.

Braff, Phyllis. *Thomas Moran: A Search for the Scenic.* East Hampton, N.Y.: Guildhall Museum, 1980.

Breuning, Margaret. *Maurice Prendergast.* New York: Whitney Museum of American Art, 1931.

Brooks, Van Wyck. *The Dream of Arcadia: American Artists and Writers in Italy, 1760–1915.* New York: E.P. Dutton, 1958.

———. "Anecdotes of Maurice Prendergast." *Magazine of Art,* October 1938.

Brumbaugh, Thomas Brendle. "A Venice Letter from Thomas P. Rossiter to John F. Kensett—1843." *American Art Journal* 5 (May 1973): 74–78.

Byron, George Gordon [Lord]. "Childe Harold's Pilgrimage." In *Byron.* Edited by Jerome J. McGann. Oxford: Oxford University Press, 1986.

———. *Marino Faliero, Doge of Venice: An Historical Tragedy, in Five Acts.* London: John Murray, 1821.

———. *The Two Foscari: An Historical Tragedy.* New York: W. B. Gilley, 1822.

Carter, Morris. *Isabella Stewart Gardner and Fenway Court.* Boston and New York: Houghton Mifflin Co., 1925. Reprinted, Freeport, N.Y.: Books for Libraries Press, 1972.

Charteris, Evan. *John Sargent.* London: William Heinemann, 1927.

Cikovsky, Nicolai, Jr. *George Inness.* New York: Praeger Publishers, 1971.

Clement, Clara Erskine, and Laurence Hutton. *Artists of the Nineteenth Century and Their Works.* 2 vols. Boston: Houghton Mifflin Co., 1884.

Cohn, Marjorie B. *Wash and Gouache: A Study of the Development of the Materials of Watercolor.* Cambridge, Mass.: Fogg Art Museum, 1977.

Coke, Van Deren. *The Painter and the Photograph from Delacroix to Warhol.* Albuquerque, N.M.: University of New Mexico Press, 1972.

Colman, Samuel. *Nature's Harmonic Unity: A Treatise on Its Relation to Proportional Form.* Edited by C. Arthur Coan. New York: Benjamin Blom, 1971.

Colman, Samuel, and Arthur Coan. *Proportional Form: Further Studies in the Science of Beauty.* New York and London: G. P. Putnam's Sons, 1920.

Cooper, James Fenimore. *The Bravo: A Venetian Story.* London: H. Colburn & R. Bentley, 1831.

———. *Excursions in Italy.* 2 vols. London: Richard Bentley, 1838.

Craven, Wayne. "Samuel Colman (1832–1920): Rediscovered Painter of Far-Away Places." *American Art Journal* 8 (May 1976): 16–37.

Curry, David Park. *James McNeill Whistler at the Freer Gallery of Art.* Washington, D.C.: Freer Gallery of Art, Smithsonian Institution; New York: W. W. Norton, 1984.

Curry, David Park, and Patricia Dawes Pierce. *Monument: The Connecticut State Capitol.* Hartford, Conn.: Old State House Association, 1979.

Dodgson, Campbell. *The Etchings of James McNeill Whistler.* Edited by Geoffrey Holme. London: Studio, 1922.

Downing, Andrew Jackson. *The Architecture of Country Houses Including Designs for Cottages, Farmhouses, and Villas, with Remarks on Interiors, Furniture, and the Best Modes of Warming and Ventilating.* New York: D. Appleton & Co., 1850. Reprinted, New York: Dover Publications, 1969.

Edel, Leon. *Henry James.* 4 vols. Philadelphia: Lippincott, 1953–69.

Edel, Leon, ed. *Henry James Letters.* Cambridge, Mass.: Belknap Press of Harvard University Press, 1975.

Eldredge, Charles C. *The Arcadian Landscape: Nineteenth-Century American Painters in Italy.* Lawrence: University of Kansas Museum of Art, 1972.

Feidelson, Charles. "James and the 'Man of Imagination.' " In *Literary Theory and Structure: Essays in Honor of William K. Wimsatt.* Edited by Frank Brady, John Palmer, and Martin Price. Pp. 331–52. New Haven, Conn.: Yale University Press, 1973.

Fernandez, Rafael. *A Scene of Light and Glory: Approaches to Venice.* Williamstown, Mass.: Sterling and Francine Clark Art Institute, 1982.

Ferriday, Peter. "Professor Moore, 1840–1930." *Architectural Review* 127, no. 758 (April 1960): 271–72.

Fine, Ruth. *Drawing Near: Whistler Etchings from the Zelman Collection.* Los Angeles: Los Angeles County Museum of Art, 1984.

Fink, Lois. "American Artists in France, 1850–1870." *American Art Journal* 5 (Novembr 1973): 32–49.

Foster, Kathleen A. "American Drawings, Watercolors, and Prints." *Metropolitan Museum of Art Bulletin* 37, no. 4 (Spring 1980): 2–5.

From Realism to Symbolism: Whistler and His World. New York: Columbia University and the Philadelphia Museum, 1971.

Frye, Northrop. *Anatomy of Criticism: Four Essays.* Princeton, N.J.: Princeton University Press, 1957.

Gerdts, William H. "The Square Format and Proto-Modernism in American Painting." *Arts Magazine* 50, no. 10 (June 1976): 70–75.

Getscher, Robert Harold. *The Stamp of Whistler.* Oberlin, Ohio: Allen Memorial Art Gallery, 1977.

———. "James McNeill Whistler's Views of Venice." Ph.D. diss., Case Western Reserve University, 1970.

Glassie, Henry. "Folk Art." In *Folklore and Folklife: An Introduction.* Edited by Richard Dorson. Pp. 253–80. Chicago: University of Chicago Press, 1972.

Gombrich, Ernst Hans Josef. *Art and Illusion: A Study in the Psychology of Pictorial Representation.* Princeton, N.J.: Princeton University Press, 1960.

Green, Eleanor. *Maurice Prendergast: Art of Impulse and Color.* College Park: University of Maryland Art Gallery, 1976.

Hale, J. R., ed. *Renaissance Venice.* London: Faber & Faber, 1974 [first published 1973].

Hardie, Martin. *John Singer Sargent.* London: Studio; New York: W. E. Rudge, 1930.

———. *Water-Colour Painting in Britain.* Vol. 3, *The Victorian Period.* Edited by Dudley Snelgrove with Jonathan Mayne and Basil Taylor. London: B. T. Batsford, 1968.

Hawthorne, Nathaniel. *Passages from the French and Italian Notebooks.* London: Strahan & Co., 1871.

Hazlitt, William Carew. *The Venetian Republic: Its Rise, Its Growth, and Its Fall, 409–1797.* 2 vols. London: Adam & Charles Black, 1915.

Heller, Nancy, and Julia Williams. "Albert Bierstadt: The American Wilderness." *American Artist* 40 (January 1976): 52–57, 96–97, 102.

Hendricks, Gordon. "Bierstadt's *The Domes of the Yosemite.*" *American Art Journal* 3 (Fall 1971): 23–31.

Hills, Patricia. *John Singer Sargent.* New York: Whitney Museum of American Art, 1986.

———. *Turn-of-the-Century America: Paintings, Graphics, Photographs, 1890–1910.* New York: Whitney Museum of American Art, 1977.

Hoopes, Donelson F. *American Watercolor Painting.* New York: Watson-Guptill, 1977.

Howells, William Dean. *Venetian Life.* London: N. Trübner & Co., 1866.

Inness, George, Jr. *Life, Art, and Letters of George Inness.* New York: Century Co., 1917.

James, Henry. *The Aspern Papers.* London and New York: Macmillan & Co., 1888.

———. *Italian Hours.* Boston and New York: Houghton Mifflin Co., 1909.

———. "John Singer Sargent." *Harper's New Monthly Magazine,* 75, no. 449 (October 1887): 683–91.

———. *Picture and Text.* New York: Harper & Bros., 1893.

———. *William Wetmore Story and His Friends: From Letters, Diaries, and Recollections.* Boston: Houghton Mifflin & Co., 1903.

———. *The Wings of the Dove.* 2 vols. New York: Charles Scribner's Sons, 1902.

Kagle, Steven E. *America: Exploration and Travel.* Bowling Green, Ohio: Bowling Green State University Popular Press, 1979.

Kennedy, Edward Guthrie. *The Etched Work of James McNeill Whistler.* New York: Grolier Club of the City of New York, 1910.

Kubler, George. *The Shape of Time: Remarks on the History of Things.* New Haven, Conn.: Yale University Press, 1962.

Lévi-Strauss, Claude. *The Savage Mind.* Chicago: University of Chicago Press, 1968.

———. *Structural Anthropology.* Translated by Claire Jacobson and Brooke Grundfest Schoepf. New York: Basic Books, 1963.

Lewis, R. W. B. *The American Adam: Innocence, Tragedy, and Tradition in the Nineteenth Century.* Chicago: University of Chicago Press, 1955.

———. *Edith Wharton: A Biography.* New York: Harper & Row, 1975.

Lindquist-Cock, Elizabeth. "Stereoscopic Photography and the Western Paintings of Albert Bierstadt." *Art Quarterly* 33, no. 4 (Winter 1970): 360–78.

Links, J. G. *Canaletto and His Patrons.* New York: New York University Press, 1977.

Long, Orle William. *Literary Pioneers: Early American Explorers of European Culture.* Cambridge, Mass.: Harvard University Press, 1935.

Lovell, Margaretta M. *Venice: The American View, 1860–1920.* San Francisco: Fine Arts Museums of San Francisco, 1984.

MacDonald, Margaret F. *Whistler: The Graphic Work—Amsterdam, Liverpool, London, Venice.* London: Arts Council of Great Britain, 1976.

Menpes, Mortimer. *Whistler as I Knew Him.* London: A. & C. Black, 1904.

Moore, Charles Herbert. *Development and Character of Gothic Architecture.* London and New York: Macmillan & Co., 1890.

Morris, Richard Samuel. *American Artists in Europe, 1800–1900.* Liverpool: Walker Art Gallery, 1976.

Mount, Charles Merrill. *John Singer Sargent.* London: Cresset Press, 1957.

Mukařovský, Jan. "The Essence of the Visual Arts." In *The Semiotics of Art: Prague School Contributions.* Edited by Ladislav Matejka and Irwin R. Titunik. Pp. 229–44. Cambridge, Mass.: MIT Press, 1976.

Nochlin, Linda. *Realism.* New York and Baltimore: Penguin Books, 1971.

Norton, Charles Eliot. *Notes of Travel and Study in Italy.* Boston: Ticknor & Fields, 1860.

Ormond, Richard. *John Singer Sargent: Paintings, Drawings, Watercolors.* New York: Harper & Row, 1970.

Owens, Gwendolyn. *Watercolors by Maurice Prendergast from New England Collections.* Williamstown, Mass.: Sterling and Francine Clark Art Institute, 1978.

Pavanello, Giuseppe, and Giandomenico Romanelli, eds. *Venezia nell'Ottocento: Immagini e Mito.* Milan: Electa, 1983.

Pennell, Joseph, and Elizabeth Robins Pennell. *The Life of James McNeill Whistler.* London: W. Heinemann; Philadelphia: J. B. Lippincott Co., 1908.

Pilgrim, Dianne Hauserman. "The Revival of Pastels in Nineteenth-Century America: The Society of Painters in Pastel." *American Art Journal* 10 (November 1978): 43–62.

Pisano, Ronald G. *A Leading Spirit in American Art: William Merritt Chase.* Seattle: Henry Art Gallery, University of Washington, 1983.

———. *William Merritt Chase.* New York: Watson-Guptill, 1979.

Pocock, Douglas Charles David, and Ray Hudson. *Images of the Urban Environment.* New York: Columbia University Press, 1978.

The Prendergasts: Retrospective Exhibition of the Work of Maurice and Charles Prendergast. Andover, Mass.: Addison Gallery of American Art, Phillips Academy, 1938.

Queen of Marble and Mud: The Anglo-American Vision of Venice, 1880–1910. Nottingham, England: Nottingham University Art Gallery, 1978.

Quick, Michael. *American Expatriate Painters of the Late Nineteenth Century.* Dayton, Ohio: Dayton Art Institute, 1976.

Ratcliff, Carter. *John Singer Sargent.* New York: Abbeville Press, 1982.

Reff, Theodore, ed. *The Notebooks of Edgar Degas: A Catalogue of the Thirty-eight Notebooks in the Bibliothèque Nationale and Other Collections.* 2 vols. Oxford: Clarendon Press, 1976.

Rhys, Hedley Howell, *Maurice Prendergast, 1859–1924.* Cambridge, Mass.: Harvard University Press, 1960.

Robert Blum Retrospective. Cincinnati, Ohio: Cincinnati Art Museum, 1966.

Ross, Denman Waldo. *On Drawing and Painting.* Boston and New York: Houghton Mifflin Co., 1912.

———. *A Theory of Pure Design, Harmony, Balance, Rhythm.* Boston and New York: Houghton Mifflin & Co., 1907.

Ruskin, John. *Modern Painters.* 5 vols. In *The Works of John Ruskin.* Edited by E. T. Cook and Alexander Wedderburn. 39 vols. London: George Allen; New York: Longmans, Green & Co., 1903.

———. *Praeterita: Outlines of Scenes and Thoughts Perhaps Worthy of Memory in My Past Life.* In *The Works of John Ruskin.* Edited by E. T. Cook and Alexander Wedderburn. 39 vols. London: George Allen; New York: Longmans, Green & Co., 1903.

———. *The Stones of Venice.* 3 vols. In *The Works of John Ruskin.* Edited by E. T. Cook and Alexander Wedderburn. 39 vols. London: George Allen; New York: Longmans, Green & Co., 1903.

Salomone, A. William. "The Nineteenth-Century Discovery of Italy: An Essay in American Cultural History—Prolegomena to a Historiographical Problem." *American Historical Review* 73 (June 1968): 1359–91.

Sanford, Charles. *The Quest for Paradise: Europe and the American Moral Imagination.* Urbana: University of Illinois Press, 1961.

Sill, Gertrude Grace. "Americans Abroad." *Portfolio* 5 (March–April 1983): 68–77.

Sims, Patterson. *Maurcie B. Prendergast: A Concentration of Works from the Permanent Collection.* New York: Whitney Museum of American Art, 1980.

Skalet, Linda Henefield. "The Market for American Painting in New York: 1870–1915." Ph.D. diss., Johns Hopkins University, 1980.

Slater, Joseph, Alfred R. Ferguson, and Jean Ferguson Carr, eds. *The Collected Essays of Ralph Waldo Emerson.* Cambridge, Mass.: Belknap Press of Harvard University Press, 1983.

Smith, Francis Hopkinson. *Gondola Days.* Boston and New York: Houghton Mifflin & Co., 1897.

Smith, Henry Nash. *Virgin Land: The American West as Symbol and Myth.* Cambridge, Mass.: Harvard University Press, 1950.

Soria, Regina. *Dictionary of Nineteenth-Century American Artists in Italy, 1760–1914.* Rutherford, N.J.: Fairleigh Dickinson University Press, 1982.

Stebbins, Theodore E., Jr. *American Master Drawings and Watercolors: A History of Works on Paper from Colonial Times to the Present.* New York: Harper & Row, 1976.

Strout, Cushing. *The American Image of the Old World.* New York: Harper & Row, 1963.

Sutton, Denys. *James McNeill Whistler: Paintings, Etchings, Pastels, and Watercolors.* London: Phaidon Press, 1966.

Sweet, Frederick Arnold. *Sargent, Whistler, and Mary Cassatt.* Chicago: Art Institute of Chicago, 1954.

Thomas Moran, 1837–1926. Riverside: University of California, 1963.

Twain, Mark. *The Innocents Abroad; or The New Pilgrims' Progress.* Hartford, Conn.: American Publishing Co., 1869.

Venice Rediscovered: A Loan Exhibition in Aid of the Venice in Peril Fund, 8th November–15th December, 1972. London: Wildenstein, 1972.

Watson, Wendy M. *Images of Italy: Photography in the Nineteenth Century.* South Hadley, Mass.: Mount Holyoke College Art Museum, 1980.

Weintraub, Stanley. *Whistler: A Biography.* New York: Weybright & Talley, 1974.

Weiss, Ila. *Sanford Robinson Gifford.* New York: Garland Publishing, 1977.

Wharton, Edith. "A Venetian Night's Entertainment." *Scribner's Magazine* 34 (December 1903): 640–51. Reprinted in *The Collected Short Stories of Edith Wharton.* Edited by R. W. B. Lewis. New York: Charles Scribner's Sons, 1968.

Whistler, James McNeill. *The Gentle Art of Making Enemies.* New York: Dover Publications, 1967. First published in 1890.

White, Norval, and Elliot Willensky. *AIA Guide to New York City.* New York: Collier Macmillan, 1978.

Wilde, Johannes. *Venetian Art from Bellini to Titian.* Oxford: Clarendon Press, 1974.

Wilkins, Thurman. *Thomas Moran, Artist of the Mountains.* Norman: University of Oklahoma Press, 1966.

Wilmerding, John. *Robert Salmon: Painter of Ship and Shore.* Salem, Mass.: Peabody Museum of Salem, 1971.

Wissman, Fronia. "Sargent's Watercolor Views of Santa Maria della Salute." *Yale University Art Gallery Bulletin* 37, no. 2 (Summer 1979): 14–19.

Wölfflin, Heinrich. *Principles of Art History: The Problem of the Development of Style in Later Art.* Translated by M. D. Hottinger. N.p.: Dover Publications, n.d.

Young, Andrew McLaren, Margaret F. MacDonald, and Robin Spencer. *The Paintings of James McNeill Whistler.* 2 vols. New Haven, Conn.: Yale University Press, 1980.

INDEX

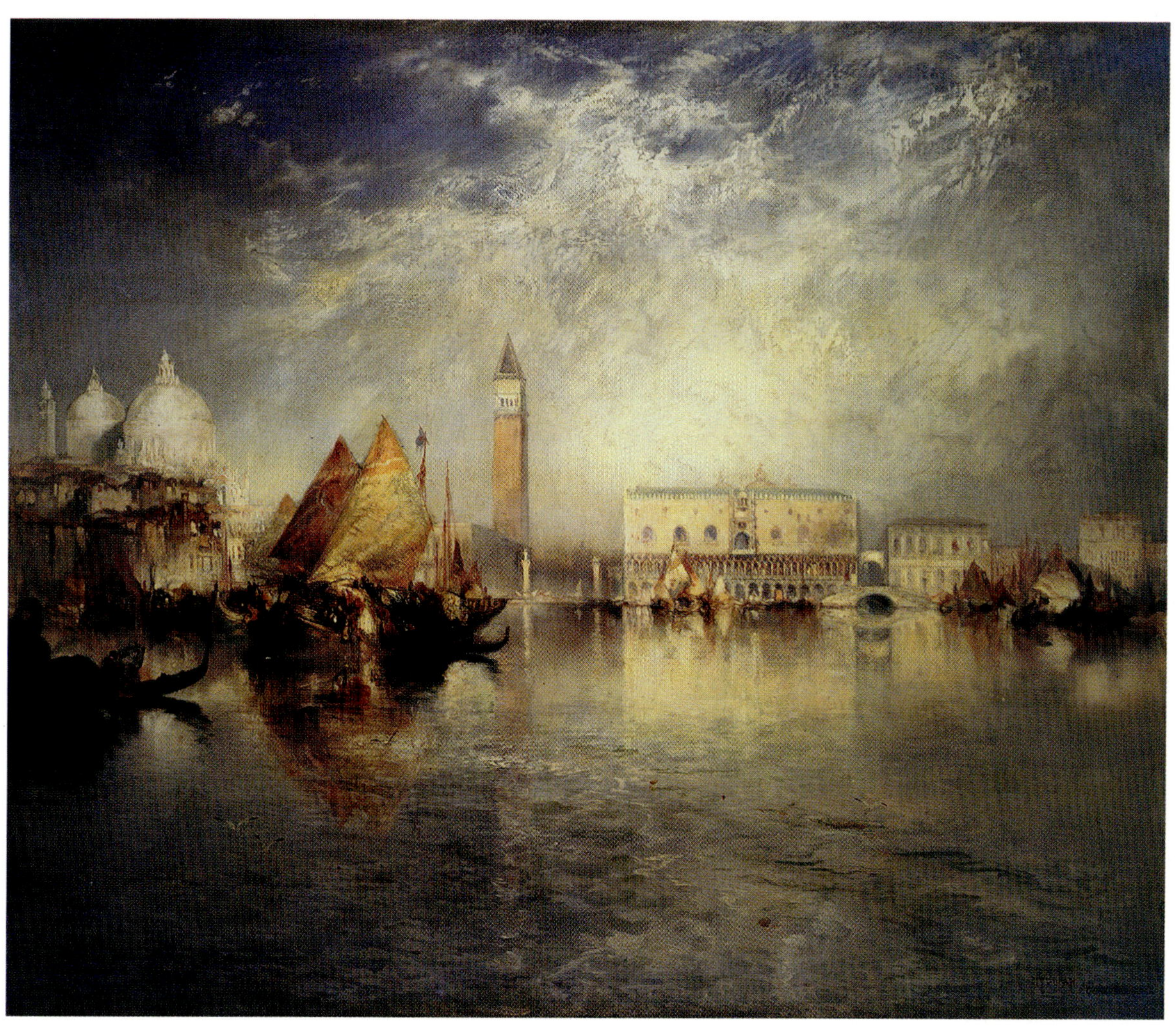

Pl. 1. Thomas Moran, *Splendor of Venice*, 1889, oil on canvas, 25¾″ × 29⅞″, Philbrook Art Center, Tulsa.

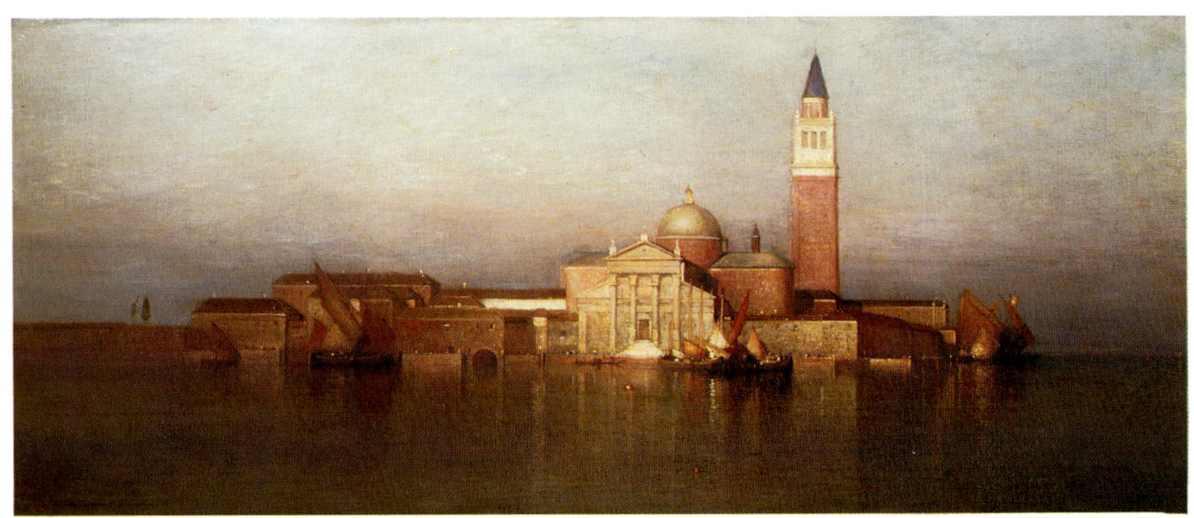

Pl. 2. Samuel Colman, *San Giorgio Maggiore*, 1902, oil on canvas, 31½ ″ × 72″, private collection; see also fig. 37.

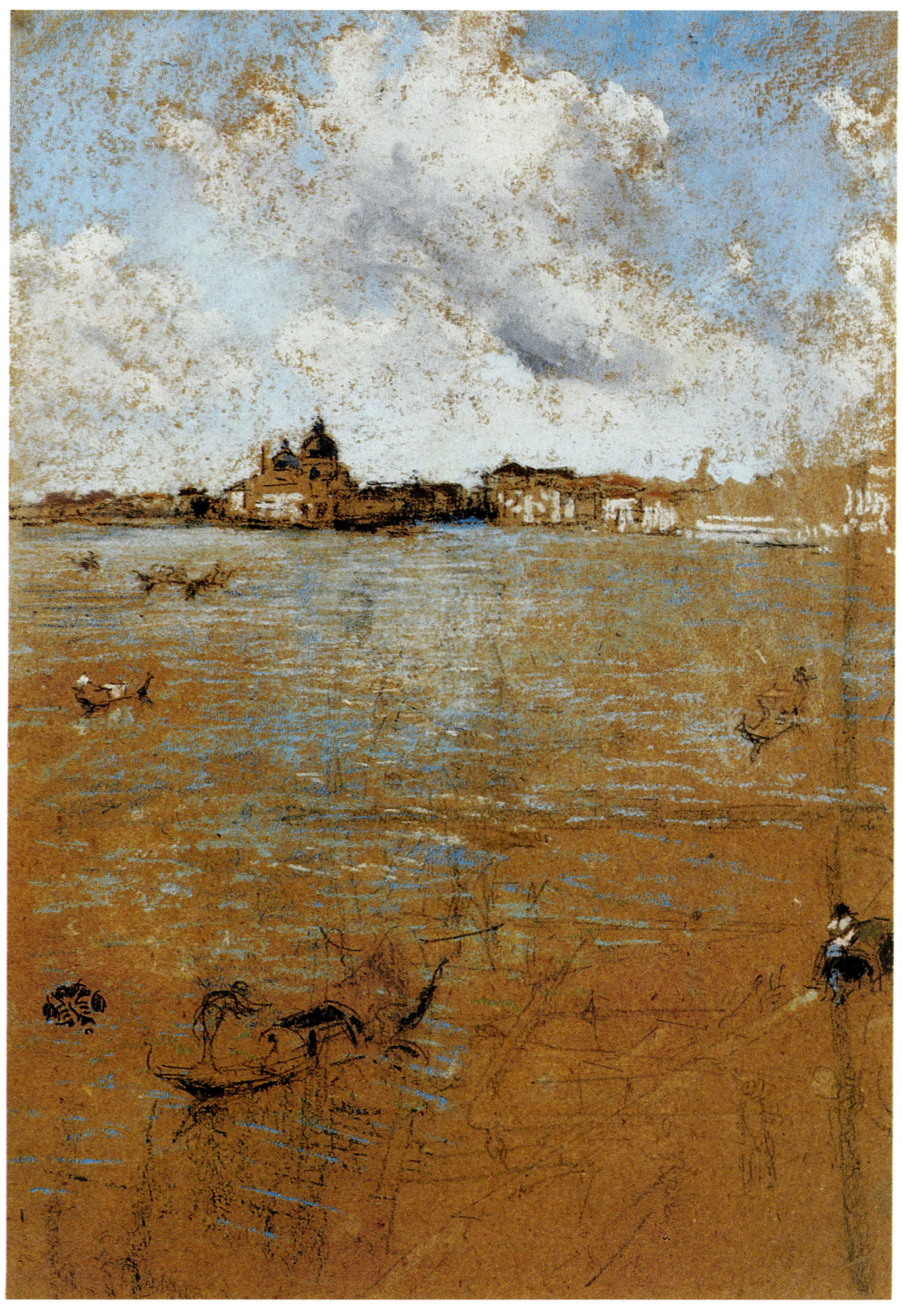

Pl. 3. James McNeill Whistler, *Venetian Scene*, ca. 1880, pastel and charcoal on brown paper, 11″ × 7½″, New Britain Museum of American Art, Harriet Russell Stanley Fund.

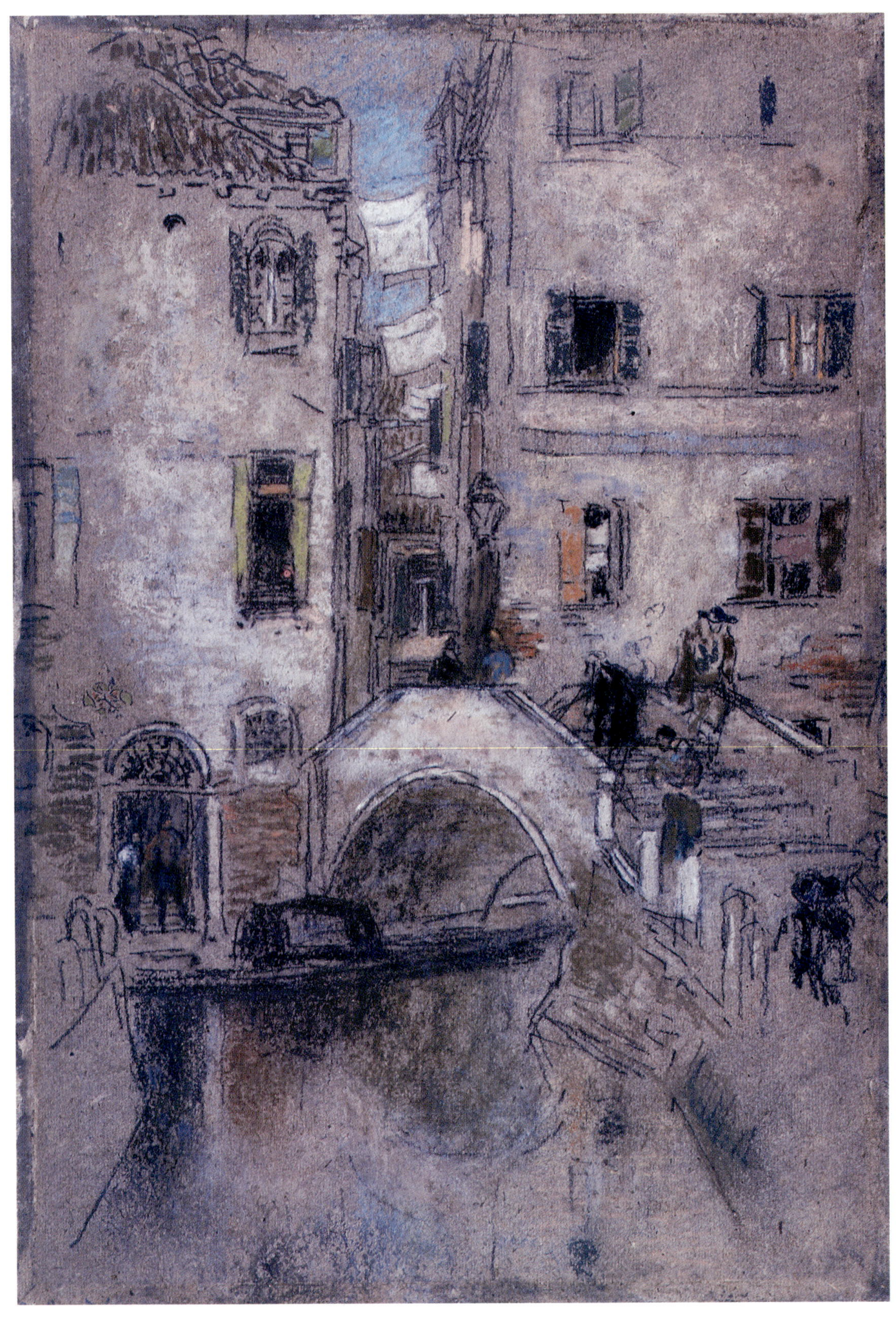

Pl. 4. James McNeill Whistler, *A Side Canal in Venice*, 1880, pastel and charcoal on brown paper, 11¼″ × 7⅝″, Burrell Collection, Glasgow Art Gallery and Museum.

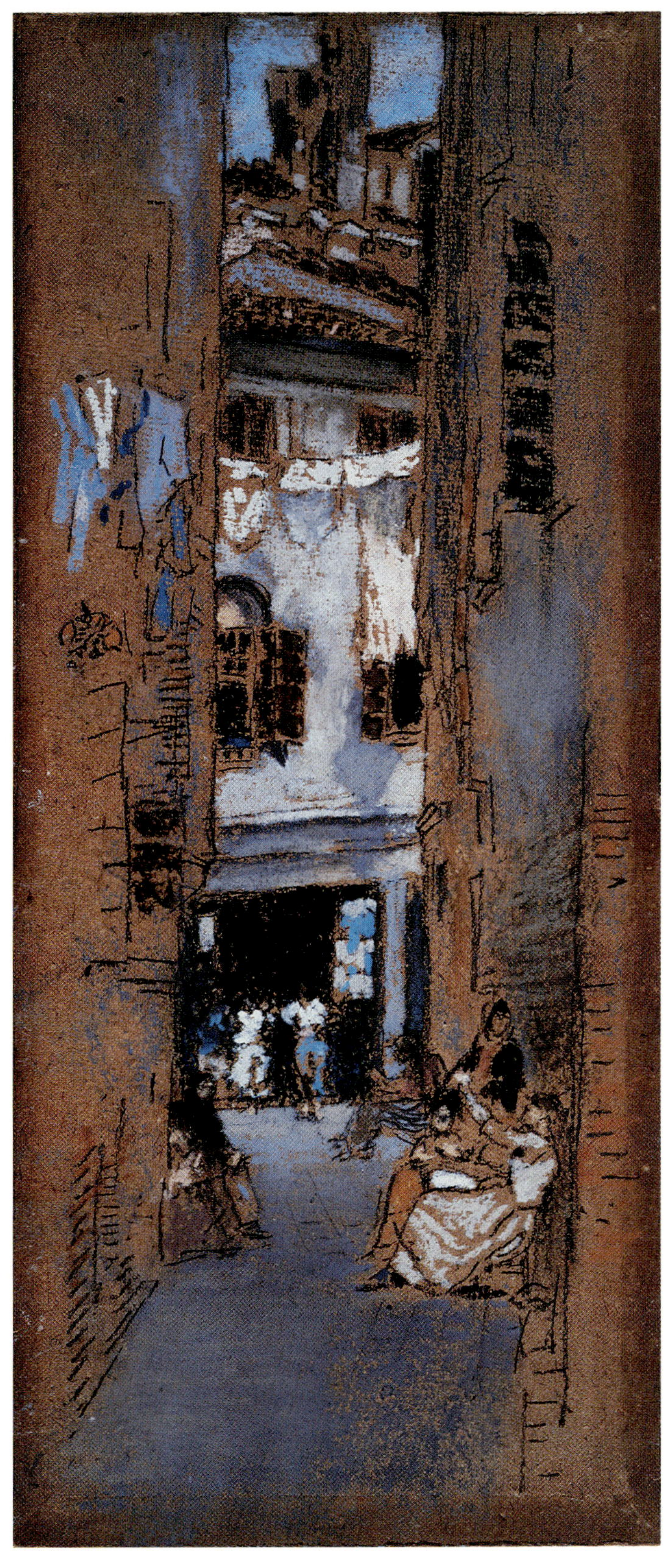

Pl. 5. James McNeill Whistler, *Bead-stringers, Venice*, 1879/80, crayon and pastel on golden-brown paper, 10⅞″ × 4⅝″, Freer Gallery of Art, Smithsonian Institution, Washington, D.C. (Acc. no. 05.124).

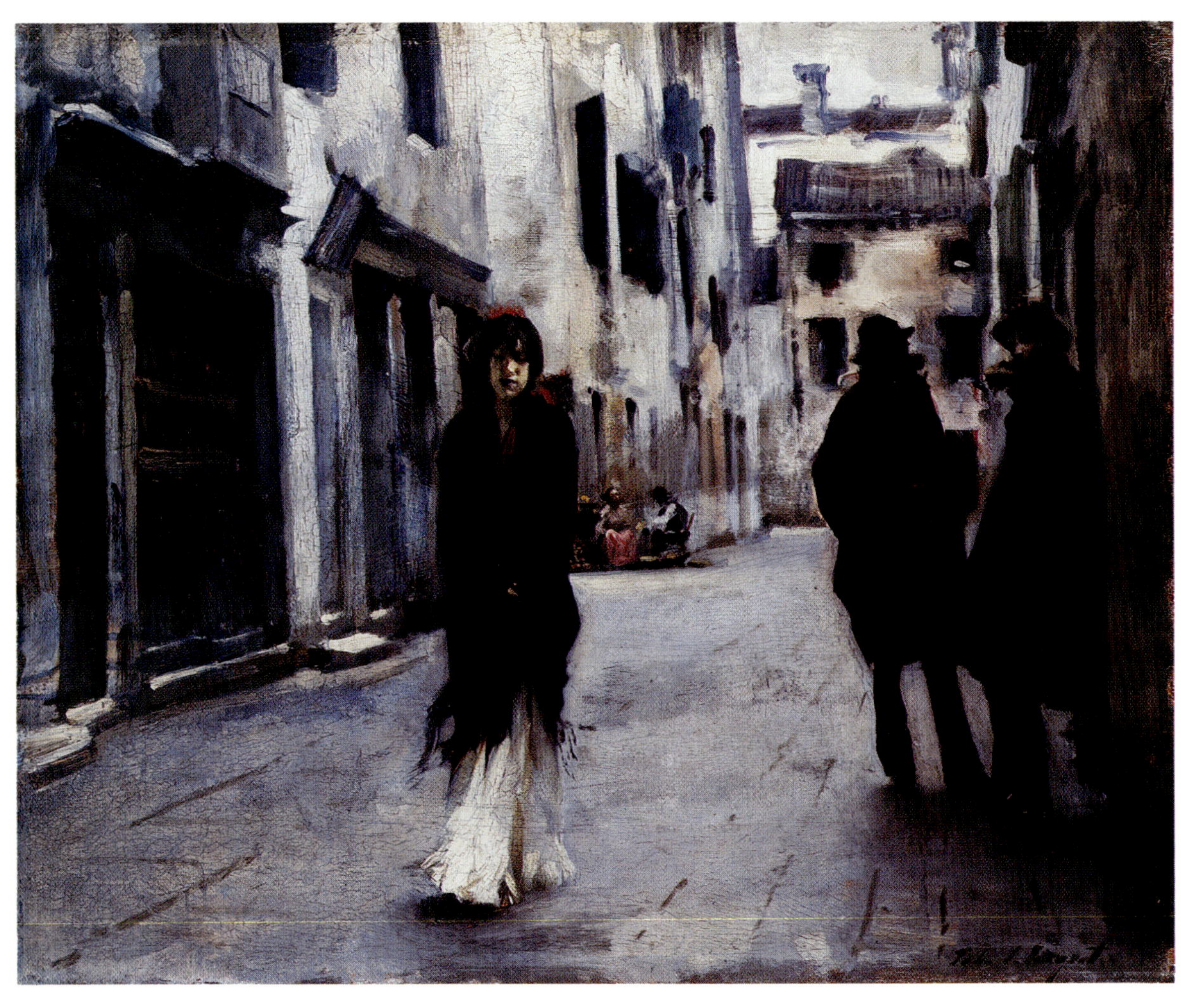

Pl. 6. John Singer Sargent, *A Street in Venice*, ca. 1882, oil on panel, 17¾″ × 21¼″, National Gallery of Art, Gift of the Avalon Foundation.

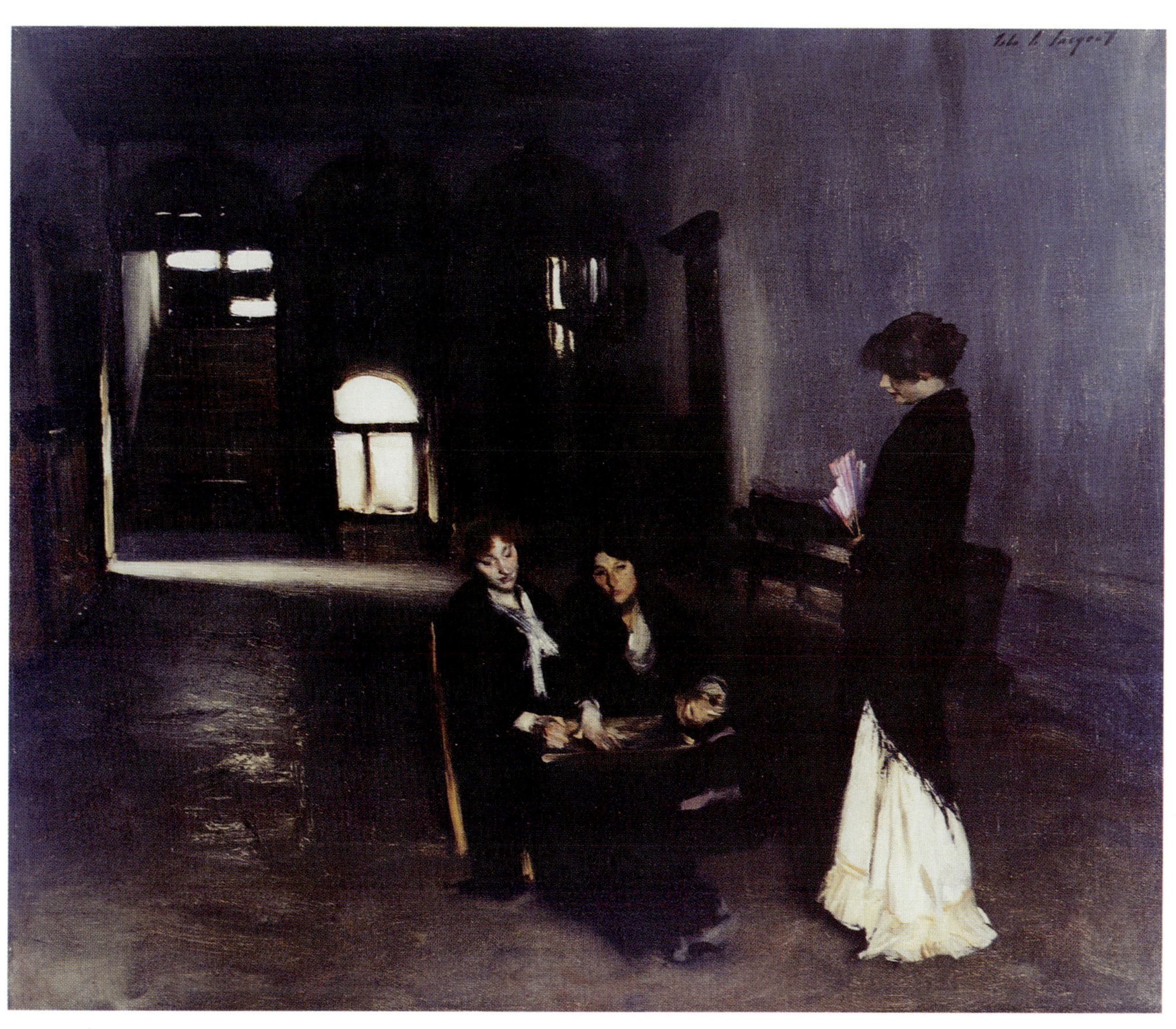

Pl. 7. John Singer Sargent, *Venetian Bead Stringers*, 1880 or 1882, oil on canvas, $26\frac{3}{8}'' \times 30\frac{3}{4}''$, Albright-Knox Art Gallery, Buffalo, New York; Friends of the Albright Art Gallery Fund, 1916.

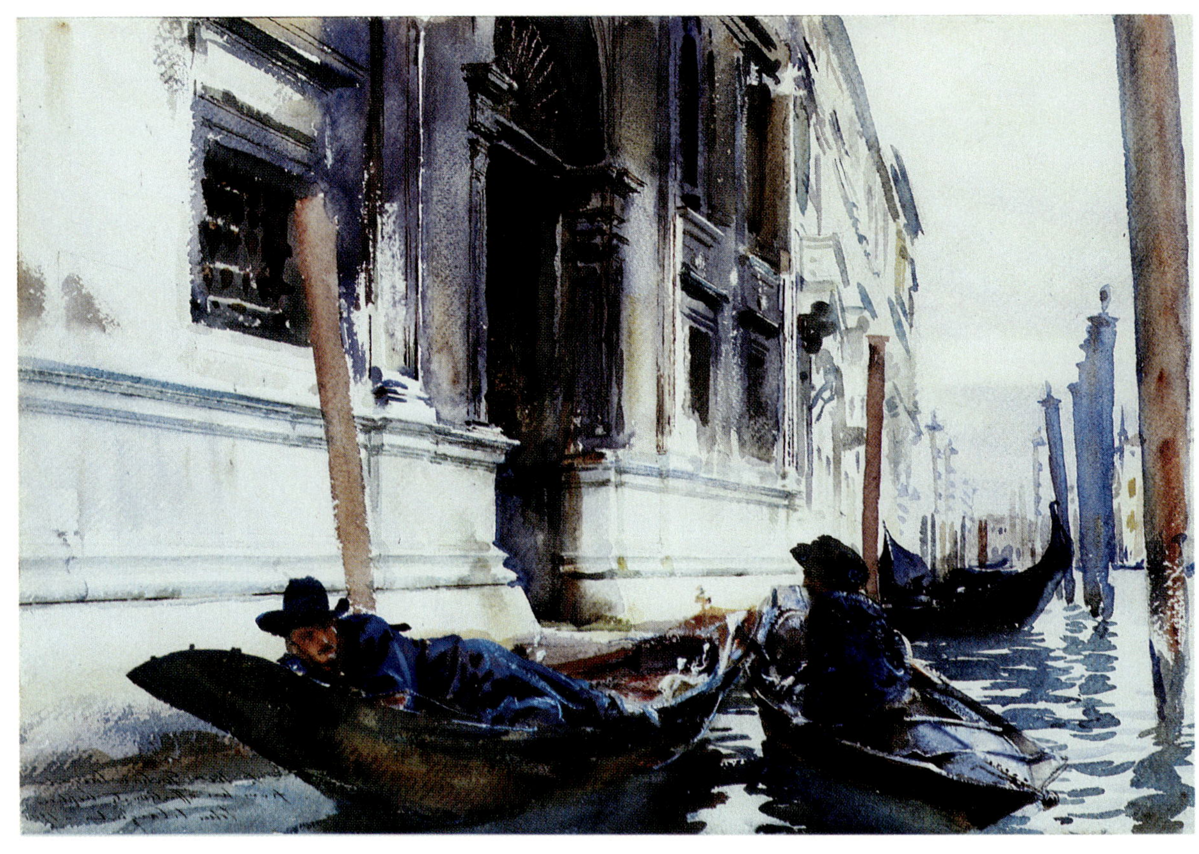

Pl. 8. John Singer Sargent, *Gondolier's Siesta*, 1905, watercolor, 14″ × 20″, Collection of Mr. and Mrs. Raymond J. Horowitz.

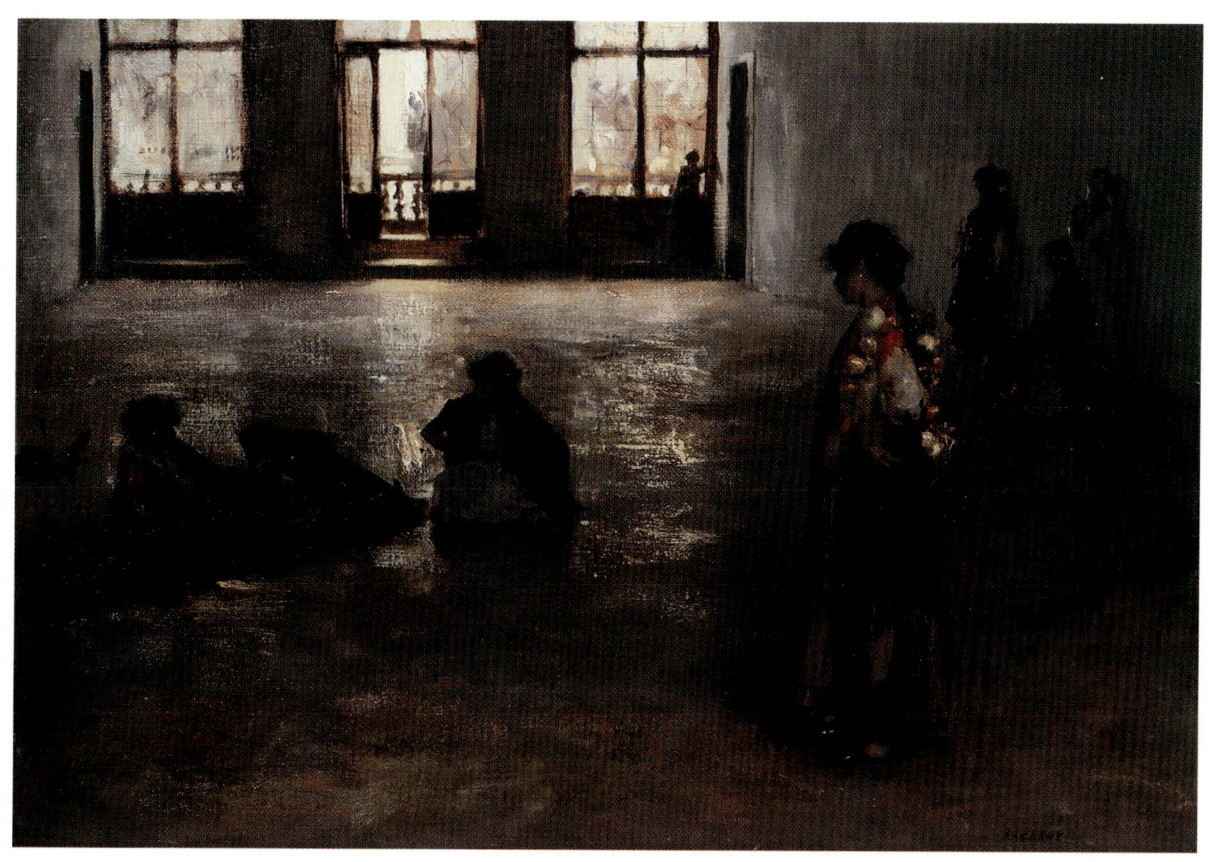

Pl. 9. John Singer Sargent, *Venetian Women in the Palazzo Rezzonico*, ca. 1880, oil on canvas, 17¾″ × 25″, Peter G. Terian.

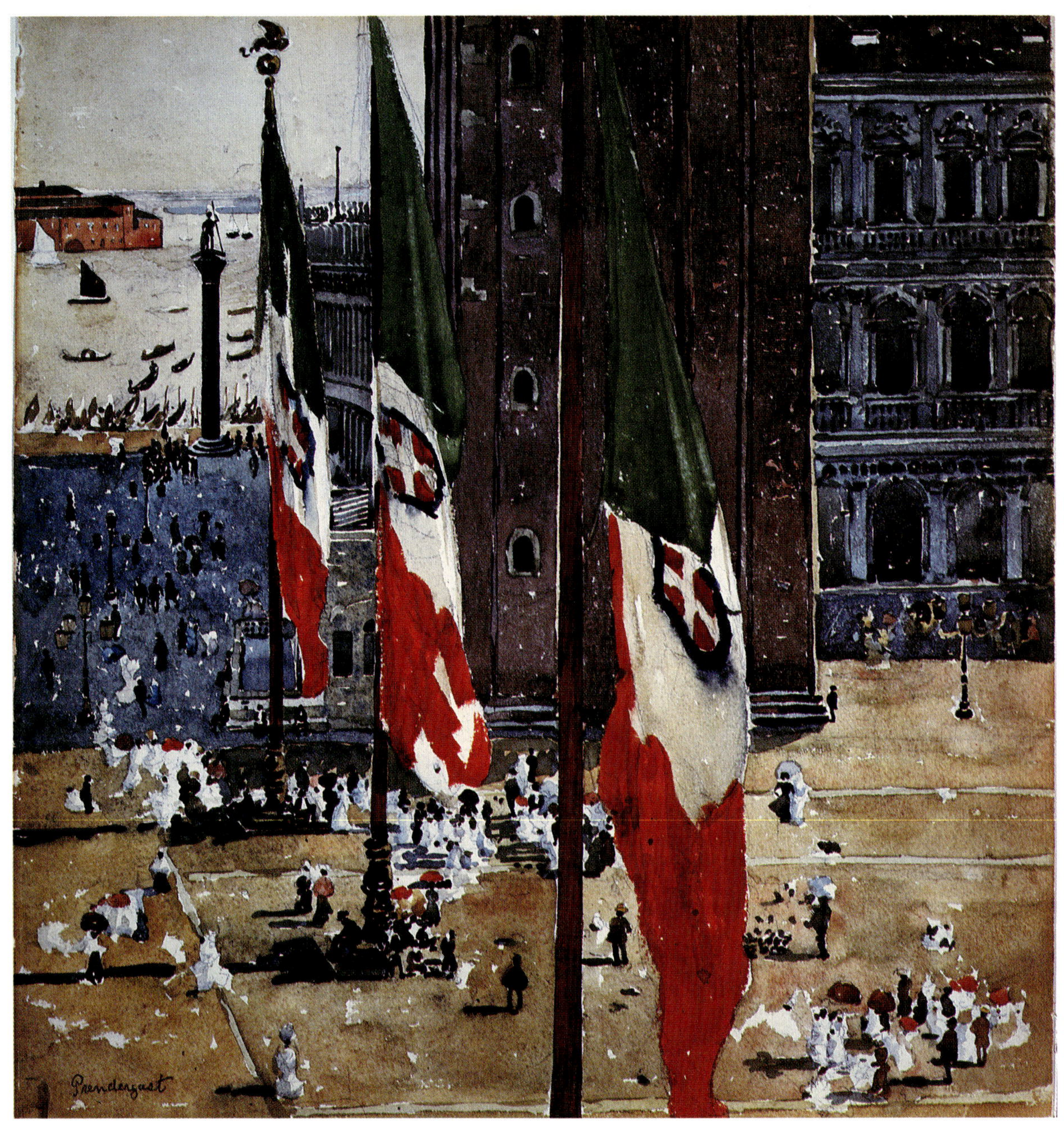

Pl. 10. Maurice Prendergast, *Piazza di San Marco*, 1898– 99, watercolor, 16$\frac{1}{8}$″ × 15″, Metropolitan Museum of Art, Gift of the Estate of Mrs. Edward Robinson, 1952; see also fig. 97.

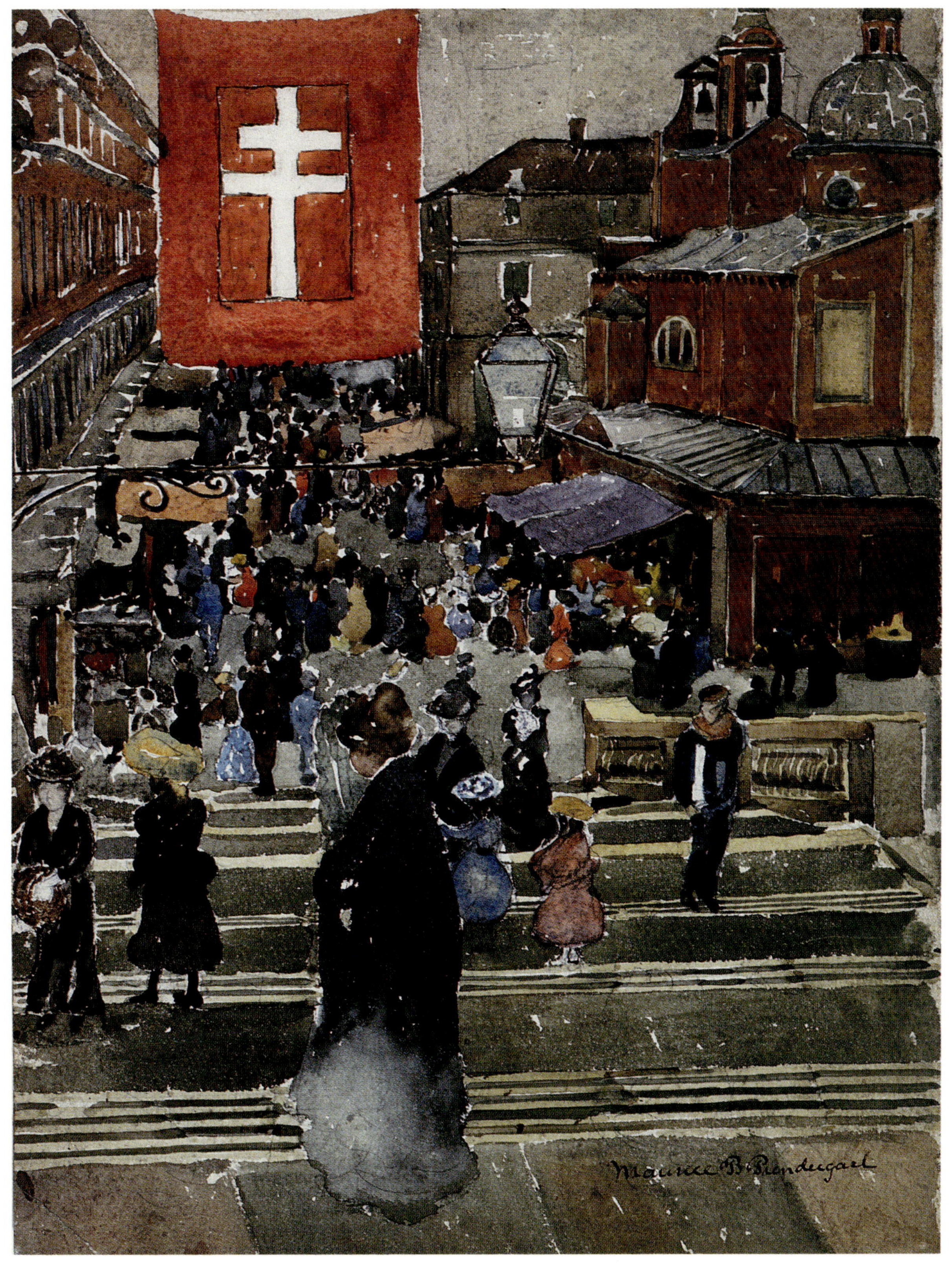

Pl. 11. Maurice Prendergast, *Market Place, Venice*, 1898, watercolor, 13⅝″ × 10″, private collection; see also fig. 98.

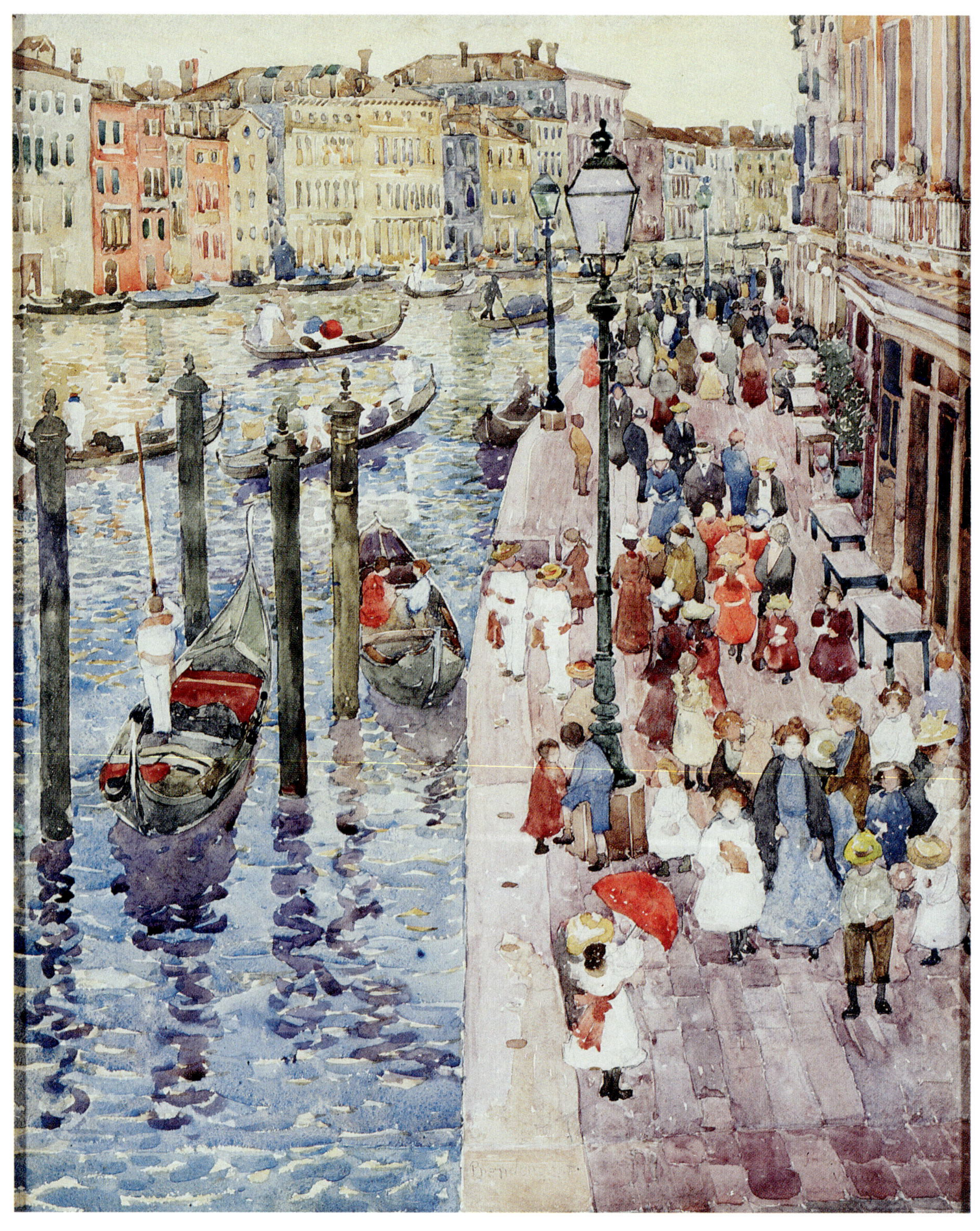

Pl. 12. Maurice Prendergast, *The Grand Canal, Venice*, 1898–99, watercolor, 17⅜″ × 13¾″, Terra Museum of American Art, Chicago, Daniel J. Terra Collection.

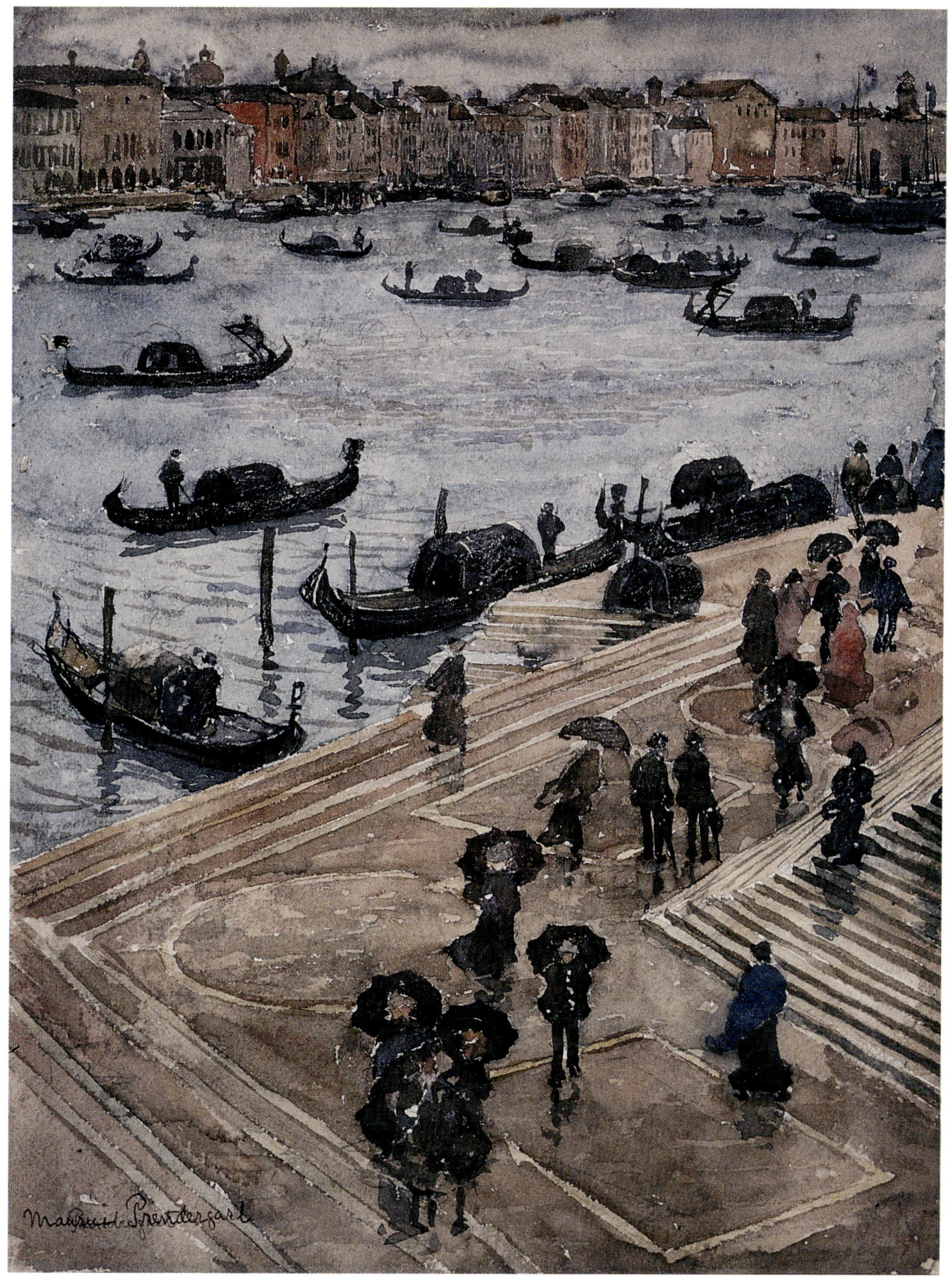

Pl. 13. Maurice Prendergast, *Rainy Day, Venice*, 1898, watercolor, 16½″ × 12½″, Wichita Art Museum, Wichita, Kansas, Roland P. Murdock Collection; see also fig. 99.

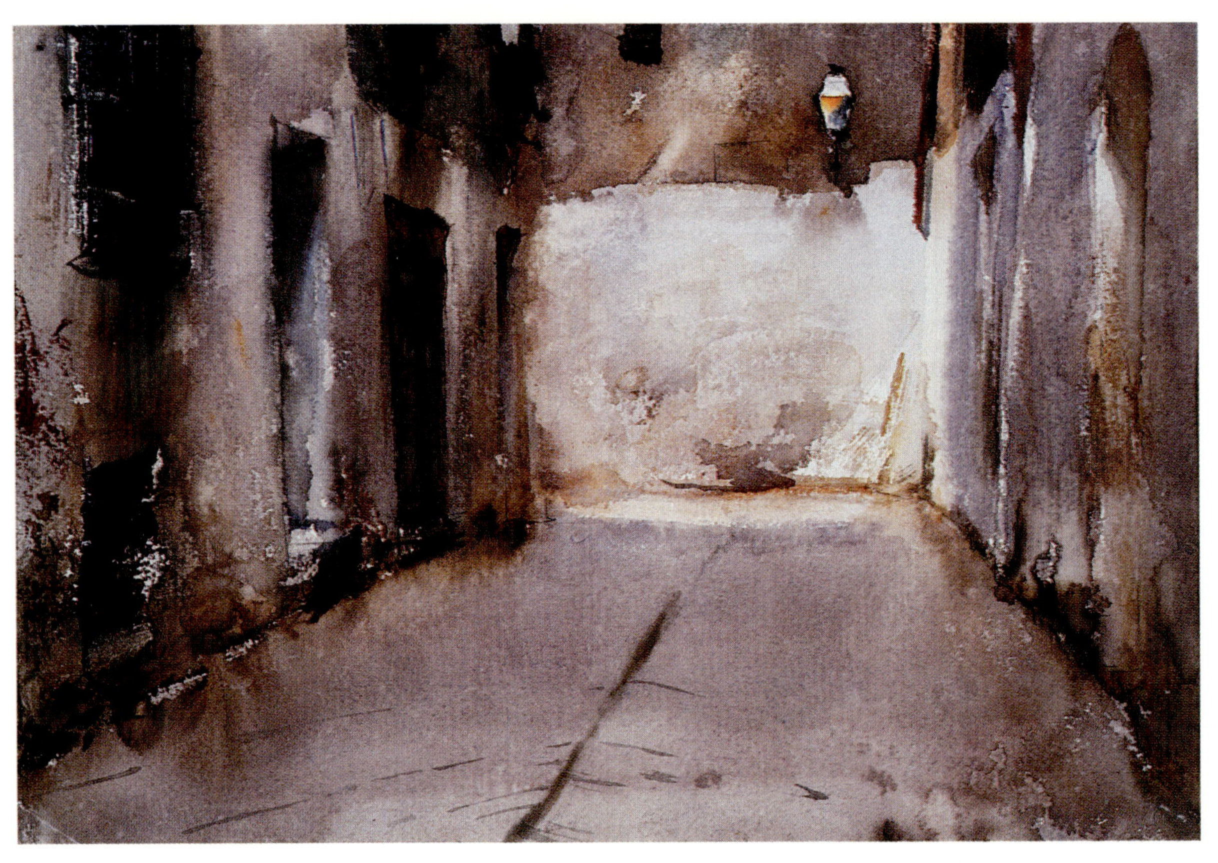

Pl. 14. John Singer Sargent, *Venice*, ca. 1905, watercolor, 9⅞″ × 14″, Metropolitan Museum of Art, Gift of Mrs. Francis Ormond, 1950.

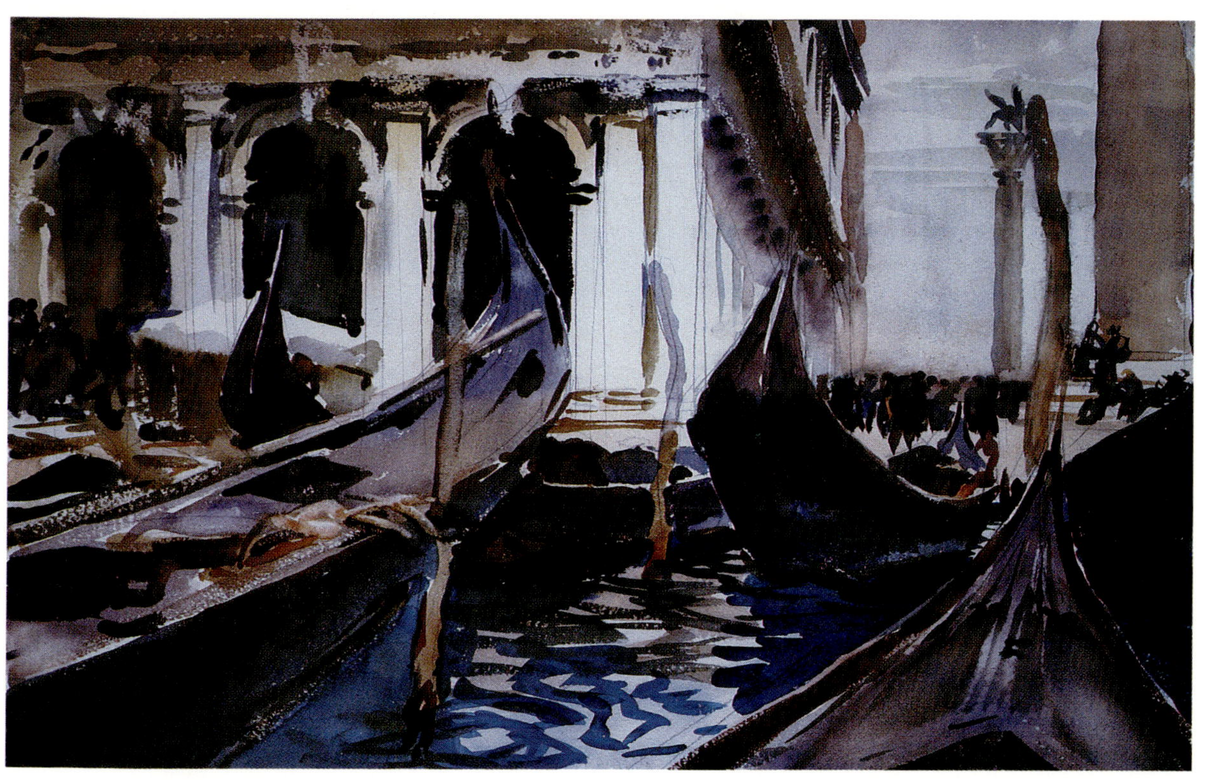

Pl. 15. John Singer Sargent, *The Piazzetta, Venice*, ca. 1904, watercolor, 13½″ × 21⅛″, Trustees of the Tate Gallery, London.

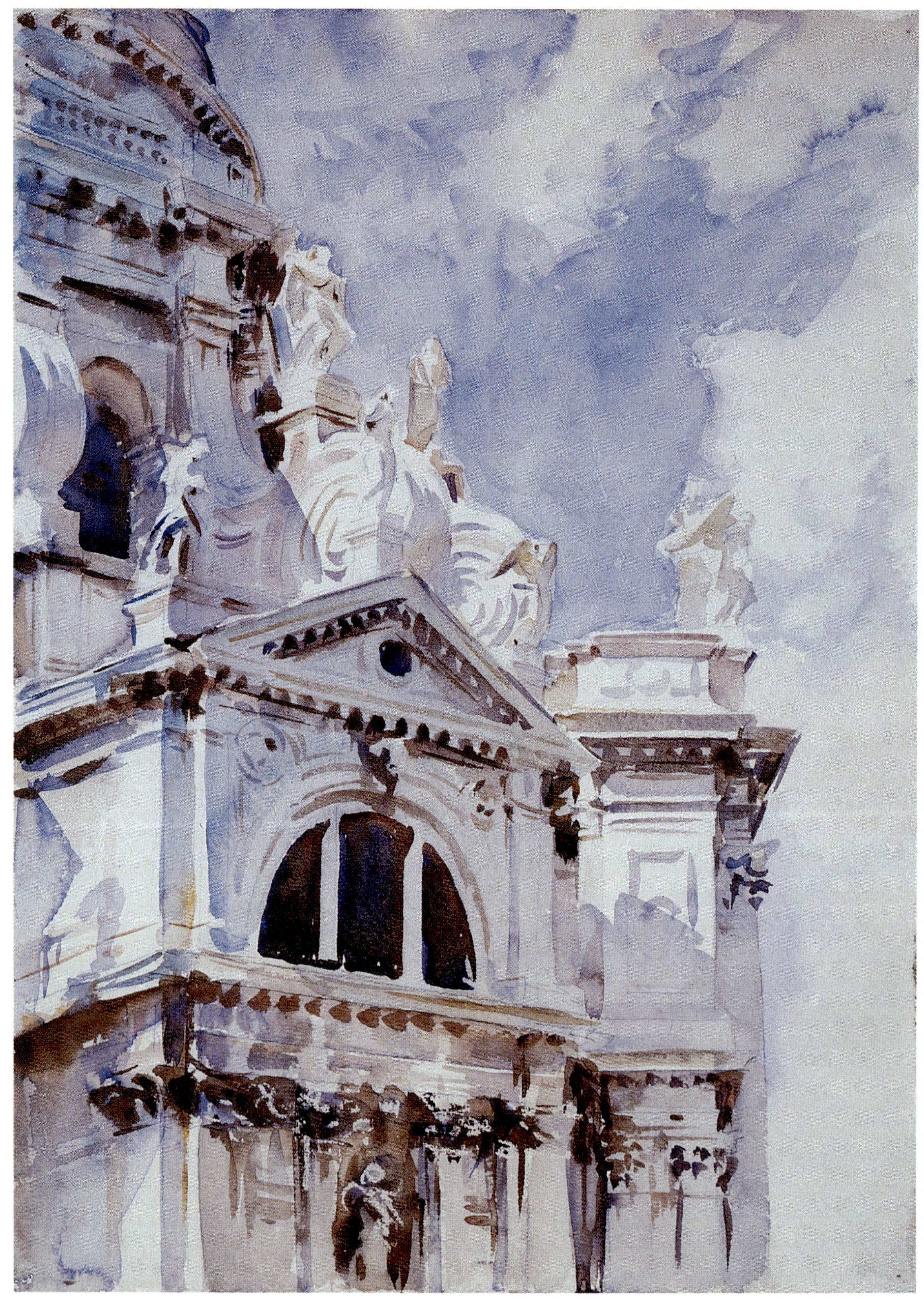

Pl. 16. John Singer Sargent, *The Salute, Venice*, ca. 1903–10, watercolor, 20″ × 14″, Yale University Art Gallery, New Haven, Connecticut, Christian A. Zabrinskie Fund; see also fig. 104.